On the Void of to Be

On the Void of to Be

Incoherence and Trope
in *Finnegans Wake*

Susan Shaw Sailer

Ann Arbor

THE UNIVERSITY OF MICHIGAN PRESS

Copyright © by the University of Michigan 1993
All rights reserved
Published in the United States of America by
The University of Michigan Press
Manufactured in the United States of America

1996   1995   1994   1993   4   3   2   1

A CIP catalogue record for this book is available from the British Library.

Library of Congress Cataloging-in-Publication Data

Sailer, Susan Shaw, 1939–
      On the void of to be : incoherence and trope in Finnegans wake /
Susan Shaw Sailer.
         p.   cm.
      Includes bibliographical references and index.
      ISBN 0-472-10414-4 (alk. paper)
      1. Joyce, James, 1882–1941. Finnegans wake.   I. Title.
PR6019.O9F593665   1993
823'.912—dc20   93-9632
                                                                  CIP

for Hazard
without whom this study would not be

Acknowledgments

I acknowledge with gratitude the long line of *Finnegans Wake* scholars without whose work mine would have been impossible. As I wrote this manuscript, I referred continually to certain texts which have been invaluable for locating passages, checking out hunches, and offering compendious *Wake*an information:

> Bernard Benstock, "A Working Outline of Finnegans Wake," in *Joyce-Agains Wake,*
> Adaline Glasheen, *Third Census of Finnegans Wake,*
> Clive Hart, *A Concordance to Finnegans Wake,*
> Clive Hart, "An Index of Motifs in Finnegans Wake," in *Structure and Motif in Finnegans Wake,*
> Roland McHugh, *Annotations to Finnegans Wake.*

Other especially helpful studies I cite in the pages ahead.

I want to acknowledge, too, the invaluable help and support my dissertation committee at the University of Washington gave me: Donna Gerstenberger, Donald Kartiganer, and Leroy Searle. Two readers for the Florida State University Press whose names I do not know read my dissertation several years ago and suggested ideas for shaping it into book form. I thank them. In its present state, Bernard Benstock and Patrick McCarthy gave my text careful and wonderfully informed readings. Their suggestions have enriched the web of connections which *Finnegans Wake* so amply invites. Hazard Adams, my dissertation advisor, deserves praise far beyond what these words can convey, not only for his guidance during the dissertation writing but also for encouraging me to undertake the substantial rewriting represented here.

I am grateful to the staff at the University of Michigan Press for their care in guiding my manuscript through production.

I want to acknowledge the *James Joyce Quarterly* for permission to reprint material that appeared originally in my article, "Conjunctions: Commentary and Text in *Finnegans Wake* II.2," 27, no. 4 (Summer 1990), and *Twentieth*

Century Literature for permission to reprint material that appeared originally in my article, "A Methodology of Reading *Finnegans Wake*," 35, no. 2 (Summer 1989). Quotations from *Finnegans Wake* by James Joyce, copyright 1939 by James Joyce, copyright renewed (c) 1967 by Giorgio Joyce and Lucia Joyce, are used by permission of Viking Penguin, a division of Penguin Books USA Inc.

Contents

Part 1. Incoherence and the *Wake*

Introduction 3

1. The *Wake* through Kristevan Eyes 11

2. The *Wake's* Language and Kristevan Metalanguage:
   A Shem and Shaun Pairing? 27

3. Writing the Body, Embodying the Writing 39

4. The *Wake* as Derridean Site 55

5. Joyce, Derrida, Heliotrope 69

6. Postal Systems: Letter and Card 81

Part 2. Tropes and Incoherence in the *Wake*

7. Troping the *Wake* 111

8. *Waking* the Tropes: A "Methodology" for Reading
   Finnegans Wake 135

9. The Limon in the Orangepeel: Fragment as Trope 159

10. The Letter: Desire as Trope 187

References 205

Index 211

PART 1
Incoherence and the *Wake*

Introduction

Wherefore let it hardly by any being thinking be said either or thought that the prisoner of that sacred edifice, were he an Ivor the Boneless or an Olaf the Hide, was at his best a onestone parable, a rude breathing on the void of to be, a venter hearing his own bauchspeech in backwords, or, more strictly, but tristurned initials, the cluekey to a worldroom beyond the roomwhorld.

—(100.24–29)

void: [noun] (1) total emptiness; an empty space or vacuum (2a) total absence of something normally present b) a feeling of emptiness or deprivation [the *void* left by his death] (3) a break or open space, as in a surface; gap

be: as a substantive verb: (1) to exist; live [Caesar *is* no more] (2) to happen or occur [when will the wedding *be*?] (3) to remain or continue (will he *be* here long?] (4) to come to; belong [peace *be* with you] (5) to have a place or position [the door *is* on your left]

be: as a copula, *be* links its subject to a predicate nominative, adjective, or pronoun so as to express attribution or identity, and by extension, value, cause, signification, etc.; it is sometimes equivalent to the mathematical sign (=)

—*Webster's New World Dictionary,* Third College Edition (1988)

Learning to read *Finnegans Wake* has changed the way I read. I suspect that is the situation for other readers of the *Wake* as well. I never had been comfortable distinguishing literal from figural, what made sense from what did not, and *Finnegans Wake* reinforced that reluctance. It showed me the roots of coherence in incoherence, and of incoherence in coherence; it washed the literal so thoroughly in the figurative and the figurative in the literal that neither has come out "clean" again.

Tradition has placed incoherence in the realm of mistake, lack, confusion; it located the figurative in the realm of "words and expressions used in ways that are out of the ordinary, serving primarily as ornament and making their appeal through novelty."[1] Neither placement worked for the way tropes and incoherence function in *Finne-*

gans Wake, where the latter is a productive force and the former, a way of thinking while, if not quite "ordinary," then at least so pervasive as to be paradigm rather than exception.

This text examines the process by which reading *Finnegans Wake* begins as incoherence that moves towards coherence. The movement results from the reader's (and writer's) activity in fusing—by applying the tropic processes of metaphor, metonymy, synecdoche, and irony—the fragments constituting the *Wake*, which Joyce termed "active elements."

I attempt to understand *Finnegans Wake* as a practice of language; first, in terms of how theories of language can address the presence of incoherence in that text and second, in terms of how tropes account for its productivity as they both enact as well as act upon incoherence. My focus is the *Wake* as "verbal substance."[2] I do not offer my text as the most recent competitor for the prize of "literary hegemony" over other critical texts dealing with *Finnegans Wake*.[3] I offer it instead as one piece of conversation in the now fifty-plus years of ongoing dialogue on the *Wake*. Although my methodology is informed primarily by reader response and deconstruction, I do not use them exclusively. I believe that each critical perspective enables distinct and valuable insights, and that though coming from differing perspectives, insights can inhabit the same text and even chapter. Thus, in chapter 9 I use a structuralist approach in examining how motifs function in the *Wake* even though my overall framework is deconstructive, the interpenetration of incoherence and coherence, tropism and "literalism." But though I see *Finnegans Wake* as a "naturally" deconstructive text, and though I work with it, especially in part 1, in deconstructive terms, I do not give a deconstructive reading of the *Wake*. One reason is that my province is elsewhere, the text's verbal substance; another is that language is a very different construct for Joyce than it is for Derrida and Kristeva, whose notions about language I find especially helpful in examining incoherence as a productive force in language. For Kristeva and Derrida, to be entangled in writing is to carry each notion and word to an interminable chain of differences, resulting in the isolation and abandonment of the subject within language. For Joyce, on the contrary, to be entangled in writing is to carry each word and notion to an interminable chain of relatedness, resulting in the enfolding of the subject in a destiny and direction shared with all other subjects.

In mentioning Joyce's name in the previous paragraph and, in the pages ahead when I quote from his letters or his notebooks, I do so not in the sense of consulting him as the authority of his writing. Rather, I see his comments in several ways: as part of the history of the reception of *Finnegans Wake,* and as copartner with the reader in forming the text. My position coincides with that of Michael Patrick Gillespie, who writes: "I strongly believe that the delineation of the paradigm laid down by the author remains a central concern, especially as it manifests itself as stylistic manipulation," and

> What I am proposing, then, is a dialectic equilibrium: a both/and condition that does not assign either to the author or to the reader the position of sole arbiter of meaning. Rather, the perspectives of artist and of audience conjoin to produce a text.[4]

I have chosen the word *incoherence* to name the effect so many readers of the *Wake* experience. But the *Wake's* incoherence names a range of responses generally delineated by the observation that one is reading words but can't "do" anything with them. Some readers feel relatively comfortable with that position; others have a near-zero tolerance for it. At academic conferences I have been struck both by the numbers of scholars who say, "*Ulysses* was hard enough, but I couldn't even get into *Finnegans Wake,*" as well as—especially at Joyce conferences—the numbers of nonacademics who read the *Wake* "for fun," sometimes even as bedtime reading. On the one hand, a chaos of words; on the other, "the pleasure of the text." And linking those two responses, the play of incoherence.

Incoherence marks one's reading of *Finnegans Wake,* and I am puzzled by responses that don't acknowledge it. Sometimes incoherence verges into chaos—that increase, at a geometric ratio, in the sense of being confused at encountering what appears to be extreme disorder. Sometimes incoherence merges with indeterminacy, the realization that limits are not fixed and that multiple signification is at work.[5] But most of the time when readers experience incoherence, what they are aware of is that they cannot connect one word with another, one sentence with another, one event with another.

Challenged to account for the text's densely convoluted language—the reader's experience of its incoherence—critics writing in the first twenty-five years following publication of *Finnegans Wake* pointed to Joyce's statement that "One great part of every human existence is passed in a state which cannot be rendered sensible by the use of wideawake language, cutanddry grammar and goahead plot."[6] But for many years the statement was accepted as self-explanatory. No studies developed the connections between Joyce's statement and the dynamics of the *Wake*'s language. Since the mid-1960s, studies exploring the nature of language have multiplied, a number of which suggest concepts that deal with incoherence in language as a component in creating signification. Such studies offer possibilities for understanding how incoherence functions in the *Wake*.

John Bishop's study *Joyce's Book of the Dark* also deals with the *Wake*'s incoherence, but its orientation differs from that of my study. Bishop's text situates the incoherence of *Finnegans Wake* as the product of the darkness shrouding the sleeper's mind and senses. Incoherence becomes the verbal equivalent of the dark, which in turn becomes the key by which the *Wake*'s incoherence makes "sense." Referring to book I, chapter 8, for instance, Bishop writes, "All of the chapter's strangest peculiarities will resolve into a stunning simplicity if we only continue to read the book as a 'reconstruction of the nocturnal life' endured by 'one stable somebody.'"[7] Bishop's statement helps differentiate my focus from his. Where he explicates how the notion of darkness underlies and explains every puzzling aspect of the *Wake*, I explore incoherence as an integral dynamics in reading the text. Part 1 examines how incoherence functions within language in *Finnegans Wake*; part 2 explores the relationship between incoherence and the pervasive tropism of the *Wake*'s language.

The first three chapters in part 1 work with Kristevan notions of language, where incoherence is rooted in the oppositional nature of the speaking subject as the effect of contradictions between the *chora*'s impulses and the *thetic*'s concerns—in other words, socialized versus biological needs. Such an understanding of incoherence views *Finnegans Wake* as the divided site of biological drives and cultural constraint. I see Kristeva's language notions as helpful in naming language operations in the *Wake* but perhaps misleading in providing a metalanguage for describing the *Wake*'s dynamics, not only because other explanations are possible, but because Kristeva's assumptions about the context in which language occurs differ so greatly from Joyce's assumptions. Nevertheless, a productive relation exists between Kristevan notions and *Wake*an figures, each "character" embodying writing as well as writing (from) the body. The five major "characters" of *Finnegans Wake* project a Kristevan biopsychological dynamics of the *Wake*'s writing, each configuring a role in the writing of the Letter.

Chapters 4 through 6 work with language notions of Derrida, for whom incoherence is rooted in the endlessly generating multiplicity inherent in language, the effect of *différance* and its "nonsynonymic substitutions"—trace, spacing, supplement, play and dissemination. Such an understanding of incoherence views the *Wake* as paradigmatic of the endless proliferation of signifiers and hence signification. Joyce in the Children's Games chapter and Derrida in "White Mythology" work with *heliotrope* as trope, and through examining how the word functions in these two texts, we can see that Joyce's language practice both coincides with and differs from that of Derrida. But since "White Mythology" is not a text in Derrida's definition of the term, it is perhaps not as useful for examining the language of Joyce and Derrida as *The Post Card*, which may be viewed as writing *Finnegans Wake* into itself as well as rewriting it. Chapter 6 explores to what extent the two texts share similar tropic structures.

Part 2, chapters 7 through 10, examines the *Wake*'s tropism, both as mental processes and as specific tropes informing the text. In *Finnegans Wake*, tropes not only enact incoherence, but they also act upon it so that their productivity, their movement, suggests connectedness that counters incoherence. Each of the "major tropes"—metaphor, metonymy, synecdoche, and irony—provides a "logic," a way of reading the text that, when used in concert, enables a "thick" reading of the *Wake*.[8] This tropic reading accepts the text's incoherence as multiple signification. The fragments that constitute *Finnegans Wake* are separate pieces that, by the reader's/writer's activity, join as "active elements" through metaphor, metonymy, synecdoche, and irony. The fragment is one of the *Wake*'s especially rich tropes, figuring the potentiality readers must actualize of the possible network of connexity among what is disconnected. Desire, another rich *Wake*an trope, is constituted by movement, time, duration, a sense of the whole, and, through the "seim anew" (215.23), affirmation and chaos. Desire is productive rather than lack and moves in two directions: it links with the word through the desired object, and it produces as well as orders the subject.

Clearly, I do not view *Finnegans Wake* as a quixotic and peculiar piece of art so specialized, so narrow, and so demanding that only Joycean academics would choose to enter it. David Hayman declares that *Finnegans Wake* is "Joyce's last and greatest work."[9] While I do not believe that ranking one monumental work against another serves a useful purpose, I think Hayman's estimate of the significance of the work is appropriate and accurate. One of this century's most profound enactments of the human family from a male view—Joyce's as well as HCE's—*Finnegans Wake* is also one of this century's earliest declarations of postmodernism in literature. I do not think it is a postmodern text per se, but it certainly is constituted of elements that define aspects of the postmodern. Consider, for instance, the following:

> Take MTV as an example. Turn it on. What do you see? Perhaps demon-like creatures dancing; then a cut to cows grazing in a meadow, in the midst of which a singer with blue hair suddenly appears; then another cut to cars engulfed in flames. In such videos, the images and medium collaborate to create a techno-logical demonstration that any text can be embedded in any con-text. What are these videos telling us, if not that the disappearance of a stable, universal context *is the context* for postmodern culture?[10]

Finnegans Wake also demonstrates the embedding of any text in any context. And the *Wake*, too, tells us about the disappearance of stability as it has been perceived for centuries, as something inherent in the institutions embedding life. The *Wake*, instead, locates it as an activity continually under construction by participants. Stability in writing/reading texts, according to the *Wake*, is the product of the writer's and reader's activity. But one of the reasons the *Wake* does not lie wholly within postmodernism is that where a postmodern perspective tends to see the particular and the local as context, Joyce conceived of the universal as context. *Finnegans Wake*, he declared, is "the great myth of everyday life."[11] In the state of sleep and dream Joyce thinks, as Richard Ellmann writes, that people "become one": "Sleep is the great democratizer: in their dreams people become one, and everything about them becomes one. Nationalities lose their borders, levels of discourse and society are no longer separable, time and space surrender their demarcations."[12] In this final decade of the twentieth century, Joyce's view appears "naive." Where his modernist perspective was attuned to what united people, a postmodernist perspective usually sees the ethnic, cultural, psychological, gender, and racial differences that separate people.

How the *Wake* constructs a dynamic stability through what may be experienced initially as incoherence is the focus of my study. The text's incoherence fosters an order different from what most readers expect, where in fact order is recognized not because it has been built in to be "found," but recognized because it has been "made"—by the joint efforts of writer and reader. This is a participatory order, a participatory stability, which—by troping the miscellany of materials the text/life gives us—the reader (of life) builds.

Balancing "on the void of to be" does not offer conventional security, demanding as it does a state of constant alertness, but it is exhilarating, a place where one can acknowledge the void as emptiness, or as absence, or as an open space to be populated as one will; where to exist, to occur, to continue, to belong, and to have a position is as near as the nearest trope, the "cluekey to a worldroom beyond the roomwhorld."

NOTES

1. Alex Preminger, ed., *Princeton Encyclopedia of Poetry and Poetics*, enlarged edition (Princeton University Press, 1974), 273.

2. The phrase is David Hayman's, from *The "Wake" in Transit* (Ithaca: Cornell University Press, 1990), 15.

3. I have borrowed the phrase from Michael Patrick Gillespie, *Reading the Book of Himself: Narrative Strategies in the Works of James Joyce* (Columbus: Ohio State University Press, 1989), 4.

4. Gillespie, *Book of Himself*, 6.

5. I use the term differently from Phillip F. Herring, who associates indeterminacy specifically with deconstruction and "Derridean principles," "where it is used to indicate a problem besetting all language and all texts." See *Joyce's Uncertainty Principle* (Princeton: Princeton University Press, 1987), xii.

6. *Letters of James Joyce*, vol. 3, ed. Richard Ellmann (New York: Viking Press, 1966), 146. Subsequent references are given in the text.

7. John Bishop, *Joyce's Book of the Dark* (Madison: University of Wisconsin Press, 1986), 338.

8. I use these tropes not in a privileging, essentializing manner, but

instead as part of the metalanguage I have chosen to discuss the process of reading *Finnegans Wake*. I could have worked with other tropes; for instance, Derek Attridge suggests that the narrative character of the *Wake* might be "just as well represented by the tropes of zeugma and bathos" ("What Constitutes Narrative in *Finnegans Wake*" [paper presented at the Thirteenth International James Joyce Symposium, Dublin, June 1992]). For my purposes, however, I found metaphor, metonymy, synecdoche, and irony more helpful for thinking about the *Wake*.

9. Hayman, *"Wake" in Transit*, ix.

10. N. Katherine Hayles, *Chaos Bound: Orderly Disorder in Contemporary Literature and Science* (Ithaca, N.Y.: Cornell University Press, 1990), 272. Subsequent references are given in the text.

11. James S. Atherton, *The Books at the Wake* (Carbondale: Southern Illinois University Press, 1959), 51.

12. Richard Ellmann, *James Joyce* (New York: Oxford University Press, 1959), 729. Subsequent references are given in the text.

Chapter 1

The *Wake* through Kristevan Eyes

Microcosm of the world, *Finnegans Wake* presents an extraordinarily multifaceted and shifting appearance. Hundreds of rhythms pulse through it, as well as hundreds of named and nameless speakers whose intonations are so well defined that we can recognize an individual voice, even if we have encountered it only once before. Certain sounds and groupings of letters and numbers are repeated endlessly and indeed, repetition is an important structuring principle of the text. Apart from repetition, patterning of various kinds can be found in the *Wake*, though patterns consistently manifest "the seim anew" (215.23), the "same," but always with a "difference." While some passages seem to offer limited coherence, the *Wake* is marked by incoherence; and when coherence does occur, it is so weltered in contradictions or inscribed in other circumstances that negate its apparent clarity that the text's "coherence" must always be viewed with suspicion. Not only difficult to categorize as belonging to any of the traditional genres, the *Wake* transgresses genre laws of both novel and epic.[1] A series of locutions demonstrating the infinite plasticity of language, the text invites readers to discover a nearly endless chain of interrelationships among a wide variety of linguistic constructs. Because these interrelationships at first elude us and then, once we have learned how to read the text, multiply at geometric ratios, *Finnegans Wake* challenges our sense of what constitutes signification, forcing us to become active participants in its production rather than allow us to capture meaning as it hides circumspectly, waiting to be discovered.

As readers, what do we make of this potential and sometimes actual chaos as these rhythms, speakers, repetitions, patterns, transgressions, and evasions interact? How can language, one of the most

11

potent forces for coherence, not only foster but indeed generate incoherence? Coming out of a background of Marxism, psychoanalysis, and semiotics, some of Julia Kristeva's formulations about language offer ways to discuss the role of incoherence in texts, which she views as the effect of the unending conflict between the two modes of language, the semiotic and the symbolic.[2]

Finnegans Wake is marked by oppositions, and Kristeva's terms phenotext and genotext provide names for two opposing effects we experience at work in Joyce's or any other text.[3] A mathematical demonstration proceeding entirely through algebraic symbols comes close to pure phenotext, while Antonin Artaud's call for theater to develop a language of gesture, incantation, and ritual focusing on the physical production of expressive sound suggests pure genotext. Kristeva insists, however, that any text is the product of both effects.

When we consider the almost countless rhythms that pulse through the *Wake,* we are confronting one aspect of the genotext, its capacity to establish distinctive rhythms. We distinguish, for instance, the rhythms that identify children's tales, such as "The House That Jack Built"; those of traditional songs, such as "Do Ye Ken John Peel"; of literary passages by other authors, such as the Quinet flower sequence; of passages from Joyce's other works, such as *A Portrait of the Artist;* of passages suggestive of the speech of characters from the *Wake* itself, such as the Anna Livia rhythms of I.8; of words famous in history, such as the Duke of Wellington's "Up, guards, and at them";[4] of names famous in conjunction with each other, such as Tom, Dick, and Harry; of conventional prayers and liturgies, such as the "Hail Mary"; of words and phrases that function as motifs in the *Wake,* such as "usquebaugh" (whiskey) and "heliotrope" and "Dear Dirty Dublin"; of riddles in the text, such as those of the Prankquean and of Shem; of verse that Joyce parodies, such as the singsong "stage-Irish" poems. We hear these and the many more rhythmic passages multiple times, so that when they recur, it is their rhythms that identify them rather than the original wordings or spellings, which tend to vary from earlier appearances as they reappear. The rhythm of "For he kinned Jom Pill with his court so gray and his haunts in his house in the mourning" (31.28–29) is immediately recognizable as "Do Ye Ken John Peel" if readers know the song.

When we consider the *Wake*'s hundreds of named and nameless speakers whose voices we distinguish from each other, we confront another aspect of the genotext, recognizable intonations. Among the named speakers, we note The Four's group voice: "The four of them and thank court now there were no more of them. So pass the push for port sake" (94.31–32) as well as their individual voices: Mark's "Ah ho!" Matt's "Ay, ay!" Luke's "Ah, dearo, dear!" and Johnny's "And so. And all." Equally characteristic is the voice that identifies The Twelve, with its latinate "-ation" constructions: "given to ratiocination by syncopation in the elucidation of complications" (109.4–5). Issy speaks in a number of voices, one of which is her breathless, plosive intonation: "Thanks, pette, those are lovely, pitounette, delicious! . . . you pig, you perfect little pigaleen!" (143.32–35). Each "character" is recognizable through his or her intonations; in fact, it is through the characteristic rhythms and intonations that we know who is speaking or spoken of since Joyce's usual practice is to not identify either by name.[5]

So it is also for the hundreds of unnamed voices that speak a phrase, sentence, paragraph, page, or section. There is the flat monotone of one of the parenthetical voices: "(There extand by now one thousand and one stories, all told, of the same)" (5.28–29); the excitable accents of the mimicking voice: "Macool, Macool, orra whyi deed ye diie?" (6.13); the platitudinous intonation of the moralizing voice: "now, patience; and remember patience is the great thing, and above all things else we must avoid anything like being or becoming out of patience" (108.8–10); the vigorous, ungrammatical accents of the black voice:[6] "You is feeling like you was lost in the bush, boy? You says. . . . You most shouts out . . ." (112.3–4); the shrill indignation of one of the commentator voices: "Figure it! The pining peever! To a Mookse!" (154.17); the sniping accents of the argumentative washerwoman: "You'd like the coifs and guimpes, snouty, and me to do the greasy jub on old Veronica's wipers. What am I rancing now and I'll thank you?" (204.29–31); the clipped intonation of the Chinese voice: "all boy more all girl singoutfeller longa house blong store Huddy" (257.7–8).

When we move from focusing on the presence of recognizable rhythms and voices to focus on the presence of repetition itself, we are involved with what Kristeva terms the chora.[7] The choric process of discontinuities—which derives from biological rhythms and drives as the text's speakers begin to articulate something, then break off, and eventually start over, again and again—repeats itself hundreds of times in the text. We can observe it, for instance, in the varied repetitions of certain words associated with sexuality, as with heliotrope and the numbers two and three. A specific instance of the chora's discontinuities effected through repeating fragmented articulations is apparent in this passage built around "hesitency," associated with lying: "But the spoil of hesitants, the spell of hesitency. His atake is it ashe, tittery taw tatterytail, hasitense humponadimply, heyheyheyhey a winceywencky" (97.25–27). The *Wake*'s recognizable rhythms and intonations as well as its repetitions of textual elements may be described, through Kristeva's language notions, as genotext effects. But the *Wake* is equally marked by phenotext effects, seen in the treatment of single pages, sections, chapters, and books. Because of the phenotext's concern for clarity of communication and its adherence to societal, cultural, and linguistic laws or constraints, we can state, for instance, that a few of the text's voices speak primarily as phenotext—as does the explicating parenthetical voice or the guidebook voice; that certain pages are constructed on the basis of a principle consistent with the phenotext, as are pages 122–23 as parody of a discussion of the "Tunc" page of the *Book of Kells;* that some chapters have a plan or format that coincides with phenotext concerns, as has II.2, with its classroom textbook layout; that one way of stating the relation between the four books of the *Wake* consistent with phenotext demands is that they model the Vico cycle that informs much of the text, book I functioning as the time of birth, book II as marriage, book III as death, and book IV as *ricorso* or rebirth.[8] While patterns such as these are present, so are competing language events, the interaction between which insures that the reader's involvement with the text is manipulated in a number of different directions at once. For this reason the phenotext is always being suppressed, undercut, or compromised.

It is the semiotic process of language warring on the symbolic that results in that suppression. In poetic language the semiotic is not only a constraint on the symbolic but "tends to gain the upper hand at the expense of the thetic and predicative constraints of the ego's judging consciousness."[9] The result, Kristeva writes, may well be "the logical thesis, disintegrated by semiotic rhythms within an infinite sentence" (*Desire*, 203).

Kristeva's statement describes most readers' experiences with the *Wake*. Because the semiotic mode of language continuously attacks the symbolic, we encounter on the one hand rhythm, intonation, and those effects generally considered "musical," while on the other we experience phonemes, sentences, and syntax. Rather than suppress the opposing tendencies of these two modes, Joyce exploits their antagonism, allowing the fact of their division to control the growth of a passage. Let us consider the following approximation of an "infinite sentence" as an example of a "logical thesis, disintegrated by semiotic rhythms":

> Now, to be an anew and basking again in the panaroma of all flores of speech, if a human being duly fatigued by his dayety in the sooty, having plenxty off time on his gouty hands and vacants of space at his sleepish feet and as hapless behind the dreams of accuracy as any camelot prince of dinmurk, were at this auctual futule preteriting unstant, in the states of suspensive exanimation, accorded, throughout the eye of a noodle, with an earsighted view of old hopeinhaven with all the ingredient and egregiunt whights and ways to which in the curse of his persistence the course of his tory will had been having recourses, the reverberration of knotcracking awes, the reconjungation of nodebinding ayes, the redissolusingness of mindmouldered ease and the thereby hang of the Hoel of it, could such a none, whiles even led comesilencers to comeliewithhers and till intempestuous Nox should catch the gallicry and spot lucan's dawn, byhold at ones what is main and why tis twain, how one once meet melts in tother wants poignings, the sap rising, the foles falling, the nimb now nihilant round the girlyhead so becoming, the wrestless in the womb, all the rivals to allsea, shakeagain, O disaster! shakealose, Ah how starring! but Heng's got a bit of Horsa's nose and Jeff's got the signs of Ham round his mouth and the beau that spun beautiful pales as it palls, what roserude and oragious grows gelb and greem, blue out the ind of it! Violet's dyed! then *what* would that fargazer seem to seemself to seem seeming of, dimm it all? (143.3–27)

Behind this barrage of words lies a question with a symbolic orientation, which we can discover by a judicious extraction of words: "Now . . . if a human being duly fatigued . . . having plenxty off time . . . were . . . accorded . . . an earsighted view of old hopeinhaven

with all the ingredient and egregiunt whights and ways to which in
the curse of his persistence the course of his tory will had been having
recourses . . . could such a none . . . byhold at ones what is main and
why tis twain . . . the sap rising, the foles falling . . . then *what* would
that fargazer seem to seemself to seem seeming of?" One translation
of that question yields the following: If a person, tired but having lots
of time, were accorded a view of life to which were attached all the
attendant problems and joys, the rises and the falls, of being human,
could such a person apprehend the unity of such a view and recognize its necessary duality? And if one could envision such an experience, what would it seem like? How could one describe the vision?
The passage suggests that *Finnegans Wake* offers such a view of life,
and the answer the text poses to its own question is "A collideorscape!" The reader recognizes that the *Wake* is a verbal kaleidoscope, and that each time one turns the viewer, a different pattern
of images and associations moves into view. The reader also understands that the text is a verbal landscape where competing possibilities for signification collide head on.

But under the attack of the semiotic mode of language, this symbolic question is buried within a barrage of alliteration, rhythmic
sequences, puns, other word plays, allusions, extraneous words that
dissolve the syntax, and references to at least several dozen themes
that develop throughout the text. The condition of a symbolic utter-
ance dissolving to incoherence by semiotic processes occurs repeatedly throughout *Finnegans Wake*.[10]

Sometimes the symbolic offers itself when least expected—as a
bit of pattern in a passage that otherwise seems to lack coherence.
One example of this presence of the symbolic occurs in the line that
opens II.3: "It may not or maybe a no concern of the Guinnesses
but."[11] These words relate neither to those that follow nor to those
that conclude the previous chapter. Neither do they reflect major
motivic threads nor do they offer syntactic coherence or tolerate paraphrase. But the initial letters of the first seven words form the phrase
"I'm no man," which recalls Ulysses as the "no man" who foiled
Polyphemus's attempts; the phrase also raises the question of who
narrates this chapter.

In conventional poetic texts the dominant mode of language, the
symbolic in the *Wake* struggles to make itself available to the reader.

Sometimes this appears as a voice projecting more syntactic coherence than what precedes or succeeds it, as in the following passage:

> Not olderwise Inn the days of the Bygning would our Traveller remote, unfriended, from van Demon's Land, some lazy Skald or maundering pote, lift wearywilly his slowcut snobsic eyes to the semisigns of his zooteac and lengthily lingering along flaskneck, cracket cup, downtrodden brogue, turfsod, wildbroom, cabbageblad, stockfisch, longingly learn that there at the Angel were herberged for him poteen and tea and praties and baccy and wine width woman wordth warbling: and informally quasibegin to presquesm'ile to queasithin' (Nonsense! There was not very much windy Nous blowing at the given moment through the hat of Mr Melancholy Slow!) (56.20–30)

But the fact of the relatively greater clarity of the parenthetical voice is quickly undercut by the fact that the voice is that of Wyndham Lewis, whose presence is detectable through words about Joyce that Lewis wrote in his *Time and Western Man*: "there is not very much reflection going on at any time inside the head of Mr James Joyce."[12] In the passage we are considering, the presence of Lewis, whose pronouncements in the *Wake* are subjected to suspicion rather than accorded the status offered, for instance, to Blake, serves to remind us that clarity as an end in itself may be a dead end.

Kristeva's claim that the semiotic and symbolic dispositions of language war continually with each other offers one way of discussing the oppositional nature of patterning in *Finnegans Wake* as well as provides a dynamics for explaining why no pattern plays a consistent role in the text. To explore why so much of the *Wake* appears to be incoherent, however, we will return to Kristeva's notion of the chora to seek an explanation that lies within a general theory of incoherence in language. Kristeva declares that only a few avant-garde poetic texts explore the full range of the signifying process to reach the chora, one of which is the *Wake*. As the place where the unity of the speaking subject "succumbs before the process of charges and states that produce him,"[13] the chora is the force behind such phenomena as HCE's stuttering as the sign of his sexual guilt, the incoherent sensual babbling of Issy's letters as the sign of her awakening adolescent sexuality, and the fury of Shaun/Jaun's tirade to Issy in III.2 as the sign of his attraction to her.

Kristeva's statement that "the very practice of art necessitates reinvesting the maternal *chora* so that it transgresses the symbolic order" (*Revolution*, 65) describes the overall functioning of *Finnegans Wake* as well as indicates how Kristeva explains the presence of undecidability in texts. In its continuous attacks on the thetic,[14] the chora is nearly always in evidence as it undermines singleness and clarity, producing instead multiplicity and indeterminacy. Virtually any sentence in the text shows its effects, as for instance:

> The stain, and that a teastain (the overcautelousness of the mas-terbilker here, as usual, signing the page away), marked it off on the spout of the moment as a genuine relique of ancient Irish pleasant pottery of the lydialike languishing class known as a hurry-me-o'er-the-hazy. (111.20–23)

The sentence begins by describing a stain on the Letter but, rapidly deflected, loses its way on the sidetracks of Irish peasant poetry and several languishing Lydias, of Joyce's *Ulysses* as well as Sheridan's *The Rivals*, falling apart quite thoroughly as it ends in a hyphenated noun phrase that offers yet a fourth direction for the sentence. Through such attacks on the thetic impulse and the symbolic mode, the chora brings wandering and fuzziness into language, which readers experience as incoherence.

Because so much of the *Wake* lacks coherence, rather than vent our frustration when the text makes no sense, we can recognize the semiotic force behind the sequences and focus on their rhythmic and intonational qualities rather than demand a meaning they are designed to avoid. The following passage is a description of HCE that occurs as part of the answer to Shem's first question in I.6 asking for the identification of a mythic figure:

> the false hood of a spindler web chokes the cavemouth of his unsightliness but the nestlings that liven his leafscreen sing him a lover of arbuties; we strike hands over his bloodied warsheet but we are pledged entirely to his green mantle; our friend vikelegal, our swaran foi. (131.18–22)

The passage does not yield a visualizable image of HCE. Nor can we compose a balance sheet opposing his "good" qualities to his "bad" since such judgments result from symbolic operations involving propositions, the formulation of which the passage disallows. Consider, for instance, what we might designate HCE's "good" traits: the fact that "nestlings liven his leafscreen"? the fact that "we are pledged entirely to his green mantle"? But neither "fact" can be formulated as a proposition. When we focus on the rhythms the passage manifests, however, we recognize an oppositional dynamics at work. On one side are the harsher consonantal sounds located in clauses whose syntax appears to invoke HCE's faults, such as -*d*, -*sp*, -*b*, -*k*; on the other are the softer sounds located in clauses whose syntax suggests his virtues, heard in -*n*, -*l*, -*f*, -*ng*. We notice the same dynamics in the intonation suggested by the voice speaking these words: taut on the one hand, commending on the other. And what both rhythm and intonation foster is the sense of opposition surrounding the figure of HCE, not only in this passage but throughout the text. Examining the lines for their semiotic qualities thus buttresses the direction we presume a symbolic reading of the passage should take, even though we cannot form the propositions required to support that reading. This pattern continues throughout *Finnegans Wake*, our ability to formulate a symbolic reading thwarted by semiotic elements but those same elements nevertheless reinforcing the suggestion of the possibility of symbolic readings.

As the moving force behind the symbolic disposition of language, the thetic usually occupies a behind-the-scenes position in texts. But in the *Wake* the act of naming is transformed from its usual status as an unnoticed given of language to a high-profile and fluid device for calling attention to textual elements. The thetic thus assumes an especially significant role in the *Wake*. We can think of such thetic acts, for instance, as the ten thunderwords, the hundreds of river names of I.8, the questions about identities raised by sigla as names, the questions raised about names when, as Glasheen puts it, "Who is who when everybody is somebody else," names consisting more of what we don't know about them than what we do, such as Lally or Lily Kinsella, the names of Joyce's texts and those of other writers, the names of songs and children's games, names of mythic and historical figures, enormous name lists such as ALP's "Mamafesta," the names of attributes of HCE/Finn in the answer to Shem's first question of I.6, the names of attributes of Shem's place of residence in I.7, and the names of the children's essay topics ending II.2.

But though the thetic plays a major role in the *Wake* through its naming function, its tendency to move toward coherence is usually submerged if not countermanded by the semiotic. What the semiotic mode of the *Wake*'s language asks is that we respond to the unexpected and the surprising in language's capacity to signify; what the symbolic asks is that we try to formulate propositions about those possibilities for signification. The following lines typify the densely heterogeneous effects Joyce achieves: "'Tisraely the truth! No isn't it, roman pathoricks? You were the doublejoynted janitor the morning they were delivered and you'll be a grandfer yet entirely when the ritehand seizes what the lovearm knows" (27.1–4). Into this single sentence Joyce weaves the strands of Irish-English political history, the position of Roman Catholics in that history, the L/R and P/Q consonant splits in the Celtic languages, the relation between progenitors and their descendants, the opposition between the dictates of rites and those of love, and the biblical passage of Matthew 6:3. The narrator of the sentence does not offer theses about these threads; instead, each forms a motif that returns throughout the *Wake* in a way that suggests the discontinuities effected by the chora. In this way—consistently offering too much connexity within and between words and sentences, and avoiding propositional statements—the semiotic tends to gain the upper hand at the expense of the thetic.

One more way in which Kristevan notions provide a dynamics for understanding *Wake*an incoherence lies in another semiotic operation, deviations from grammatical and syntactical rules. Among such deviations, Kristeva names three having special importance for the *Wake*. The first involves movement away from phonemic to phonetic bases, thus shifting emphasis from meaning to what Kristeva terms the drive-governed bases of sound production. This shift occurs, for instance, in the recurrent rhythmic passages, where the reader recognizes rhythmic sequences encountered previously in the text even though the words through which the rhythms move may differ from those in the original sequence.

The second deviation is overdetermination of a lexeme by significations it doesn't have in conventional usage. One of the most important operating principles of the *Wake,* this deviation recurs through-out the text in nearly every sentence, as Joyce coins portmanteau words, integrates foreign words into sentences, and combines words, as in this example: "And they viterberated each other, *canis et coluber* with the wildest ever wielded since Tarriestinus lashed Pissasphal-tium" (157.1–2). Here, "viterberated" suggests at least four compo-nents: vituperate, Viterbo (the papal residence in Italy), berate, and the German word *weiter,* meaning "further." The Latin terms trans-late as "dog" and "serpent," coming from a writing by Leo XII. "Pis-sasphaltium," according to the eleventh edition of *Encyclopedia Britan-nica* via McHugh, is a word used by ancient writers for "asphalt." Its first syllable also names the act of urinating, for which dogs, though not serpents, are notable. Through the sound of its first two syllables, "tarriestinus" suggests not only "terra," the earth upon which the serpent crawls, but also "Tara," or Ireland, at one time supposedly overrun by serpents until ridded of them by St. Patrick. Since the "they" of the passage under discussion refers to the Mookse and the Gripes, these significations all contribute to the complex overdetermi-nation of this pair.

The third deviation Kristeva addresses is syntactic irregularity such as ellipses, nonrecoverable deletions, and indefinite embed-dings.[15] Again, the *Wake* abounds in examples of such irregularities. Let us examine two briefly: "Here one might a fin fell" (52.36–53.1) and "I hope it'll pour prais the Climate of all Ireland I heard the grackles and I skimming the crock on all your sangwidges fippence perleg per drake. Tuk" (141.36–142.2).

The first is recognizable for at least two associations: a place so quiet that one might hear a pin drop, and the fall of Finn. Either way, however, the sentence is marked by ellipsis, lacking a main verb for "might."[16] The second example shows either ellipses or nonre-coverable deletions, evident in the lack of a connective between the first five words and the second five of the first clause, and the lack of coordination or subordination between the first and second clauses.

In a Kristevan reading of *Finnegans Wake,* then, incoherence is the product of the semiotic's warring upon the symbolic, the effects of which appear in manifestations such as grammatical and syntactic lapses, the repetition of rhythmic and intonational patterns, disconti-nuities resulting from the breaking off of these and their subsequent return followed by recurrent breakings off and returnings. These effects call to readers' attentions the physical, sensual nature of language.[17]

The dynamics of incoherence suggested by Kristevan notions about language fosters a reading of *Finnegans Wake* that focuses on oppositional relationships. Such oppositions operate at all levels of Joyce's text: within and among words, sentences, paragraphs, sections, chapters, books; within and among the "identity" of "characters";[18] between the darkness of night and the coming light of day. Given the continuous battle between semiotic and symbolic, the generation of opposition is endless. Incoherence as the product of semiotic versus symbolic processes suggests that behind the *Wake*'s oppositions lie unconscious needs battling conscious efforts at controlling them. The chora stores energy resulting from instinctual drives for later release; the thetic expresses social, cultural, and linguistic constraints; the speaking subject is the site of their collision. Readers of the *Wake* continually encounter such collidings. As he presents his innocent version of the affair in the park, HCE simultaneously reveals the pressure of his guilt; relinquishing her riverself to the stream following in her stead before flowing into the sea that will swallow her, ALP exhibits the pain and fear of death while accepting the course she must take; as carrier and deliverer of letters, Shaun both resists and attempts to carry out his role.[19]

Kristeva's notions about language offer a dynamics for understanding incoherence as a producer of the signification *Finnegans Wake* establishes. But they also raise some questions about the extent to which these notions and the assumptions behind them mesh with notions and assumptions behind the *Wake*'s language. With that concern, we move to chapter 2.

NOTES

1. Harry Levin declares, in fact, that the *Wake* is "unclassifiable": "The class of unclassifiable books is a well-recognized *genre*, particularly in English: *Finnegans Wake* belongs on a shelf with *The Anatomy of Melancholy*, *Don Juan*, *Sartor Resartus*, *Moby-Dick*, and *The Golden Bough*." See *James Joyce: A Critical Introduction* (Norfolk, Conn.: New Directions, 1941), 165.
2. Any text, for Kristeva, is the effect of the dialectical interplay between two warring dispositions of language, the semiotic and the symbolic. The

semiotic results from the nonverbal articulations arising from the body's response to biological drives; the symbolic results from the efforts of the "speaking subject" (in the phrase "speaking subject" Kristeva has a double intention: to indicate that a person defines and extends oneself through language, and to refuse the notion of autonomy, which tends to be associated with the term "the individual") to communicate meaning, which it does through naming objects and forming propositions about them.

3. Those effects of language which originate in the drives and operate within the semiotic component appear in the text as what Kristeva terms the genotext—as nonlinguistic elements such as rhythms, intonations, and other aspects of sound as a physical medium of expression; those originating in conformity with societal, cultural, and linguistic laws and other constraints and operating within the symbolic disposition of language appear as phenotext, those aspects of the text that may be specified as propositions.

4. Readers may recognize that "Up" also wanders in from *Ulysses*.

5. Edmund Epstein notes in *The Ordeal of Stephen Dedalus* (Carbondale: Southern Illinois University Press, 1971) that Joyce
> intended that his characters in *Finnegans Wake* should display characteristic rhythms in their speech; in one of his drafts for book 1, chapter 6 of the *Wake*, he notes that Issy's speech rhythm is to be trochaic, Shaun's spondaic, and Shem's pyrrhic. The other characters in the *Wake* have their characteristic rhythms also. (18)

6. Answering the question of whether the voices of blacks and Asians in the text are stereotyped in ways different from those of Irish and English voices may require linguistic and sociological analysis. Until such work has been done, I will defer judgment on the issue. I would like to note, however, that the text's voices present "symphonic" qualities, where each has its own "timbre." Certainly, Joyce was more concerned with written words as transcribed sound than with the sociology of words. That he could maintain such a position places him as a modernist writer.

7. The motive force behind the semiotic disposition in language, the chora converts drive discharges into stases so that their energy becomes available for creative expression. Nonverbal articulations emanate from the chora, whose expressivity is marked by rhythms derived from the instinctual drives and analogous to both vocal and kinetic rhythm. Though it has neither unity nor identity, the chora is subject to a regulating process that differs from the conventional laws governing the symbolic. It is regulated by temporarily articulating something, then breaking this off and starting over, again and again. The chora is a precondition of the thetic, or the thesis-formulating agency of mind. But the chora works not with the thetic but against it, in its refusal of both identity and unity, warring against the signifying order called for by linguistic and other conventional laws. It is this effort at transgression that gives rise to creativity.

8. Other formulations about the patterning among the four books of the *Wake* based on Vico's notions about cyclicity include W. Y. Tindall's claim that book 1 "is Vico's divine age, the second his heroic age, and the third his

human age. The fourth book is the reflux that leads to the divine again." See
James Joyce: His Way of Interpreting the Modern World (New York: Charles Scribner's Sons, 1950), 72.

9. Julia Kristeva, *Desire in Language*, ed. Leon S. Roudiez, trans. Thomas
Gora, Alice Jardine, and Leon S. Roudiez (New York: Columbia University
Press, 1980), 134. Subsequent references are given in the text.

10. Joyce of course did not write a relatively "symbolic" first draft of
Finnegans Wake and then obscure it with invasions of the "semiotic" in later
drafts. Examining the first draft available in Hayman's *A First-Draft Version
of Finnegans Wake* indicates that even in an early stage in the writing of this
section, the semiotic is warring successfully on the symbolic.

11. Bernard Benstock notes that "this fragmentary opening is based on the
Farsi storytelling opening, one of several in *Finnegans Wake* that duplicates
'Once upon a time . . .'" (private correspondence).

12. Roland McHugh, *Annotations to "Finnegans Wake"* (Baltimore: Johns
Hopkins University Press, 1980), 56. Subsequent references are given in the
text.

13. Julia Kristeva, *Revolution in Poetic Language*, trans. Margaret Waller
(New York: Columbia University Press, 1984), 28. Subsequent references are
given in the text.

14. By this term, Kristeva indicates the proposition-forming tendency of
the symbolic component of signification to effect communication with others
according to grammatical, linguistic, and social law.

15. Julia Kristeva, "The System and the Speaking Subject," *Times Literary
Supplement*, 12 October 1973, 1249.

16. However, when "might" is read as "night" the syntax holds up perfectly, and it makes sense as a parallel reading.

17. I do not want to imply that the base of language in *Finnegans Wake* is
oral. As David Hayman writes,

Clearly, the *Wake*, a book that has been heavily fetishized by deconstruc-
tionists, is not simply a pointed reminder of oral procedures. Far from
undermining the deconstructive thesis and in keeping with the hyper-
paradoxes of his novel, Joyce's method ultimately prioritized the written
word. (*"Wake" in Transit*, 10)

Rather than declare the written word the victor, I would say that in the *Wake*,
written and spoken procedures war on each other, maintaining a productive
balance.

18. Because HCE, ALP, Issy, Shem, and Shaun realize so few expectations
readers have of novelistic characters, I cannot use the word directly. However, the term sigla is not adequate to convey the powerful emotional effects
ALP and the rest of her family generate in readers. I therefore place the term
"under erasure," though hereafter I will not enclose it in quotation marks.

19. Shari Benstock discusses this dual effort on Shaun's part:

Entrusted to Shaun, who is the embodiment of canonical and common
law, the letter catches him in a double bind: the need to deliver the letter
and the desire to suppress it. That is, the postal system itself has an

investment in seeing to it that the letter both arrive and not arrive at its destination. Thus Shaun delivers the letter always into the wrong hands (which are also the right hands), insuring that it is continually deflected, diverted, displaced, and detoured. (604)

See "Apostrophizing the Feminine in *Finnegans Wake*," *Modern Fiction Studies* 35 (1989): 587–614.

Chapter 2

The *Wake*'s Language and Kristevan Metalanguage: A Shem and Shaun Pairing?

The continual attack of the semiotic component of language upon the symbolic offers a dynamics that can account for the productive role of incoherence in *Finnegans Wake*. Related Kristevan processes also describe language operations encountered in reading the *Wake*. We could describe that text, for instance, as a polyphonic novel, the polyphony marked by ambivalence and the disruption of monosemy through a "pulverizing and multiplying unity through rhythm" (*Desire,* 175). The result "produces an infinite fragmentation that can never be terminated" (*Desire,* 174). Then, too, the phrase "desacralized sacred" that Kristeva applies to Beckett's *Not I* (*Desire,* 158) applies equally to the *Wake*'s inversions of the sacred, the Lord's Prayer parodies, for example, or Shaun's stations of the cross. For her, laughter makes symbolic adherence to laws and restraints dialectical by introducing "the aggressive, violent, liberating drive" (*Revolution,* 222, 224). The antithesis between the sacred and the polyphonic novel in its denial of theologization, the dynamics of laughter as investing a new order while dissolving the old: we recognize these operations on every page of *Finnegans Wake*.

Another area where Kristeva's notions seem to describe *Wake*an practice is the kind of art that certain modern poetic texts achieve. In such works, Kristeva indicates, mimesis operates to undermine the symbolic order of prohibitions and respect for restraints by forcing both writers of these texts and their readers to function in perspectives that transgress monotheistic religions as well as Western science viewed as a linear process leading to certain, singular truth. But as it shatters the old symbolic unity, the poetic text develops "new signifying devices" that act to bind the shards of the old into "a new reality" that corresponds more closely to the objective conditions in which the speaking subject as reader or writer exists. This is the poetic text's ethical function, which it accomplishes "only when it pluralizes, pulverizes, 'musicates' these truths, which is to say, on the condition that it develop them to the point of laughter" (*Revolution*, 233).

In its treatment of sexuality and the sacred as well as in other areas, *Finnegans Wake* transgresses prohibitions and restraints. Through laughter, it forces the sacred into secular transubstantiation, holds forbidden sexual practices up to laughter, denies hierarchical values. And the language Joyce developed for the *Wake* remains so new that, as Richard Ellmann remarks, we are still learning to be Joyce's contemporaries (*James Joyce*, 3).

A number of areas of significant match exist, then, between the *Wake* as language practice and Kristeva's notions: the relation between laughter and the sacred, the role of these two in the text's ethical stance, the creation of new ways of signifying, opposition in language that supports polyphony rather than monosemy.

But we also need to examine areas where the match is less extensive and, perhaps, where no match exists. Several statements on this and the preceding page, for instance, have a questionable applicability to *Finnegans Wake*. The notions of objective and subjective, though interactive, are separable for Kristeva, and their distinction is significant for her sense of what constitutes reality. In the *Wake*, however, Joyce does not distinguish between objective and subjective. Perhaps this can be explained on the basis of the *Wake* as nightbook, where we never move outside the dreamer's mind.[1] But neither in *Ulysses* does Joyce distinguish objective from subjective. In fact, the parallax that operates consistently throughout that text equates subject with object, since the object takes shape only through the view of a subject, lacking a condition sui generis. Speaker and spoken about, seer and seen, so thoroughly interpenetrate that what results is amalgam. For Kristeva, though, the language one speaks and the historical period in which one lives condition and form the speaking subject; and even though the speaking subject as writer of the modern text in turn conditions and modifies both language and evolving history, nevertheless subject and object are separable both theoretically and practically.

Another area of questionable match lies in how Joyce and Kristeva each view the products of opposition. For Kristeva, the collision between the semiotic and symbolic produces an endless process of infinite fragmentation where the further one traces the line of fragmentation, the further removed the most recent branchings are from earlier oppositions. We experience such fragmentation as nonreversible change. For Joyce, the process is ongoing in which opposition works toward unity which in turn works toward opposition, the cycle repeating again and again, the result being, as the text announces, "the seim anew." The return of the same carries a difference; it is, after all, "anew," but as significantly, it is "the seim." The text is a congeries of fragments whose interaction models the cycle of opposition/unity through the return of "the seim anew."

Further, perhaps the *Wake*an dynamics of coherence and incoherence is not that, or not exclusively that, of semiotic invasion of the symbolic. Although in the brief sentence examined in chapter 1, "Here one might a fin fell," there is no doubt that some kind of syntactic distortion exists, either ellipsis or substitution, we may question whether this effect is necessarily due to invasion by the semiotic as well as whether it is an effect of incoherence. Of course Kristeva so defines the realms of semiotic and symbolic that all coherence is an effect of the latter operation, all incoherence that of the former. But is plurality of signification necessarily incoherence? And is it necessarily the effect of the drives? In Kristevan dynamics, the instinctual drives cause the semiotic mode of language to interfere with the symbolic efforts at unambiguous communicability to the end that incoherence results. But if coherence is the signifying linkage of parts, parts need not link in only one way. So long as each possible linkage maintains a dialogue with its context, modifying, confirming, assessing or in some other way commenting on the larger units in which the linkage takes shape, such plurality is neither more nor less coherent than singular signification. Thus, for "Here one might a fin fell," we may try out these possible readings: at this location, one evening Finn fell; in this condition, that of being "human only, mortal" (186.5–6), anyone might fall; as HCE begins his recounting of the "crime in the park" incident, his listeners are so quiet one might have heard a pin fall; Finn, or an avatar, is "one mighty fine fellow." Because each of these readings can dialogue with the sentence's immediate context as well as the themes and motifs of the *Wake*, the sentence may be considered coherent, despite its syntactic irregularity.

Let us consider another instance where an apparent incoherence may be explained by a dynamics other than intrusion by the semiotic. Kristeva's description of "the logical thesis, disintegrated by semiotic rhythms within an infinite sentence" (*Desire*, 203), seems apt for a number of Joyce's gargantuan sentences, such as the question resulting in the answer "A collideorscape!" (143.3–27), considered in the previous chapter. Kristevan analysis of that question finds a relatively straightforward symbolic question buried by a barrage of semiotic operations. But if we recognize the syntax of the question as a long periodic sentence that we tend to lose because we are following the movement from one word to the next, we may question the need for Kristeva's semiotic/symbolic dynamics to discuss the passage's counterpointing of coherence and incoherence.

Incoherence reflecting the writer's deliberate mediation, which perhaps operates independently of the conflict between drives and constraints in the speaking subject, the products of fragmentation differing significantly for Joyce and Kristeva, their differing stances on the objective/subjective distinction: these issues measure significant separations between the two writers. But they do not negate the issues of significant match in how each understands and uses language: the *Wake* as polyphonic novel, the role of laughter in disrupting the sacred, the importance for both Joyce and Kristeva of opposition in language, the recognition each gives to new ways of signifying.

Weighing the extent to which Kristeva's language notions match *Wake*an language practices leads to the following provisional formulation: Kristeva's notions name some aspects of the *Wake*'s language, but as sole explanation of the dynamics through which that language operates, they are problematic, not only because alternate explanations are possible but also because of differing assumptions Joyce and Kristeva hold about language. Let us explore this thesis by examining the operation of three terms that are important to both writers: textual negativity, history, and laughter.

For Kristeva laughter is the means by which the speaking subject escapes the control of social prohibitions; it is the product of an impossible contradiction between the force of the instinctual drive and the demands of the social/cultural order. Neither the speaking subject nor any audience that may be privy to it experiences this contradiction as humorous. A weapon in the service of social/ethical progress and a psychological tool for the speaking subject, Kristevan laughter is a dynamics that brings the new as an unstable synthesis of material contradictions that have fragmented the old; it announces itself, as Kristeva quoting Lautréamont indicates, through a sense of pain and the ridiculous:

> Laughter is what lifts inhibitions by breaking through prohibition (symbolized by the Creator) to introduce the aggressive, violent, liberating drive. Yet when this contradiction takes place within a subject, it can hardly be said to make him laugh: "My reasoning will sometimes jingle the bells of madness and the serious appearance of what is, after all, merely grotesque (although according to some philosophers, it is quite difficult to tell the difference between the clown and the melancholic man, life itself being but a comic tragedy or a tragic comedy." (*Revolution*, 224)

Although Joyce shares with Kristeva the recognition that laughter produces polyphony, for him the root of laughter is the identity of contraries, the connectedness of disparities, the capacity for unity within fragmentation as well as the fragmenting of unity. Joycean laughter addresses opposition as a dynamics that brings return of the same but with a difference; it announces its presence through wit and humor.

Further, in Kristeva's thought certain practices of poetic language use music and rhythm to oppose sense "through nonsense and laughter" (*Desire*, 142). But in Joyce's *Wake*, rhythm and music, nonsense and laughter, are an integral part of sense. One does not find, on the one hand, sense, and, opposing it, rhythm and music and nonsense and laughter, but instead an equation where sense equals all its components. In *Finnegans Wake* sense is additive, though the sum of its addends may be impossible to tally except in the metaphors the text projects of its own summing up, such as a "collideorscape" (143.28) or "Our wholemole millwheeling vicociclometer, a tetradomational gazebocroticon" (614.27–28). In Kristeva's thought, sense is the ally of the symbolic and the upholder of social/cultural prohibitions, always open to attack and destruction by nonsense. Kristeva's defiant laughter precipitates ongoing revolutions in speaking subject and society that differentiate the future from the past; though also defiant, Joyce's laughter attests to ongoing revolutions between generations and between cultures, but the result is "the seim anew" (215.23), which results in the simultaneity and inter-changeability of past, present, and future, not in the sense that past, present, and future are identical but that the same components con-stitute each.

Kristeva interprets history from a materialist, Marxist perspec-tive, where the dualism in language reflects the dualism of the con-text in which it takes place: "the production of the symbolic function [is] the specific formation of material contradictions within matter itself" (*Revolution*, 119). Both writer and written are immersed in history so that each inevitably "entails the taking into account of social and historical conditions" (*Desire*, 100). The speaking subject articulates thought within an objective ideology, meaning being pro-duced through the speaking subject in response to "concrete social contradictions." This production becomes artistic practice only if the practice articulates "the social struggles of a given age" (*Desire*, 232). Signification both operates through the subject/writer and modifies him as he attempts to express "the ideological and political expecta-tions of his age's rising classes" (*Desire*, 232). Kristeva's belief that art plays an ethical role through making dialectical the "truths" of the ruling classes means that for her, art is in service to social concerns but not subservient to them. Such a belief separates her from the position that

> commit[s] art to serving as the representation of a so-called pro-gressive ideology or an avant-garde socio-historical philosophy. The latter view denies the specificity of "art," which is its posi-tion between metalanguage or contemplation on the one hand and the irruption of drives on the other. (*Revolution*, 233)

For Joyce, though art may serve social concerns, it is the artist's sense that defines those concerns rather than "the ideological and political expectations of his age's rising classes." When Stephen de-clares his intention to forge "the uncreated conscience of my race," this forging will occur in "the smithy of my soul."[2] Though we do not assume that Joyce speaks through Stephen here, a continuity exists between Stephen's locating the need for change in the artist's perception and Joyce's concern, several decades later, that the expected outbreak of World War II would distract readers' attention from the about-to-be-published *Wake* (Ellmann, *James Joyce*, 733).[3] For Joyce, the artist through the artistic work deals with a time different from the time of history which, he declared, "repeats itself comically."[4] Like the flowers that appear, disappear, and reappear through the rises and falls of civilizations, art, Joyce believed, has the capacity to "quadrille[d] across the centuries and whiff now whafft to us, fresh and made-of-all-smiles as, on the eve of Killallwho" (15.10–12). The time in which we think we experience history is composed of differentiated past, present, and future, but the time of art, like the time of history if properly understood, is "that chef of seasoners" which makes "his usual astewte use of endadjustables and whatnot willbe isnor was" (236.27–28).

This is a time in which "history, literature and myth have equal validity," a time that derives from Bruno's statement that "'the actual and the possible are not different in eternity.'" The circular history of *Finnegans Wake*, in which "every part tends to change its identity all the time,"[5] merging myth and history, past and present and future, is simply not Kristeva's linear history, in which the past cannot be returned to since the present destroys it in evolving from it, just as the future, in evolving from the present, will destroy it in turn.

In addition to history and laughter, the term negativity names another concept that is important to both Joyce and Kristeva, and yet the way each understands and uses the term differs significantly. Joyce and Kristeva each employ terms that indicate the merging of opposites. The dynamics of the Kristevan operation are indicated in her statement that

> although repeated rejection [a form of negativity] is separation, doubling, scission, and shattering, it is at the same time and afterward accumulation, stoppage, mark, and stasis. In its trajectory, rejection must become positive: rejection engrammatizes, it marks One in order to reject it again and divide it in two again. (*Revolution*, 171)

This is similar to Joyce's expression of Bruno's idea of the relation between opposites:

> His [Bruno's] philosophy is a kind of dualism—every power in
> nature must evolve an opposite in order to realise itself and
> opposition brings reunion etc etc.[6]

For both Joyce and Kristeva, oppositions not only merge, then separate to merge again in an ongoing process, but they consistently
operate together, warring on each other. Neither can operate without
the other, and neither takes priority over the other. We see this in the
functioning of Kristeva's chora and thetic, semiotic and symbolic,
genotext and phenotext, as well as in Joyce's invader and invaded,
time and space, penman and postman.

But for all their similarity, Joyce's merging of opposites and coincidence of contraries is also a very different notion from Kristeva's
negativity. One difference may be located in the fact that for Kristeva
negativity is a force apart from what it shatters and rebinds, whereas
Joyce's comparable term denotes no separate force but rather the
relation between the opposites themselves. Kristeva declares that
negativity is the "fourth 'term' of the dialectic" (*Revolution*, 109), a
"process of charges and stases" and hence a process arising from the
chora, entirely distinct from negation, "the act of a judging subject"
(*Revolution*, 28), and hence a process of the thetic. Negativity links
the "real" and "conceptual," objective and subjective. Rather than
destroy, it affirms by "reactivat[ing] new organizations." It culmi-
nates in ethics, not an ethics that obeys laws but an ethics that cor-
rupts and absorbs laws "by what Hegel calls the aesthetic" (*Revolution*, 109–110). Because in *Finnegans Wake* Joyce does not distinguish
between real and conceptual, objective and subjective, his merging
of opposites links items having the same ontological status. That is
to say, myth has the same reality status as history; neither is more
objective or conceptual than the other. But they are opposites, and
because of that each takes its identity from the other, becomes the
other, separates from the other in an unending cycle. This continual
process of merging and separation results in the possibility for
unity—not as a permanent hostage to sameness, but as the other side
of fragmentation and separation.

Kristeva declares that the subject is "constituted by the law of
negativity and thus by the law of an objective reality." This frees the
subject, who is "no longer 'outside' objective negativity as a transcen-

dent unity" (*Revolution*, 110–11). That is, by registering conflicts between biological/social instincts and biological/social restraints in the subject, negativity constitutes the subject as it responds to this conflict. That negativity is objective insofar as the biological drives and social restraints exist whether or not the speaking subject ceases or continues to exist. But because the subject is "submerged in negativity," that "objective negativity" is not external to the subject and so the subject can function neither as "a transcendent unity"[7] nor be submitted to external control as "a specifically regulated monad" (*Revolution*, 111). The subject, then, is constituted by negativity as it mediates between the drives and restraints, inner and outer, and through the mediation effected by negativity, it modifies both inner and outer.

But with Joyce's *Wake*, as we have observed before, no inner/outer distinction exists, any more than a real/conceptual distinction exists. Such integration may be an effect of the text's projection as dreamer's dream or a Blakean insistence on the identity of vision and envisioned. The significant factor is that Joyce's "coincidence of contraries" results in the "seim anew" in psychology as in myth/history rather than, as with Kristeva's negativity, a temporary resolution in the "material contradictions within matter itself" (*Revolution*, 119), whether that matter is psychological or historical.

Another difference between Joyce's and Kristeva's merging and separating opposites lies in the realms in which these may be noticed. For Kristeva, negativity is observed "only in modifications of the function of negation or in syntactic and lexical modifications," Lautréamont's *Maldoror* showing the former and Mallarmé's *A Throw of the Dice* the latter form of negativity (*Revolution*, 124). Through these effects of negativity as seen in linguistic modifications, the subject succeeds "in remodeling the historically accepted signifying device by proposing the representation of a different relation to natural objects, social apparatuses, and the body proper" (*Revolution*, 126).

This sounds very much like a description of the language of *Finnegans Wake*. There is no doubt that through the linguistic modifications he developed for the *Wake's* night language, Joyce does represent a different relation to natural objects (river and mountain and human beings), social apparatuses (the similar dynamics of love and war, theology and psychology), and the body proper (the body as writer and written on, the body as divided site of both lagging performance and endless desire).

But once again we find an unbridgeable gap between the capacity of Kristevan concepts to give names to some aspects of the *Wake*'s language practices, and the very different assumptions the *Wake* models and Kristeva makes about the outcomes these concepts name. Kristeva finds that by "remodeling the historically accepted signifying device," the subject as writer of poetic language changes not only textual representation but the self, readers of that language, and hence society and history. But Joyce does not assume such change. He not only denies it through his notion of the "the seim anew," but Kristeva herself recognizes that he denies it, declaring that Joyce's writing provides a "strictly verbal analysis," as opposed to Lautréamont's *Poems*, which "stresses the need for an attitude rooted in practice" (*Revolution*, 218). For Kristeva, the text attains its essential dimension as "a practice calling into question (symbolic and social) finitudes by proposing new signifying devices" (*Revolution*, 210), where practice for Kristeva involves "acceptance of a symbolic law together with the transgression of that law for the purpose of renovating it."[8] Kristeva believes that in his *Poems*, Lautréamont purposes renovating the symbolic law his text transgresses, whereas she finds in *Finnegans Wake* transgression of symbolic law not for the purpose of renovating it but rather as the effect of verbal analysis. Though Kristevan negativity is observed in linguistic modifications, its import lies in the ramifications these modifications have upon writer and readers and, through them, upon the understanding and changing of the social contradictions current during a specific historical time.

Joyce's "coincidence of contraries" is expressed linguistically but applies to a domain not bounded by the linguistic, indicating a law that Joyce believed operates in the macrocosm, whose movement he mirrors through linguistic mergings: tree and stone, left and right banks of the Liffey. For him, the merging of opposites and their subsequent fragmenting indicates the nature of experience at all levels, its status as simultaneous "ones" and yet also "twain." For Kristeva, as we noted earlier, when negativity "engrammatizes, it marks One in order to reject it again and divide it in two again" (*Revolution*, 171). Despite her disclaimer, Kristeva's negativity serves the historical necessity of expressing material contradictions. Although she rejects the view of art held by "a so-called progressive ideology or an avant-garde socio-historical philosophy" because it denies "the specificity of 'art,' " Kristeva's view of art, while claiming that its specificity "is its position between metalanguage or contemplation on the one hand and the irruption of drives on the other" (*Revolution,* 233), allows that specificity little wider realm of operation than that of those she condemns.

What relation obtains, then, between Kristeva's notions of language and the language of *Finnegans Wake*? The tentative thesis offered earlier seems to hold: Kristeva's notions can name some aspects of the *Wake's* language practices, but as explanation of the dynamics of those practices they are problematic, not only because alternate explanations are possible, but also because of the very different assumptions the *Wake* models and Kristeva holds about the context in which language occurs. A surprisingly large number of linguistic operations are common to both *Finnegans Wake* and Kristeva's notions about language: polyphony, opposition in language, the relation of laughter to the sacred, the development of new signifying devices, the dynamic relation between language and history, the merging and separating of opposites. But because text and theory work with these concepts in such different ways, a metalanguage for the *Wake* deriving from Kristevan notions could mislead about the effects of *Wake*an incoherence rather than open an understanding of how it functions. Language practices in *Finnegans Wake* and Kristeva's concepts about language are a Shem and Shaun-like pairing since, significantly opposed to each other, these oppositions attract to merge and then separate again, only to merge and separate again and again.

NOTES

1. Kimberly J. Devlin offers a persuasive argument for "the single-dreamer theory" rather than multiple dreamers, locating the dreamer in HCE "not because he is the central 'speaker,' but rather because he is the central 'spoken of': with a compulsive predictability, the topic of discussion returns to him—or, if not to him, to a familial extension of him, to his wife, his sons, or his daughter." See " 'See ourselves as others see us': Joyce's Look at the Eye of the Other," *PMLA* 104 (1989): 889. See also Devlin's *Wandering and Return in Finnegans Wake* (Princeton: Princeton University Press, 1991), chap. 5.

2. Joyce, *A Portrait of the Artist as a Young Man* (New York: Viking Press, 1956), 253.

3. Joyce's response to the impending war is difficult to assess. Richard Ellmann quotes Joyce in the introduction to Stanislaus Joyce's *My Brother's Keeper* (London: Faber & Faber, 1958), 23 as saying, "Don't talk to me about politics, I'm only interested in style." Umberto Eco claims that this remark "leaves us perplexed concerning his human character, but it represents an example of an aesthetic and austere choice without half measure, that arouses in us, if not admiration, fright" (*The Aesthetics of Chaosmos: The Middle Ages of James Joyce*, trans. Ellen Esrock [Cambridge: Harvard University Press, 1989], 86). For discussion of Joyce's politics, see Richard Ellmann's "Joyce and Politics" and "Political Perspectives on Joyce's Work," in *Joyce & Paris: 1902. . . . .1920—1940. . . . .1975*, ed. J. Aubert and M. Jolas (Lille: Publications de l'Université de Lille 3 / CNRS, 1979), 31–32 and 101–23.

4. Quoted in Jacques Mercanton, "The Hours of James Joyce," in *Portraits of the Artist in Exile*, ed. Willard Potts (Seattle: University of Washington Press, 1979), 234.

5. The quotations in this and the preceding sentence come from Atherton's *Books at the Wake*, 36.

6. *Letters of James Joyce*, vol. 1, ed. Stuart Gilbert, rev. ed. (New York: Viking, 1966), 226. Subsequent references are given in the text.

7. Unity is a negative term for Kristeva, the product of symbolic restraint and hence contrary to the interests of the age's rising classes in that it is an instrument of social control. When synthesis occurs through operation of the dialectic, that synthesis is temporary, already on its way to becoming the new thesis to be attacked by a new antithesis. Kristeva valorizes splitting and fragmenting in that they mark the advance of the rising classes. For Joyce, however, unity balances fragmentation. It marks the possibility for a temporary and unstable whole which is neither privileged nor disdained. Unity names one member of the pair of opposites that become each other, separating into multiplicity which we experience as fragmentation, the fragments then joining again, endlessly.

8. Kristeva, "System and Speaking Subject," 1249.

Chapter 3

Writing the Body,
Embodying the Writing

We have reached an impasse, it seems. On the one hand, Kristeva's modes of semiotic versus symbolic offer a dynamics that can account for the productive role of what we as readers experience as language's incoherence in *Finnegans Wake;* on the other, Joyce and Kristeva differ significantly in the assumptions each makes about the contexts in which language operates.[1] But the fact that Joyce's ideas about the relation of language to history differ from Kristeva's does not discount the capacity of Kristeva's theories to illuminate Joyce's practice. For example, though Joyce's notion of history involves its interpenetration by myth, Kristeva might declare that Joyce's views of history themselves occurred at a precise historical moment and illustrated the relationship between status quo and avant-garde, the relation of rising to established class, at that moment.[2] For another, though Kristeva's notion of history involves the Marxist notion of its linearity with the concomitant notion of *Aufhebung*, Joyce might have responded that Kristeva's views of history were part of the great myth of nonreversible materialist progress dominating much of nineteenth- and twentieth-century thought.[3]

Similarly, that dynamics other than those of Kristeva's warring semiotic versus symbolic modes of language can offer a model of incoherence as productive neither validates those others nor invalidates the Kristevan model. Given the overdetermination operating everywhere in the *Wake,* it is no surprise that multiple factors motivate the play of what readers experience as incoherence. Thus Kristeva's notion that the body's instinctual pulsations do battle with social structures that work to regulate those fluxes is a helpful formulation of the factor of bio/psychodynamics. John Bishop's thesis that the *Wake's* incoherence is a function of the novel's being set within the mind of a sleeping person is insightful for the textual factor, in which questioning the writer's shaping of text involves answering those questions in terms of the text itself. And, when we come to them in the next chapter, Jacques Derrida's notions about language's inevitable differing and deferring from itself offer the factor of (Saussurian) linguistic dynamics for the production of incoherence.

But for now our concern remains with Kristeva's dynamics of incoherence. Kristeva has been much interested in Joyce's writing because, as she writes,

> to Joyce belongs the formidable superiority of having explored, mimed, known, and brought to light . . . the details of identification's mechanism, one that presides over the Imaginary's genesis, and consequently over its realization—which is what all fiction is.[4]

Identification she defines as "the capacity of the speaking being to identify with another subject or object, or a part or a trait thereof" (167) and as the "movement by which the subject comes to be, insofar as he makes himself one with, identical to, an Other" (172). Love assumes two forms, Kristeva claims, both of which are "variants of identification, the one paternal and symbolic, the other maternal, having to do with the drive" (178). As an analyst, Kristeva sees both forms "united in the artist's experience, leading him to transmute 'consubstantially' his psychic life into his characters and their adventure" (178). The text a writer generates is thus written out of and into his/her body, giving rise to the Kristevan term, "text-body" (171). Any poetic language, then, is a writing of the body, a body writing, a writing the body; any poetic text is an embodiment of writing.

But *Finnegans Wake* embodies writing and writes the body explicitly, whereas most other texts do so implicitly. The Letter constantly referred to—as being multiply written, found in a dungheap, variously interpretable, about to be delivered—serves as synecdoche of the *Wake* itself.[5] And its five major characters figure a Kristevan biopsychological dynamics of its writing, each of whom is directly involved in the writing of that Letter. Since readers are invited to experience the *Wake* as synecdochic of all writing, that dynamics figures the act of writing itself. The same characters also embody writing as constituted of five parts: its subject, splintered; the elusive pursuit by memory through desire of this subject; the writer, suspect by social standards; the (limited) social transmission of that writing; the words desiring transmission, sensual signifiers eluding capture.

As subject of that writing, HCE—mountain, land and city, father, husband, lover, civic leader, pub keeper, the Everyman of all history—circles throughout the text of Letter and *Wake*, aware he has fallen from a past more "productive" than the present, aware of guilt but maintaining innocence. Seen in her varying textual roles as river Liffey, mother, wife, and lover, ALP embodies the fertile, unconscious, engendering flow of memory and desire. The rival but inseparable twin sons Shem and Shaun body forth a doubleness in writing, Shem as vulnerable artist, writing on his own body with ink made from his own bodily excretions, and Shaun as the social transmission of that writing, jealous because he does not receive recognition for his role in "delivering" the Letter, suspicious of the writing his efforts keep in currency. Younger version of her mother and the desire of both her father and her brothers, Issy embodies sensual, material words, the pleasure of their play.

As that material substance, Issy incarnates sensual delight for Shem, Shaun, and HCE. (Issy cannot do so for ALP since she is ALP's younger form.) And for all three, she remains elusive, enjoyed in perception, beyond harnessing. The lines "Jaun, after those few pre-limbs made out through his eroscope the apparition of his fond sister Izzy" (431.13–15) show the attraction to Issy, as figure of verbal sensuosity, of Shaun as figure of the social transmission of writing. The Children's Games chapter, II.1, shows the desire for Issy of Glugg, the immature form of Shem-as-writer, who cannot yet guess the nature of her sensuality. As subject of writing, HCE also needs the material sensuosity of words. Through Issy's power, he takes shape through which others may read him. Aware of this interaction, Issy voices the dynamics thus: "He fell for my lips, for my lisp, for my lewd speaker. I felt for his strength, his manhood, his do you mind?" (459.28–29). Without a subject, words as material sensuosity lack a focus on which to act. And without the material of words, the subject does not exist for others or for self. As sensual material she is "naturally" concerned with writing; thus she finds in grammar and syntax expressions of sexuality, the metaphor for her own concretion as the word made flesh. Thus, she says about herself, as the Barthes-like pleasure of the text, "You may go through me! Never in all my whole white life of my matchless and pair. Or ever for bitter be the frucht of this hour! With my whiteness I thee woo and bind my silk breasths I thee bound!" (148.27–30).

As social transmission of writing, Shaun is the postman. Formulating his role in the coming-to-be of the Letter, he gives primacy to his role: "Letter, carried of Shaun, son of Hek, written of Shem, brother of Shaun, uttered for Alp, mother of Shem, for Hek, father of Shaun" (420.16–18). But for all the addresses to which he has attempted to make delivery (see 420.18–421.11), the Letter remains undelivered, though the expectation that it will arrive is a defining event of book IV. Nevertheless, delivery lies more in moving backward through time than forward. As barrel, Shaun falls into the river and floats backward toward his beginnings; and it is in that direction that he carries his potentiality as well as his incapacity for delivery. He himself acknowledges that movement whereby he gains his strength: "I am, thing Sing Larynx, letter potent to play the sem backwards" (419.24–25). (Such movement backwards in time for delivering the Letter suggests an interesting parallel with Derrida's *The Post Card*, where Freud is figured writing to Socrates, a parallel that will be developed in chapter 6.) Let us underline the movement by which *Finnegans Wake* figures the transmission of writing: it is a Letter written in the present, continuously written and rewritten in the present, but taken to old addresses, no-longer-in-existence addresses for delivery. Writing addresses the past, then, but the past cannot receive itself as seen by the present, though the present must continue to write and attempt delivery.

Although uttered in jealousy, Shaun comments accurately on his brother's nature. As writer, Shem requires the partnership of ALP, the flow of memory and desire, to help him tap into Issy, the material substance of words: "She, the mammy far, was put up to it by him [Shem]" (421.35). Shem's writing, according to Shaun, has a paradoxical double nature: both obscene in that everything Shem writes comes from the experiences of his body,[6] and plagiarized in that everything Shem writes is taken in form or style or phrase from previous writers. In Shaun's words: "Every dimmed letter in it is a copy. . . . The last word in stolentelling!" (424.32, 35)

and . . . this Esuan Menschavik and the first till last alshemist wrote over every square inch of the only foolscap available, his

own body . . . reflecting from his own individual person life un-
livable, transaccidentated through the slow fires of consciousness into a dividual chaos. (185.34–186.5)

In writing from the writing of others, Shem links his concerns
with the history of writing: each piece of writing bears within itself
the history of where and how it has come from elsewhere. But in
writing from the body, from his material existence, Shem opts for a
human context for his words that though "perilous" is "potent" and
"common to allflesh" (186.5): "Reading off his fleshskin and writing
with his quillbone [Shem wrote] a most moraculous jeeremyhead
sindbook for all the peoples" (229.30–32).

Shem's impulse toward writing, ALP figures the engendering
flow of memory and desire that feeds the writer. Unbounded, containing all, without end or goal, the river of memory flows on, resurrecting some images, submerging others, distributing its gifts without regard for effect or appropriateness. ALP, for instance, "skalded
her mermeries on my Snorryson's Sagos" (551.4) and dredges up
from the silt of past experience the image of HCE as "a youth in his
florizel, a boy in innocence, peeling a twig, a child beside a weeny-
white steed" (621.29–31) and, a few pages later, as "the
pantymammy's Vulking Corsergoth" (626.26–27).

"In the languo of flows" (621.22), ALP's movement involves a
"letting on to meself always. And lilting on all the time" (627.20–21).
But it also involves an ending that is at the same time a beginning:
"Coming, far! End here. Us then. Finn, again! Take. Bussoftlhee,
mememormee!" (628.13–14). Literally and metaphorically, after *fin*
comes *again*, just as ALP's phrase "It's Phoenix, dear" (621.1) declares
both a finishing and a resurrecting.

As subject of writing, HCE focuses the efforts of ALP, Shem,
Shaun, and Issy to give him verbal sensuosity written out of memory
and desire, out of writing's history and the writer's body/life, trans-
missible through expectation but always deferred, a gift/burden from
the present to the past in response to the burden/gift of the past to
the present. As that focus, HCE is the Letter/text's "central 'spoken
of': with a compulsive predictability, the topic of discussion returns
to him—or, if not to him, to a familial extension of him, to his wife,
his sons, or his daughter."[7] Or, as HCE expresses this, "I am known
throughout the world wherever my good Allenglisches Angle-

slachsen is spoken" (532.9–11). Desiring recognition for his achievement, HCE is continually beset by guilt about vaguely sexual sins.
Protesting his innocence, he manifests his guilt: "On my verawife I
never was nor can afford to be guilty of crim crig con of malfeasance
trespass against parson with the person of a youthful gigirl frifrif
friend chirped Apples" (532.18–21). But whether innocent or guilty,
petty of achievement or great, the subject of writing is always a "tall
tale" told by "croon[ing] paysecurers" (366.28), who persecute,
prosecute, pay to secure, and pay to cure the subject who, never an
object in his own right, is defined by the interest others have in him.

The *Wake*'s five major characters, then, embody writing as constituted by five parts: the subject, "resurrected" in words through memory and desire by a writer whose writing is delineated by the experiences life has "written" upon him/her, transmitted by a delivery
system. But in addition to embodying writing as material substance,
these five characters also configure a biopsychological dynamics of
writing that invites comparison with Kristeva's notions about language: ALP as chora, HCE as thetic, Shem as the semiotic, Shaun as
the symbolic, Issy as the jouissance of language.

As energy regulated in accordance with constraints imposed on
the body by family and social structures and generated by the drives,
the chora has neither unity of meaning nor identity but instead is
"the place where the subject is both generated and negated, the place
where his unity succumbs before the process of charges and stases
that produce him" (*Revolution*, 28). These descriptors fit ALP in her
roles as unending river flow, generating matrix, and disappearing
mater. When Anna Livia comments,

> By earth and the cloudy but I badly want a brandnew
> bankside, bedamp and I do, and a plumper at that!
> For the putty affair I have is wore out, so it is, sitting, yaping
> and waiting for my old Dane (201.5–8),

she recognizes that her flow as river needs restraint in the form of
new banks, a restraint that is both external to her waters and yet
necessary for her recognition as river.

Locus of the subject's generation and negation through his
unity's succumbing before the process of charges and stases that
produce him, ALP holds in the flow of her energy the vision of what

HCE has been and can be as well as the fear of his present absence. As that flow she has neither unity of meaning nor identity; witness the multiplicity of identities in the "many names" by which "her untitled mamafesta memorialising the Mosthighest has gone" (104.4–5). Efforts to establish unity of signification for the river gifts she bears her 111 children is futile. As flow that can be defined by her river banks, modified as she is giving to her husband or being taken into her father sea, ALP is choric energy, continually immersed in the cyclic motility of gathering as little rain cloud (her young form; Issy takes the cloud as one of her shapes), falling as rain (another of Issy's forms), moving through canals and streams (her 111 children) to flow into the river Liffey, losing her own identity as Liffey through flowing into her father the Irish Sea, evaporating into droplets, forming clouds, condensing into rain and thus continuing the cyclic flow. This movement is analogous to Kristeva's designation of the chora as a dynamics of "effectuat[ing] discontinuities by temporarily articulating them and then starting over, again and again" (*Revolution*, 26).

In her configuration of language, Kristeva opposes the thetic to the chora. Formed through proposition and judgment, the thetic is "that crucial place on the basis of which the human being constitutes himself as signifying and/or social" (*Revolution*, 67). Continually forming himself by offering propositions and evading judgments about himself, HCE manifests himself as social, thus signifying. Figured as force for civilization, HCE waxes eloquent about his accomplishments: "I sent my boundary to Botany Bay and I ran up a score and four of mes while the Yanks were huckling the Empire" (543.4–6), and "from the farthest of the farther of their fathers to their children's children's children they do inhabit it and hold it for me unencumbered and my heirs . . . with all the liberties and free customs" (545.16–19).

At the local level as well, HCE pronounces as to what constitutes happiness for citizens: "Obeyance from the townsmen spills felixity by the toun" (540.25–26). Identifying the thetic with positioning oneself in relation to a notion, Kristeva notes that "even if it is presented as a simple act of naming, we maintain that the thetic is already *propositional* (or syntactic) and that syntax is the ex-position of the thetic" (*Revolution*, 54). Where ALP's nature as fluid motion is consonant with her river identity, so HCE's as positional and positing is consonant with his mountain, land, and city identity. He continually positions himself in relation to accomplishments that he hopes may offset his guilt and to the "innocence" that bespeaks that guilt. Hopeful of a superior stature—one of his identities suggests divinity: he is "heavengendered" (137.14) and he walks "Head-in-Clouds" (18.23); another suggests nobility ("as an earl, he counts" [128.5–6])—HCE sees himself as ALP's "zoravarn lhorde and givnegenral" (243.10), similar to the thetic's efforts to govern the chora's flow that disregards rule and convention.

Coming into play through the effects of the chora as the symbolic does through the effects of the thetic, the semiotic mode of language is rhythmic, intonational, and "heterogeneous to meaning and signification." It constantly tears open the symbolic, introducing "wandering or fuzziness into language" (*Desire*, 133, 136), and thus remodels language, opening it to creativity. These statements describe Shem, his greater alliance with his mother than his father, his insistence on a plurality of possibilities, his continual transgression of rules.

From Shaun's stance in rule- and convention-governed language, Shem's writing is a farce, "a farced epistol to the hibruws" (228.33–34), and "acomedy of letters" (425.24). Whether to highbrows or Hebrews, Shem's writing might as well be Greek to Shaun since Shem "would wipe alley english spooker, multaphoniaksically spuking, off the face of the erse" (178.6–7). His linguistic transgressions spill over into other areas governed by convention, so that Shaun, upholder of all convention, feels called upon to condemn his brother as "always blaspheming" (177.23) and a "mental and moral defective" (177.16). But the upshot of Shem's words, when he speaks on his own behalf after Shaun's verbal mauling, is that "he lifts the lifewand and the dumb speak" (195.5). The corresponding action for Shaun is that "he points the deathbone and the quick are still" (193.29). The effect of transgressiveness, reading metaphorically, is life enhancing, en-"voicing" silence. Correspondingly, the effect of adherence to convention is death enhancing, silencing voice.

The symbolic concerns itself with communicativeness in the form of sentences and sequences that follow from recognition of boundaries set by social, cultural, and linguistic constraints. Such operations are consistent with Shaun's activities: his identity with his father, his attempts to control what he perceives as Shem's defiance of laws, his insistence on social and religious prescripts. Thus, Shaun is the text's commandment giver and sermon deliverer. In his version of the Ten Commandments, Shaun declaims, "First thou shalt not smile. Twice thou shalt not love. Lust, thou shalt not commix idolatry" (433.22–23). His sermons prescribe lust by proscribing it.

Openly inviting all to desire and enjoy her, endlessly available in potentiality, Issy configures the jouissance of language, its sensuality. The following are some of her siren songs to the reader:

> Can't you read by dazzling ones through me true? Bite my laughters, drink my tears. Pore into me, volumes, spell me stark and spill me swooning. . . . Transname me loveliness, now and here me for all times! (145.18–21)

and

> I was listening to every treasuried word I said fell from my dear mot's tongue (146.26–28)

and

> Is it not divinely deluscious? But in't it bafforyou? *Misi, misi!* Tell me till my thrillme comes! I will not break the seal. I am enjoying it still. (148.1–3)

Kristeva's notion of jouissance includes the notion of a "*totality* of enjoyment—simultaneously sexual, spiritual, physical, conceptual," but a total joy without mystical connotation.[8] The Issy whom Shaun addresses in his sermons of III.2 (see 432–54) is such a totality, though a comic one, in line with the comic/cosmic vision of *Finnegans Wake,* which in itself is another manifestation of Kristevan jouissance, "simultaneously sexual, spiritual, physical, conceptual."

"The aim of this practice [the texts of Joyce, Céline, Artaud]," writes Kristeva, is

> not only to impose a music, a rhythm—that is, a polyphony—but also to wipe out sense through nonsense and laughter. This is a difficult operation that obliges the reader not so much to combine significations as to shatter his own judging consciousness in order to grant passage through it to this rhythmic drive constituted

by repression and, once filtered by language and its meaning, experienced as jouissance. (*Desire*, 142)

Issy figures such a jouissance. She is not the product of "combine[d] significations," and even less that of the reader's "judging consciousness"; rather, she figures the place where the reader/Shem-Shaun arrives after breaking through that judging consciousness to reach the choric "rhythmic drive" that, after being "filtered by language and its meaning" the reader experiences as a totality of joys simultaneously sexual, spiritual, physical, conceptual.

Several other Kristevan formulations involving jouissance help delineate Issy's role here. "Art—this semiotization of the symbolic—thus represents the flow of jouissance into language" (*Revolution*, 79); and "poetry becomes an explicit confrontation between jouissance and the thetic, that is, a permanent struggle to show the facilitation of drives within the linguistic order itself" (*Revolution*, 81). Thus, HCE as thetic, Shem as semiotic, and Shaun as symbolic all seek Issy. (ALP of course does not seek Issy because, as chora, ALP *is* Issy's parent form.) As jouissance, Issy is the pleasure Shem would manifest through his writing; the danger Shaun must warn against in his sermons and yet be powerfully drawn to; the child HCE would control by incorporation with himself, with the result that, after a time, Issy would give birth to a product no longer herself: "Rawmeash, quoshe with her girlic teangue. If old Herod with the Cormwell's eczema was to go for me like he does Snuffler whatever about his blue canaries I'd do nine months for his beaver beard" (260.n1). If as thetic HCE is "the linguistic order itself," then Issy as jouissance is "the facilitation of drives" and the *Wake* as poetry or poesis is the site of Issy's operating within HCE and his efforts to come to terms with her. Joyce thus genders writing as female and male, both in its biological/psychological dynamics as well as in its materialization as the flesh made Word.[9]

Just as each character embodies writing as well as writes the body, so too does the Letter bear the double identity of material object and play of signifiers. Throughout the *Wake* but especially in I.5, we encounter a near surplus of information about the Letter's material characteristics. It rejects the use of quote marks and abjures other punctuation marks as well though uses its own system to show the reader when and how long to pause ("please stop," "stop," "full stop"). We learn some details about the appearance of letter and envelope, including the tears, puncture marks, and stains. The Letter's words, we are told, run up, down, transversely, diagonally, and circularly upon the page. Written in a universal language, it can't be read in the usual terms; instead, it has its own Morse code of script, which must be learned on its own terms in process of reading the Letter. Problems with accurate typesetting obscure an already difficult text. Its presence is certainly real though its meaning is equally certainly unclear. It is a product of the arbitrariness of signs as well as the inevitable parallax involved in the multiplicity of perspectives from which it may be read. Given such circumstances, small wonder that its "ideal reader" will suffer "from an ideal insomnia" (120.13–14).

Embodying writing as the play of signifiers unfixed by signifieds, the Letter demonstrates the sign as the play of difference. "Maggy's tea" becomes "majesty, if heard as a boost from a born gentleman" (116.24–25); and "maggers" is a variant of "the more generally accepted *majesty*" (120.17). The difference between "maggers" and "majesty" is socioeconomic in origin. Addressing the king who is passing along the highway and sees his vassal in a curious state of attire, complete with hoisted flowerpot perched on top of a pike, Humphrey Chimpden responds to the king's question with "Naw, yer maggers, aw war jist a cotchin on thon bluggy earwuggers" (31.10–11). The difference between "majesty" and "Maggy's tea," however, has another origin. Homonyms, they show metaphoric substitution in that here, majesty *is* Maggy's tea, Maggy's tea *is* majesty; and they show metonymic combination in that Maggy's tea or the consummation of sexuality (the *Wake*'s teastains having consistently sexual connotations) is associated with the large-scale capacity for pleasure and power of majesty. Further, majesty has religious connotations in the *Wake* in addition to those of royalty, an example of which may be seen in the opening of ALP's letter to HCE: "Dear. And we go on to Dirtdump. Reverend. May we add majesty?" (615.12). Shaun's words, "His Diligence Majesty, our longdistance laird that likes creation" (457.23–24), seem to point to the God of creation. And in her closing monologue, ALP, inviting HCE to arise, suggests,

We might call on the Old Lord, what do you say? There's something tells me. He is a fine sport. Like the score and a moighty went before him. And a proper old promnentory. His door always open. For a newera's day. (623.4–7)

While the "Old Lord" clearly suggests Jarl van Hoother, who learned from the Prankquean to keep his door open, the capitalized "Old Lord" also suggests the Lord of Christianity, Jesus, whose "door" is always "open" to "sinners" that they may begin a "new era." As "the Allmaziful" (104.1), the Letter is the maze of difference; as "untitled mamafesta" (104.4), it is feast and festival of maternal generative power giving birth to difference rather than a manifesting of paternal thetic proposition.

The Letter not only has multiple authorships but also multiple "versions" existing in varying degrees of completeness. Given all this multiplicity, when we speak of the Letter, what are we talking about? Clive Hart identifies the "Boston, Mass." letter as the "main motif-complex," mentioning that *"Finnegans Wake* contains other letters, however, whose relationship to the main motif-complex is more tenuous," giving as examples of the latter those at pages 201 and 308. Hart lists as "Major Statements" of the "Boston, Mass." letter the following: those on pages 11, 111, 113, 116, 279.F1, 280, 301, 369–70, 413, 457, and 615.[10] Page 308 contains the "Nightletter" from "jake, jack and littlesousoucie" to "Pep and Memmy," reminding the parents that their time for control is ending ("youlldied") and that the younger generation intend to take over ("the babes that mean too"). The Letter on page 413 may be a speaking rather than a writing. Here Shaun is being interviewed by The Four and their ass, and so Shaun's words are probably spoken, the letter Shaun declaims to his inquisitors being one that he *would* write. In any case, Shaun here addresses himself "to the Very Honourable The Memory of Disgrace, the Most Noble, Sometime Sweepyard at the Service of the Writer." Actual or intended letter, Shaun shows here that Shem is not alone in plagiarizing and "stolentelling," drawing heavily on material written by, to, and about Swift. In the Letter Shaun incarnates HCE in his role of protesting innocence in relation to women but actually manifesting his guilt:

This, my tears, is my last will intesticle wrote off in the strutforit about their absent female assauciations which I, or perhaps any other person what squaton a toffette, have the honour to had upon their polite sophykussens in the real presence of devouted Mrs Grumby when her skin was exposed to the air.

About this passage, we can observe that in delivering a version of HCE's guilt, Shaun is running true to form as "post man," delivering the message of another.

Issy writes several letters, at pages 279 and 457–58, both of which are "pepette" love missives to potential lovers, both of which are "whisperings" rather than "writings": "Tizzy intercepted, flushing but flashing from her dove and dart eyes as she tactilifully grapbed her male corrispondee to flusther sweet nunsongs in his quickturned ear" (457.27–29). As with Shaun, here too Issy runs true to form as the material sensuosity of words, choosing the sense of hearing as the format for her letter.

Three of the letters are ALP's: on pages 113, 201, 615. Of these, the first and third show her efforts, respectively, to explain (away) and ask forgiveness for HCE's supposed crime. The second presents her river need for new banks. Although the first is clearly in letter format, the second and third appear in spoken format. These letters, too, are written out of the body/text identity of their writer/ speaker.

Four of the letters are forms of the "Boston, Mass." "traumscript" (623.36) or "transhipt" (111.09): on pages 111, 280, 301, 369–370. Each of these addresses "maggy" or one of its variants and is a condensation of formulas in social letter writing, wishing the other party well, reporting family news, beginning and closing with conventional forms, and so on. "Maggy" is elusive to identify, but for a first association we may note that it is a variant of "maggers" and thus a form of "majesty." Adaline Glasheen has this to say about the Maggies and Maggy:

> [They] steadily interchange with Magdalene (q.v.), and may go back to Maggy Magee (q.v.), who is present in some versions of "Finnegan's (q.v.) Wake." The letter from Boston is addressed to a single "Maggy" or "Majesty" (q.v.). The letter is from one part of a dissociated female personality to another—see Sally, Christine Beauchamp; and perhaps the split personalities are equivalent to Magdalene's seven (q.v.) evil spirits. . . . The Maggies are also Proust's madeleine (q.q.v.); and in "The Mime" the

Maggies are the cake which Angel and Devil (q.q.v.) would take as a prize.[11]

When we talk about the Letter, then, we are speaking of a composite that has at least five different perspectives of parallax: the children's view of the relation between generations as power shift, the male's discomfort and defensiveness about sexual guilt (HCE through Shaun's voice), and the female's relation to that guilt: Issy "inviting" it, the correspondent to "Maggy" domesticating it, and ALP exonerating it.

Besides the parallax of perspectives, which is a matter of writing the body, the various forms the Letter takes has another component, the embodiment of writing. At least three factors appear to be involved. First, the Letter's varying appearances instance the signifier's primacy over the signified and the signifier's signification taking its shape from its temporary recipient/writer, as Lacan shows for Poe's "The Purloined Letter."[12] Second, each variant of the Letter embodies its writer in the sense that the writer's letter is written out of and into the writer's body. Third, the embodiment of writing is often the embodiment of speaking. We noted earlier, for instance, that Issy's and Shaun's letters may be a speaking as well as a writing; this is the case with ALP's letters, too, though not for the "maggy" letters.

We have arrived, in other words, at language as the play of difference: the supplementarity of writing and speaking, the trace as embodiment of parallax. It is time to move from Kristevan to Derridean notions about language as we continue to consider incoherence as productivity in *Finnegans Wake*.

NOTES

1. For a study of the relation between writing and the body that takes a perspective different from what I do in this chapter, readers may want to examine Gabriel Josipovici's *Writing and the Body* (Princeton: Princeton University Press, 1982). Whereas I work with the body as site of biopsychological metaphor and synecdoche, Josipovici explores more literal connections between the body and writing.

2. I am indebted for this idea to an unknown reader for the *South Atlantic Review*. I had sent an earlier version of the present chapter 2 to that journal, and one of the readers offered the insight, which I have used here.

3. *Aufhebung* means "lifting up," but it also contains the opposed meanings of "conserving" as well as "negating." Thus, *Aufhebung* involves the

lifting to a "higher" degree of comprehensiveness what had been two opposed areas, in which both are conserved though negated in this new synthesis. This, of course, is the thesis-antithesis-synthesis paradigm, on which Marx, drawing on Hegel, based his notion of class struggle.

4. Julia Kristeva, "Joyce 'The Gracehoper' or the Return of Orpheus," in *James Joyce: The Augmented Ninth*, ed. Bernard Benstock (Syracuse: Syracuse University Press, 1988), 168. Hereafter in the present paragraph, pages referring to this article will be placed in parentheses.

5. Suzette A. Henke makes a closely related claim when she writes that "each of the multiple versions of the letter serves as a textual paradigm for the *Wake* itself, acting as a semiotic microcosm of the linguistic macrocosm in which it has, like a puzzle or rebus, been playfully embedded" (*James Joyce and the Politics of Desire* [New York: Routledge, 1990], 185).

6. The body in *Finnegans Wake*, as in *Ulysses*, is the carnivalesque body Mikhail Bakhtin writes of as "deeply positive. It is presented not in a private, egotistic form, severed from the other spheres of life, but as something universal, representing all the people." When Shaun dwells on the obscene in Shem's writing from and of the body, readers may understand this as the degradation Bakhtin defines, a de-grading, a "coming down to earth, the contact with earth as an element that swallows up and gives birth at the same time. To degrade is to bury, to sow, and to kill simultaneously, in order to bring forth something more and better" (*Rabelais and His World*, trans. Helene Iswolsky [Cambridge: M. I. T. Press, 1968], 19, 21).

7. Devlin, "Joyce's Look," 889.

8. See Leon S. Roudiez's introduction to *Desire in Language*, 16.

9. Joyce's figuring of writing is sexist in that it identifies the female as object of others' desire and defines her largely through unconscious processes while at the same time identifying the male as subject for others, and creator, albeit with help from the female muse, as well as transmitter of that subject. Joyce's writing is not sexist insofar as the female role in writing is equally significant with the male role. Kimberly Devlin formulates the *Wake*'s Letter itself as configured on both gender lines:

This final bifurcation of ALP's letter along gender lines hints that female writing within androcentric structures is inevitably a double document, containing both an official and repressed text: the former speaks the language of male desire, telling the father what he might like to hear, while the latter tells a different story, one that is at odds with patriarchal imperatives and concerns—or perhaps has nothing to do with them at all. This dualistic letter mentioned within the final monologue is a miniature of the monologues as a whole, for ALP's speech . . . is indeed a double document, uttered in conflicting tongues as it were. (*Wandering and Return*, 161).

10. Clive Hart, *Structure and Motif in "Finnegans Wake"* (Evanston, Ill.: Northwestern University Press, 1962), 232. Subsequent references are given in the text.

11. Adaline Glasheen, *Third Census of Finnegans Wake* (Berkeley and Los Angeles: University of California Press, 1977), 181.

12. See Jacques Lacan, "Seminar on 'The Purloined Letter,'" trans. Jeffrey Mehlman, in *Contemporary Literary Criticism,* 2d ed., ed. Robert Con Davis and Ronald Schleifer (New York: Longman, 1989), 301–20.

Chapter 4

The *Wake* as Derridean Site

The competing domains of Kristeva's trios—genotext, semiotic, chora; phenotext, symbolic, thetic—imply a reading of *Finnegans Wake* in which the *Wake*'s language signifies the needs and desires of the unconscious in competition with those of the conscious of the speaking subject, incoherence understood as product of that competition, the impact of semiotic processes confronting symbolic operations. Like Kristeva in not deliberately setting out to construct a theory of language, Jacques Derrida creates terms and employs notions that nevertheless do offer an account of language. And this account implies a somewhat different reading of the *Wake* from Kristeva's, one that emphasizes the uncontrolled proliferations its language generates rather than, as in Kristeva's, the oppositional nature of its processes. Again like Kristeva's, this account allows incoherence a productive role in signification, but rather than locate the site of incoherence in the dualism of the speaking subject, Derrida locates incoherence in language, where it becomes another name for the indeterminacy inherent in language not stabilized—and not capable of being stabilized except through the violence of metaphysical constructs—by rooting it in a transcendental signified. This incoherence/indeterminacy is visible in the capacity of written words to escape the limits of interpretation, calling instead for openness and multiplicity. As does Kristeva, Derrida denies the capacity of his terms to be systematized since, like Kristeva's and Joyce's uses of names that designate processes, each of Derrida's terms accumulates additional associations and significations as the reader encounters it in successive contexts. But in exploring the language of *Finnegans Wake* through these notions, using them to observe incoherence at work there, it will be helpful to consider Derrida's ideas as though the successive accumulations of significance can be layered here.

Derrida's notions of *text* and *différance*, with what Derrida calls its "nonsynonymic substitutions" of *supplementarity, trace, spacing, play,* and *dissemination,* are especially helpful in addressing the incoherence that readers experience in the endless multiplicity of the language of *Finnegans Wake.* Virtually any sentence from the *Wake* testifies to its status as *text.*[1] Composed of thousands of texts, *Finnegans Wake* appears well on its way to generating other thousands that will carry on its textuality. If the text shows us something not formulatable as a proposition, the *Wake* illustrates this in an exemplary manner. The vast play of humor as one response to the condition of existing in a secular universe, the abundance of language as gift giving, as in ALP's gifts to her 111 children, the *Wake's* numerous reflexive statements: all of these exemplify a showing forth of language as metaphoric and polysemic. No single interpretation can be abstracted from the text and shown to have primary significance. Thus, besides functioning as the expression of humor, the appearance of laughter in the text may express the braying of a donkey or the recitation of vowels. No one of these may be said to take precedence over the others. Besides offering metaphors that suggest the nature of the text, reflexive passages set forth motifs woven throughout the *Wake* as well as participate in its diachrony. Again, none of these functions is more central than another.

"Cryptic" and "undecidable,"[2] *Finnegans Wake* continually forces readers to confront what Saussure claimed was the arbitrary nature of language.[3] In erasing the boundaries between words, Joyce takes for granted this arbitrariness through his expansion of the capacity of signifiers to signify, as in the puns, portmanteau words, and transformations of word clusters such as the "dear dirty Dublin" series or the "half a tall hat" series. Any of the *Wake's* sentences models the signifier's liberation from subservience to an underlying teleology and announces the role of the signifier as generator of more and more signifiers/signifieds. If the *text's* meaning is deferred, *Finnegans Wake* has been exemplifying this trait since fragments of it began to appear in print in the mid 1920s. Although critics have explored many aspects of the text since that time, its meaning continues to defer itself. One of the many reflexive passages addresses this deferral, expressing it as a waiting:

> When the messanger of the risen sun, (see other oriel) shall give to every seeable a hue and to every hearable a cry and to each

spectacle his spot and to each happening her houram. The while we, we are waiting, we are waiting for. Hymn. (609.19–23)

While we can discuss the passage, we cannot interpret it with closure. What we can do is note associations appropriate to the passage, such as the condition of indefinite waiting it speaks to, its themes of messengers (Shaun), the status of Ireland (*Oriel* as an ancient Irish principality), the sight-sound relation, the suggestion of HCE ("every hearable a cry"), the status of religious observations in a secular world (hymn). But having noted these associations, we cannot offer propositional meaning. The lines instead suggest and intimate and show forth, Joyce's polysemy indefinitely deferring the possibility of containable meaning.

Derrida's notion of *différance* and its "nonsynonymic substitutions" provides a second model for understanding the *Wake*'s endlessly generating multiplicity, its incoherence. Neither a word nor a concept but instead an operation, *différance* is everywhere active in the operations of *Finnegans Wake*: the ten "thunderwords," the text's characters,[4] words that "structure" chapters, such as *heliotrope*, and Joyce's use of Vico's four-stage cycle in the development of nations: gods, heroes, citizens, *ricorso*.

Whether we are speaking of the *Wake*'s characters, its "plot," its syntax, or its words, we find the disruption and division by which *différance* manifests itself. For Joyce as for Derrida, the double gesture of using a term while simultaneously revealing its contradictions is necessary. It takes a variety of forms in *Finnegans Wake*: using enough of a word to make it recognizable but changing it enough so as to deny its referentiality; restructuring a word, phrase, or sentence to make it deny what it suggests ("my bosthoon fiend"); inverting through parody those forms and concepts traditionally considered "sacred" and honorific.

For Joyce as well as Derrida there is no name, no operation, no entity that is not marked by otherness. Names, operations, and entities continually slide into and merge with each other. Readers cannot stabilize any term through the creation of absolute oppositions based on the presence of a transcendental signified because Joyce deconstructs the possibility for any word or concept to take on a metaphysically stable role. *Différance* as scission and division is seen especially clearly in the fact that the characters of *Finnegans Wake* become not the sum of their parts but the differings and deferrings of their fragmentation. Some of The Four's associations instance this: elders of the text and patrons of the "mime," they are also monks of an ancient Irish order, the four magic objects brought to Ireland by the Tuatha Dé Danaan, the four compass directions, the elements of earth-air-fire-water, the four Irish provinces, and the four evangelists.

The characters and "plot" of *Finnegans Wake* inhabit the condition of being "always already." We meet The Four, for instance, on page 13, where rather than presenting a sense of their physical appearance or their primary roles in the text, a narrator thrusts upon us their multiple roles and associations, overwhelming us with their bewildering fragmentation. Not until page 368 does a narrator give readers a sense of the physical appearance of The Four; but this, like their introduction, serves to enforce our sense of their fragmentation. They are treated as always already existing as traces incapable of assuming presence. As new readers of *Finnegans Wake*, we may have approached the text with the expectation that its realms would swallow us, at least temporarily, during which time we would develop a strong sense of the presence of its characters, setting, plot. This did not happen, of course. Instead, we find that though the narrators continually suggest places and times—the Willingdone Museyroom, the midden heap, Shem's room, 1132, 566, dusk, dawn—the continual destruction of continuity by the insertion of overlapping and juxtaposed fragments of varying lengths subverts and thwarts our orientation to seek textual presence.

As *différance* continually breaks up in a chain of nonsynonymic substitutions, so do the text's characters and motifs. The text's males merge with and substitute for each other, as do its females, yet each remains distinct for us. Thus, although HCE, Shaun, the Cad, Hosty, and the three soldiers in the park all replace each other, each has his own particular operations, just as do Issy, Nuvoletta, Isolde, Alice, Sosie, and Isis.

Supplementarity[5] offers another means for thinking about the *Wake*'s endless capacity to proliferate possibilities for interpretation. Our early associations with Shaun, for example, include his being the "good" half of the twins as opposed to the "bad" Shem. But this view is supplemented by others, such as Shaun's insufferable boorishness and advocacy of an objectionable ethics, advising his brother, for instance, that "he prophets most who bilks the best" (305.1–2). Nor is the new whole allowed to stand. In another of his associations, Shaun incarnates the future leader, hope of his people; and this is no more than half an ironic identity since the ass, representing some wiser framework than most other characters, recognizes Shaun's potential for good.[6] But neither does the new whole stand—in fact, it is not a whole but a chain of supplementation—since it too is supplemented in its turn.

Of the associations that cluster about Shaun, we cannot say that one is primary to his identity whereas the others are secondary. They link with and imply each other. And as supplementarity never reaches the condition of completeness and unity, neither will the supplementarity that creates Shaun, which means that he cannot help but be identified with Shem as well as with an extraordinarily broad range of other associations. In just this way, any term in the *Wake* links with other terms.[7] Supplementarity names the relation between Shem and Shaun. Though narrators position them as opposites, throughout the text they exchange places with each other, shown graphically in II.2 when the twins change sides during "half time." Neither appears without the direct or indirect involvement of the other; thus they imply and contain each other. Numerous statements throughout the text address this requisite condition between "opposites," as for instance, "This one once upon awhile was the other but this is the other nighadays" (561.5–6). Derrida's supplementarity is a dialectics of the rigorous questioning of the history of two opposing notions, with discovery through play of that point within circularity at which they intersect to become each other's *différance* and supplement. The *Wake* presents a number of instances of this process. St. Patrick as representative of a cultural awakening in Ireland and the Archdruid as upholder of the old ways both find themselves becoming colors in a village church window illuminated by the dawn. For all their opposition to each other, Burrus and Caseous are both sought by Nuvoletta, who desires to have each of their attentions but succeeds in capturing that of neither. Much as the Mookse arrogates his own supremacy and the Gripes abases himself, each is carried off to bed as an infant figure by a strong woman. In all three instances, the same force works upon and moves the opposing pair toward a point of intersection.

Joyce repeatedly acknowledged the importance for his development of *Finnegans Wake* of Giordano Bruno's notion of the coincidence of contraries. The question arises of the relation of Bruno's contraries to Derrida's supplement. Clearly, some parallels exist, as evidenced in these statements of Bruno:

> On this diversity and opposition depend order, symmetry, complexion, peace, concord, composition and life. So that the worlds are composed of contraries, of which some, such as earth and water, live and grow by help of their contraries, such as the fiery suns

and

> The beginning, middle, and end of the birth, growth, and perfection of whatever we behold is from contraries, by contraries, and to contraries; and wherever contrariety is, there is action and reaction, there is motion, diversity, multitude, and order.[8]

When we begin to discuss Bruno's ideas, however, gaps appear between how and why his contraries and Derrida's supplementarity operate. Bruno saw the function of opposites as bringing about a new unity, but Derrida denies the possibility of unity. Bruno joins both Joyce and Derrida, however, in wanting to eliminate transcendence in explaining causation, choosing instead to locate the causes of human and natural events internal to the world rather than in the external causation both Plato and Aristotle had posited. But the very conditions making possible and necessary for Bruno the coincidence of opposites—the basic unity of all that exists, including the transient and the permanent, within the infinite unity of Being—align him with metaphysics and acceptance of the transcendental signified. That such is Bruno's position is clear from his statements that "contraries coincide in this one and infinite" and "the principle of being is one."[9] Derrida, of course, recognizes transience and multiplicity. That the soul can attain union with the One is the basis for Bruno's belief that people can achieve truth. On the contrary, Derrida declares we can grasp only truths, which are necessarily partial and fragmentary. For Bruno, reality is a unitary process in which matter is both content and form. While Derrida too is anti-idealist, he also deconstructs materialism, and for him reality is marked by *différance* rather than unity.

Judging by the use Joyce makes of contraries in *Finnegans Wake*, he has displaced Bruno's contraries into Derridean-like realms where no metaphysical unifying principle, no singular truth, no reality as a unitary process serves a transcendental signified; instead, the necessary attraction of opposites functions as the play of *différance*, manifesting differing, deferral, fragmentation, and polysemy. And yet, for Joyce the possibility remains that as artist he can construct a unified work of art. Derrida's later work, such as *Glas*, suggests that he may be positioning philosophy and juxtapositional art as supplementary, although his rejection of the possibility of unity remains as strong as ever. Joyce sees polarities as Blakean negation, whether they take the form of Shem/Shaun or unity/difference. Blakean opposition contains negation, as HCE comprehends the forms of Shem and Shaun and *Finnegans Wake* comprehends unity and difference, where the copula of metaphor asserts a coupling that draws negations or polarities into dynamic interaction that lies beyond the semantic-semiotic problem of opposition.

Trace, another of the nonsynonymic substitutions for *différance*, also provides some contexts for understanding the *Wake*'s operation of incoherence as endless multiplicity. If the trace functions to eliminate truth as a stable and continuing presence, then each of the *Wake*'s characters undermines its capacity to show itself as a present, unified whole through the play of its traces. ALP as nagging wife, insisting that HCE close up the pub and come to bed, denies ALP as the young seductress who lured and won HCE in the potency of his youth. Both of these deny ALP as gift-giving mother of 111 children. And all three refuse the ALP who flows bitterly, fearfully, into her father/ocean, renouncing for a while a separable identity. In the same way, a narrator moves Shaun through the play of traces as he successively modulates from Shaun to Jaun to Haun to Yawn.

Joyce's handling of time in the *Wake* has generally puzzled readers. If we take the trace as paradigm for time's functioning, however, we can begin to approach an understanding.[10] Each moment is a trace that manifests its connectedness to moments from the "past"—even to the distant past—as readily as to moments nearer at hand. The play of traces denies linear chronology, moving us between Eocene and Pleistocene, ancient Rome, the Middle Ages, the 1920s and 1930s, sometimes within a single sentence. Nor does a given year represent only the time to which it seems to point; in fact, sometimes it refers as readily to space as to time.

The configuration of associations that cluster about 1132 offers an instance of this. Sometimes a narrator implies it designates a specific year, as "in the year of the flood 1132" (387.23). As it first appears in the *Wake* on page 13, 1132 is followed by the abbreviation for Anno Domini; yet in the paragraph containing it, no reference is made to an historical event. A number of critics have suggested possible events which occurred in this year, trying to understand why Joyce named 1132 rather than some other number, among them the birth of Lawrence O'Toole and the unification of Ireland. Another way of exploring the significance of 1132, however, is to investigate its relation to other numbers in the text. Several possibilities suggest themselves. The year of Finn MacCool's death is traditionally given as 283. The *Wake* has four historians. One way to view 1132 is as the product of these two numbers. 1132 is linked several times with 566; another way of deriving it is as the product of two—a number Joyce associates with females—and 566. But 1132 also has associations with the characters of the text: ALP and HCE are each 1 and 1; side by side, they form 11, the cabalistic number of regeneration; they have twin sons and their daughter has a double personality; altogether they have three children; within the law of falling bodies, 32 suggests the fall, in all its senses.[11] Also, 1132 reduces to 7 ($1 + 1 + 3 + 2 = 7$), and 7 reduces to 1 ($7 + 6 + 5 + 4 + 3 + 2 + 1 = 28$ and 28 [$2 + 8$] reduces to 10 and 10 [$1 + 0$] = 1). To attempt understanding of 1132, then, is to join in the play of traces. As 1132 moves throughout the *Wake*, it accumulates associations involving the spatiality of time and the temporality of space. Their interrelations constitute the play of traces. One of the final narrators puts the matter in this way:

> Shamwork, be in our scheining! And let every crisscouple be so crosscomplimentary, little eggons, youlk and meelk, in a farbiger pancosmos. With a hottyhammyum all round. Gudstruce! Yet is no body present here which was not there before. Only is order othered. Nought is nulled. *Fuitfiat!* (613.13–14)

If the trace is that through which the present increases itself even as it disappears, an especially vivid illustration of this is ALP's act that by ending rebegins the text: her disappearing into the arms of her ocean/father and erasing her present self, to reappear in the text's next moment, its beginning, as "riverrun," where her otherness, always and already a textual effect, comes into play: as a near homonym of "reverend," an unspecified addressee of her letter (see 615.12) and, as a near homonym of the German *Erinnerung* or remembrance as McHugh indicates (*Annotations*, 3), the operation of memory. Rather than the presence of a thing, then, there is its trace, the simulacrum of a presence that dislocates, displaces, and refers beyond itself.[12]

Trace and supplementarity model the operations of contradiction and paradox we encounter while reading *Finnegans Wake*. If the trace is the sum of all possible relations which inhabit and constitute the sign, then we will not expect a *Wake*an character to take on a unified identity but will recognize it as infinitely expansible. This will be so in part because whereas the word is controlled by a teleology that governs it, the trace is not controlled and hence enjoys its capacity to generate multiplicity. This aspect of trace allows us to begin answering the question of what Joyce does in erasing the margins of a word so that the word becomes multiple in its suggestiveness. Following a word's successive forms as Joyce plays it across several chapters—as, for instance, *heliotrope* across II.1 and II.2—shows us at least as much about the text's construction as does a "plot" synopsis of those same chapters. To make this statement is to recognize that the signified is only trace and always in the position of signifier, as a glance at any of Joyce's portmanteau words shows.

Spacing names another of Derrida's terms whose description fits Joyce's writing practices.[13] Examining any of the *Wake*'s sentences reveals the existence of gaps. Within one sentence we are likely to experience portmanteau words, words from several languages besides English, allusions to other texts including songs and advertisements in addition to popular and classical literary works, syntax that refuses to resolve itself into the logic we expect, and puns that make sacrilege of the sacred, asserting the humor of the scatological.

For Joyce as well as Derrida, the mutual interpenetration of space and time is of interest. This is especially noticeable in Professor Jones's lecture, the Mookse and Gripes tale, and the Burrus and Caseous exchange. These three sections develop the answer to the eleventh question of I.6, would Shaun help to save his brother's soul if Shem asked his help: "if the fain shinner pegged you to shave his immartial, wee skillmustered shoul . . . would you?" (149.7–10).

Since the time-space relation is central to all three sections, a connection seems to be suggested between the problem of saving or refusing to save souls and the interchangeability of time and space, to which numerous passages refer.

> Is this space of our couple of hours too dimensional for you, temporiser? (154.25–26)

> Dime [time] *is* cash [space] and the cash system . . . means that I cannot now have or nothave a piece of cheeps in your pocket at the same time and with the same manners as you can now nothalf or half the cheek apiece I've in mind. (161.6–11)

> Of course the unskilled singer continues to pervert our wiser ears by subordinating the space-element, that is to sing, the *aria*, to the time-factor, which ought to be killed, *ill tempor*. (164.32–35)

But although a connection is suggested, we cannot formulate it, with the result that we are left with the gap between thoughts. Interpretation can explore but cannot bridge that gap.

Another nonsynonymic substitution of *différance, play*[14] also marks the movement of *différance* throughout *Finnegans Wake:* in the "nonlogical" relation between the dozen questions of I.6 and their answers; in the proceedings between St. Patrick and the Archdruid; in the relation among marginalia, footnotes, and text in II.2; in the movement from any one chapter or part of *Finnegans Wake* to the next. But though the *Wake* involves play to a much greater extent than nearly any other text, this play can never be completely free since it operates under certain laws which it, like all other forms of play, must find ways to transgress. The *Wake*'s transgressions are legion. Violations of virtually every convention we may have held about literature force themselves upon us until we tend to call for the relief of intact conventions: conventions about what a novel should do and be; about what an epic is; about the nature of connexity; about grammar, diction, and syntax; about the relations between one language and another; about spelling; about the process by which we come to find meaning in a text; about the nature of humor; and the list goes on. For any pattern we think we can find in the *Wake*, the text confounds us because of its degree of play, whether we are speaking of a pattern in the language, in the treatment of a character, in the "structure" of a chapter, a book, or the whole text. *Finnegans Wake* suggests all kinds of patterns, but as we pursue them, they evaporate, leaving us with either an inaccurate though impressive-sounding generalization or a generalization that has to be so highly qualified as to have deconstructed itself as a paradigm.[15] *Play* names the process of what happens to language in the absence of the transcendental signified. In the center of the discourse—outside of which nothing exists, according to Derrida, since the author is just a name with no special ability to interpret the meaning of the text, and no telos exists to govern and stabilize meaning—what we have is laughter, which frees the discourse from becoming a system. As the recognition of laughter, of the limitation of rules, play is one way of discussing the significance of the laughter punctuating the *Wake*, as in such passages as these.

> Loud, heap miseries upon us yet entwine our arts with laughter low!
> Ha he hi ho hu. (259.8–10)

> Hohohoho, moulty Mark!
> You're the rummest old rooster ever flopped out of a Noah's ark. (383.8–9)

> Mattheehew, Markeehew, Lukeehew, Johnheehewwheehew! Haw! (399.30–31)

But *Wake*an laughter is not only laughter; the "Haw," here, is also the bray of a donkey; the "ha he hi ho hu," the recitation of vowels.

As "the rain . . . of unsummable meanings" we encounter in a text, *dissemination*, the last of the nonsynonymic substitutions for *différance* that concerns us, gives a name to the experience most readers undergo in reading *Finnegans Wake*. Geoffrey Hartman notes that dissemination acknowledges "we no longer live in a world defined by certain writings having testamentary force. . . . There is no way to canonize or close a series whose very character is centrifugal and disseminative."[16] Joyce's use of texts in the *Wake* is such an acknowledgment, where Dion Boucicault's *Arrah-na-Pogue* and "The House That Jack Built" share equal billing with the Lord's Prayer and the Apostles' Creed.

Strongly marked by otherness, the notions of text and *différance*, with its "nonsynonymic substitutions," give names to effects we experience in reading *Finnegans Wake:* incoherence as our experience of the endless proliferations that language generates, incoherence as our name for the multiplicity that as readers we must do something productive with or find ourselves overwhelmed by. Once we can use incoherence productively, that is, when we can produce out of it, with it, then we no longer speak of incoherence. Incoherence in this view names an initial stage of experiencing overabundance or supersaturation. It indicates the condition of not yet being able to produce order but does not imply lack or failure.

Beyond giving names to reading effects, text and *différance* also offer a dynamics for the way language operates in *Finnegans Wake.* The *Wake*'s language is not exceptional to language processes in this view; rather, it is representative and paradigmatic of them. In foregrounding what most other writings work to deny, the *Wake* requires us to confront our assumptions about meaning, reading, connexity. Where Kristeva's warring terms suggest an oppositional reading of *Finnegans Wake* with the speaking subject torn between chora and thetic demands, semiotic and symbolic expression, Derrida's terms of text and différance suggest an endlessly proliferating reading of *Finnegans Wake* as the continual production of signifiers marked by continual deferral of signification and pervasive intertextuality.

NOTES

1. Derrida views language as an arbitrary construct rather than a truth-claiming referent to preexisting reality. Books, according to him, claim to tell the truth about things and about the nature of the world; *texts* comment on other texts. Where a book presents the truth about a totality identifiable as a relatively determinable content, a *text* is an act of writing that recognizes itself as necessarily incomplete and tied to other texts, both to those upon which it comments as well as to others.

2. These are Barbara Johnson's terms for describing a text. See her "Rigorous Unreliability," *Critical Inquiry* 11 (1984): 280.

3. Saussure had claimed that the relation of signifier to signified is arbitrary. Kristeva, via Benveniste, corrects this formulation:

Basically, as Benveniste has noted, it is not the relationship between the signifier {*oks*} and the signified "ox" that is arbitrary. The link {*oks*}-"ox" is necessary: the concept and the sound-image are inseparable and are in an "established symmetry." What is *arbitrary* is the relation between this sign (signifier/signified): {*oks*} and the reality it names, in other words, the relation between the language symbol in its totality and the real outside it that it symbolizes. (*Language: The Unknown*, trans. Anne M. Menke [New York: Columbia University Press, 1989], 16)

4. If by character one has in mind constructs appearing in fiction and definable by discrete identity, self-consistency, uniqueness and separability from other characters, then *Finnegans Wake* has no characters. In using the term character, I redefine it so as to designate an umbrella name for a cluster of related processes. Thus, ALP designates such processes of flow, self-renewal, nurturing of others; HCE designates such processes as accretion, cultural construction, the subject as desiring and guilty. Similarly, though the notion of plot as the linearly sequential ordering of narrative events must be put under erasure, textual situations occur in which such a word is helpful. At such times, I will designate the double gesture as "plot."

5. One of Derrida's substitutions for *différance*, the supplement adds something that was missing, but when added, it reconstitutes the thing to which it was added. Though the supplement has been considered secondary to and coming later than what it supplements, Derrida insists that the supplement is inseparable from and implied by the thing it supplements.

6. The ass, in its functions as intermediary and interpreter and in its associations with points of intersection and places that hold humans, suggests a human rather than a divine perspective, one that recognizes that human limitation and potential are concurrent with each other rather than mutually exclusive. The ass's wisdom, accordingly, recognizes the relation of supplementarity between opposites rather than acknowledges presence resulting from the hierarchizing of the privileged members of binary oppositions. Joyce perhaps noted such an ass in the biblical ass of Balaam. See Numbers 22:21–31.

7. Derrida's notion of supplementarity has much in common with Umberto Eco's notion of unlimited semiosis. See, for instance, Eco's mapping of the *Wake*an term "meanderthaltale" in *The Role of the Reader* (Bloomington: Indiana University Press, 1979), 75.

8. The first quote comes from Bruno's *On the Infinite Universe*, in *Cause, Principle, and Unity*, trans. Jack Lindsay (Westport, Conn.: Greenwood Press, 1962), 33. The second comes from Bruno's *The Expulsion of the Triumphant Beast*, also quoted in Lindsay's translation of *Cause, Principle, and Unity*, 34.

9. Bruno, *Cause, Principle, and Unity*, 147, 149.

10. One way the trace closes off the possibility of presence-as-truth is its relation to both "past" and "future." This relation reconstitutes the present not as a moment isolatable from other moments but as a link that signifies only in relation to other links. Such relatedness extends not only to contiguous but also to widely separated links.

11. Bernard Benstock brought to my attention the notion of 11 as the cabalistic number of regeneration (private correspondence).

12. Jacques Derrida, "Differance," *Speech and Phenomena*, trans. David B. Allison (Evanston, Ill.: Northwestern University Press, 1973), 156.

13. As the visibility of the trace, spacing is recognition of the gaps that lie between and within thoughts. Whereas traditional interpretation attempts to minimize these gaps by making connections that may be implied only in the most indirect ways by the text, spacing opens the gaps as wide as possible. The result is the disruption of the text's coherence and stability, the establishment of its undecidability.

14. Not a logic in the usual sense of the word, play is nevertheless the logic that allows the text "free play," as opposed to the logic of dialectics, which depends on a telos that orients author and reader as to the desired and predetermined effect or result.

15. This is an example of play as the operation that prevents a word, concept, or enunciation from summarizing and governing, from the theological presence of a center, the movement and textual spacing of differences. See Jacques Derrida, *Positions*, trans. Alan Bass (Chicago: University of Chicago Press, 1981), 14.

16. Geoffrey H. Hartman, *Saving the Text* (Baltimore: Johns Hopkins University Press, 1981), 80, 63.

Chapter 5

Joyce, Derrida, Heliotrope

The fit between Derrida's terms of text and *différance* and the language practices of *Finnegans Wake* suggests a similarity in the verbal operations of Joyce and Derrida, each writer using words in ways that manifest *différance* and textuality. Because *heliotrope* is a word both make significant use of, it invites exploration as a measure of the extent of this similarity. For Joyce, *heliotrope* is the focus around which the movement of II.1 plays, although the word as such does not appear until the following chapter. *Heliotrope* is the color that Glugg must guess in the children's game Joyce called "Angels and Devils or colours." It names the color of the drawers his young love Izod is wearing, and though she provides several dozen hints and clues to guide him to the correct answer, Glugg fails to "read" the information Izod offers him. *Heliotrope*, here, names the situation of frustrated desire.[1]

In "White Mythology," *heliotrope* is important in Derrida's argument that figures of speech and especially metaphor permeate the philosophic text rather than are excluded by it. Though metaphors are concepts, Derrida shows that like all conceptual knowledge, they are neither clear nor certain. *Heliotrope* functions as Derrida's metaphor for metaphor as he deconstructs the notion that philosophemes are essentially independent of figurative language and hence express knowledge more directly than do other kinds of language. With it, too, he deconstructs the notion that a metaphor for metaphor exists in an originary and founding sense.

The associations that the two *heliotropes* gather about themselves follow from their contexts. Derrida's *heliotrope* begins as movement toward the sun, "naturally" generating the extension to light as knowledge and dark as ignorance. Because differentiating between ignorance and knowledge has been a major concern of philosophy, it appears that the sun "fathers" philosophic metaphor as the source out of which other metaphors spring. *Heliotrope* thus names the trope of metaphor. The movement of *heliotrope* describes the movement of metaphor, not only in its turning toward an object of attraction in giving a name that is not its own to the thing, but also in its movement away from that attraction. Just as the sun hides itself, eclipses itself, so the metaphor conceals and obscures as it erases the line dividing the thing's given name from its metaphoric name. *Heliotrope* recognizes the steady quality of the attraction between two names but also measures the inherent unsteadiness, the capacity of metaphor to be not-itself, to be other. *Heliotrope* thus names the capacity of language for polysemy.

Occurring within the context of a children's guessing game, Joyce's *heliotrope* measures another movement of attraction, that of one sex for the other. Typical of many children's games, "Angels and Devils" allows youngsters to try out adult roles in play form, the roles here of love and courtship.[2] But childhood is marked by impotence in a variety of forms, and Glugg is trapped in a child's sexual impotence, shown by his being unable to guess the color of Izod's drawers.[3] Though he lusts after Izod and though Izod desires him to "know" her through the several dozen hints she provides through anagrams and conundrums, Glugg cannot "penetrate" the sexual knowledge Izod offers. Joyce's *heliotrope*, then, names a stage of sexuality as well as measures the tendency of language toward polysemy.

Both *heliotropes*, however, are strongly marked by *différance*. For neither the *heliotrope* of "White Mythology" nor that of the Children's Games chapter is it possible to fix meaning as stable presence. Joyce's *heliotrope* never appears as such in the chapter of which it operates as absent center but rather occurs only in the form of anagrams, variations on anagrams, and conundrums. Not until the following chapter does it announce itself in its "natural" or "correct" form, when Shem—who had played the role of Glugg—provides the answer he had previously sought in the form of a marginal note that comments ironically on the opposing text: "In snowdrop, trou-de-dentelle, flesh and heliotrope" (265.L1). The answer has been deferred from one chapter to the next, corresponding to the appropriate stage of Shem's development: in II.1, Shem-Glugg functions as a child at play; in II.2, as an adolescent greatly occupied with sexual knowledge. Joyce does not allow an "originary presence" to develop about the word as he plays it through the games chapter but rather keeps it in a condition of fluid motion. Not only does the color move physically as Izod dances, broods, and leads the Flora girls from one area to another; but it moves psychologically as the sign of Izod's burgeoning sexuality and socially as the indicator of Izod's leadership of the Floras, herself the flower named heliotrope.

Derrida's *heliotrope* is as strongly marked by *différance* as is Joyce's. Although not absent from the essay in the sense in which Joyce's word absents itself from the chapter, the *heliotrope* of "White Mythology" certainly "eludes the grasp of a pure, self-present awareness":[4] *heliotrope* as sensory sun is the prime, unitary, nonmetaphor around which other figures turn and is simultaneously the divided, composite metaphor that itself requires other metaphors to describe its nature and actions; it is at once the source of metaphor and of the inevitably catachretic nature of metaphor. Derrida's *heliotrope* defers itself through the cycle in which it continually engages, constructing its own destruction and then resurrecting itself to new metaphor. Metaphor self-destructs, that is, either because it mistakenly attempts to make itself coordinate with a truth that exists apart from syntax but must necessarily fail in this effort since it can exist only within language; or else because it unfolds toward polysemy without limit and thus explodes the opposition between the metaphoric and the "proper" meaning. But given the "natural" tendency of language to metaphor, *heliotrope* can neither stay frozen in timeless truth nor remain shattered by infinite polysemy. In resurrecting to new metaphor, it begins the cycle again. Finally, Derrida's *heliotrope* denies the possibility of the sun to function as originary metaphor. Although it would seem "natural" to consider the sun as the father of all figures since all figures turn around it, it is impossible that a metaphor for metaphor should exist. If there were a central, fundamental metaphor, monosemy would be the result; but since all language leads to polysemy, metaphor exists only as the plural *metaphors*. Rather than the sun be an originary metaphor, it requires metaphor to define itself as it "casts" its rays, "travels" in its elliptical orbit, "hides" behind clouds, and so on.

The "nonsynonymic substitutions" for *différance* offer even more instructive means than their parent term for assessing the difference between how Joyce and Derrida use *heliotrope*. Both writers view *heliotrope* as supplementary. Derrida's sun as composite and metaphoric adds itself to and replaces the sun as unique, unitary, and nonmetaphorical. Joyce's Chuff adds himself as sight and space and son/sun to Glugg as hearing and time and dark. Neither one of the members in the pairs Glugg/Chuff and nonmetaphoric sun/metaphoric sun is prior to the other; they exist rather as each other's supplement.

Derrida and Joyce both treat *heliotrope* as trace rather than as word. Derrida's sun gives rise to nonmetaphor that divides to recognize its inherently metaphorical nature; *heliotrope* names itself as the movement of figures about the sun both literally and metaphorically; but *heliotrope* names a flower, an herb, a stone, besides its sun-related significations. Derrida's *heliotrope* thus appears only as signifier. So does Joyce's, since it occurs only as anagram or conundrum, each appearance pointing toward new signifiers. Though several dozen exist in the chapter, two will serve as examples here. One of the conundrums Izod offers Glugg explains the articulation of the word he seeks: "Clap your lingua to your pallet, drop your jowl with a jolt, tambourine until your breath slides, pet a pout and it's out" (248.8–10). Another conundrum describes the physical surroundings in which *heliotrope* exists as a color which Izod wears:

> In the house of breathings lies that word, all fairness. The walls are of rubinen and the glittergates of elfinbone. The roof herof is of massicious jasper and a canopy of Tyrian awning rises and still descends to it. A grape cluster of lights hangs therebeneath and all the house is filled with the breathings of her fairness. . . . There lies her word, you reder! (249.6–14)

The word as physically produced sound, the word as indicating the female genital environment: these are only two of the significations *heliotrope* receives in the chapter.

For Joyce, spacing takes on a role of primary importance throughout II.1, as indeed it does throughout the *Wake;* but for the Derrida of "White Mythology," the notion is not especially significant since in the essay he moves in relatively traditional ways from one thought to another.[5] The three anagrams that follow one another exemplify the importance of spacing for Joyce: "O theoperil! Ethiaop lore, the poor lie" (223.28).[6] Not only do anagrams represent the spacing inherent in words as arbitrary constructs of letters, but this succession of anagrams illustrates spacing in relation to the associations each one calls forth. We jump from the peril into which the *Wake* casts theology and the peril with which *theos* can threaten the *Wake* into the lure and lore of Ethiopia and from there into the at least double recognition that a lie can be a poor one and that the poor can lie.

   Play as an operation on *heliotrope* functions differently in "White Mythology" than in II.1. Derrida puts *heliotrope* into play as both the metaphor of metaphor and the recognition that there can be no originary metaphor, that metaphor is always plural. He ends the essay with the insistent reminder that *heliotrope* has been put into play rather than fixed as center: "The heliotrope can always be *relève*.[7] And it can always become a dried flower in a book. . . . Heliotrope also names a stone." In contrast with this decentering of Derrida's *heliotrope*, Joyce makes of his a center, though an absent one. The immature sexuality or unconsummated desire that *heliotrope* projects never veers off into otherness, never contradicts its own operations. Though Joyce plays with the word, he does not put *heliotrope* into play in the Derridean sense. If this is so, then Derrida must be wrong, or else I am wrong and Joyce's *heliotrope* is only the illusion of a center. Here is a text which admits the practices of supplementarity and spacing but rejects play—and yet these terms, while nonsynonymic, are substitutes for each other. But is *heliotrope* only the illusion of a center? If it were, we could locate other possible identities for *heliotrope* that would exist outside the sphere of sexuality. Such is not the case, however. At this point let us harbor the possibility that Derrida's formulation of the relation among his terms is flawed. As we shall see, the confusion deepens when we consider the last of the nonsynonymic "substitutions."

   The same sharp difference that divides Joyce's from Derrida's use of *play* concerning *heliotrope* also obtains in their use of *dissemination*. For Derrida, a *book* conveys truth about a subject matter, whereas a *text* disseminates itself, refusing summarizable formulas. But "White Mythology" tends to convey a "truth": that philosophy does not project a univocal reality that exists in an absolute presence beyond and independent of words but rather it projects the polysemy of metaphor that exists in a world necessarily formed and shaped by the language used to represent that world. Now while monosemic truth *is* deconstructed by metaphoric polysemy, nevertheless to declare this is to formulate the "thesis" of Derrida's essay, a condition that a *text* must avoid. On Derrida's own terms, then, "White Mythology" exists as *book*, not as *text*. On the other hand, a thesis for the Children's Games chapter cannot be formulated. Like the cosmos of which it is microcosm, as is any part of the *Wake*, it IS; but its meaning is not expressible as a thesis or series of theses that declare a truth. The chapter thus disseminates itself, while Derrida's essay does not. What we have in Joyce's Children's Games chapter, then, is a *text* with a center, but that operates without play in the Derridean sense, yet nevertheless disseminates itself. And in "White Mythology" we have a decentered *book* that engages its chief term in play and yet projects a meaning. What we have encountered, I claim, is that Derrida has been caught up in the play of *différance* that denies his assertion that *supplementarity, trace, spacing, play,* and *dissemination* may be substituted for each other. Although the attributes Derrida attaches to each term describe some problems with multiplicity that the language of modern texts generates, Derrida has misformulated the relationship among those terms that, rather than operate in a substitutive manner, instead operate relatively independently, metonymically rather than metaphorically.

Significant similarities as well as striking differences also exist between Joyce's and Derrida's treatment of *heliotrope* as operation. Using Aristotle's definition of metaphor as the transport of names, Derrida makes *heliotrope* the metaphoric name for this act. Joyce's game of "Angels and Devils or colours" presents metaphor in action, as Glugg attempts the correct transport of names but produces only bad metaphor in his three rounds of efforts to guess Izod's color. Derrida speaks of metaphor's opening "the wandering of the semantic" as it loosens the truth relation between metaphor and referent.[8] Again, the children's game may be viewed as this wandering in action, both in the hints Glugg fails to "read" from Izod, and from the "wandering" of *heliotrope* in its various anagram and conundrum forms.

Derrida writes of the sun as father of metaphor and, since unique, nonmetaphorical, but subsequently shows that the sun is also divided, composite, and metaphorical in its dependence on figures to describe its own motions. A comparable situation of opposites as supplementarity exists in the Children's Games chapter, where Chuff as Sungod attracts all the Flora girls about him in heliolatry, making Chuff primary and unique; Joyce subsequently shows that

Chuff has failed to command the attention of Izod, who sits nearby, moping over Glugg's failure to "read" her signs, unaware of the potency of Chuff's beams, causing Chuff now to be divided in his effects.

Derrida notes that the philosophical metaphor turns toward the sun in its association of light with knowledge and dark with ignorance, making the philosophical metaphor "analagous to the heliotrope" (250). Joyce's Flora girls turn towards their sungod in heliolatry, drawn by the pure and nonsexual Chuff. But Izod yearns for Glugg, who is associated with darkness, to claim her. Here the dark is associated with sexuality rather than the more traditional ignorance. Ironically, the Flora girls turn towards Chuff in heliolatry while Izod wears heliotrope in a "dark" or "hidden" area.

For Derrida *heliotrope* is intimately associated with metaphor: "metaphor means heliotrope, both a movement turned toward the sun and the turning movement of the sun" (251). Joyce, on the other hand, associates *heliotrope* with synecdoche rather than metaphor. Heliotrope as the color of Izod's drawers is synecdochic of the potent attraction of "dark" and "hidden" sexuality, a sexuality that for children is powerfully desired but not consummated. Derrida writes that "insofar as it structures the metaphorical space of philosophy, the sun represents what is natural in philosophical language" (251). Correspondingly, we may assert that for Joyce, "Insofar as it structures the synecdochic space of the unconscious, sexuality represents what is pervasive and omnipresent in unconscious language," a statement recalling Kristeva's claim, and behind hers, Freud's, that sexuality structures the unconscious. But at this point we encounter a significant departure from what Derrida does with the sensory sun/metaphor connection to what Joyce implies about the sexuality/synecdoche connection.

Derrida's sensory sun "does not furnish poor knowledge solely because it furnishes poor metaphors, it is itself solely metaphorical," since it "bears within itself the means to emerge from itself" as it "accommodates itself to 'artificial' light, eclipses itself, ellipses itself" (251). *Heliotrope* as metaphor for the trajectory of metaphor is based on the sun's double nature of being *itself* as sensory sun and being *other* as eclipsed and darkened. Though synecdochic of the unconscious, sexuality does not bear "within itself the means to emerge from itself" since its drives and desires show a steady state of operation not only throughout the Children's Games chapter but throughout the *Wake*. Joyce's *heliotrope* as synecdoche of the unconscious, then, is based on the nature of sexuality to be only itself, never other. This implies that sexuality is (uniquely) before language, that it is not submitted to the chain of signifiers.

For both Joyce and Derrida, however, *heliotrope* involves cyclic return. Because the movement of the sun presents the movement of metaphor, each necessarily indicates the return of the same. As Derrida writes,

> Does not such a metaphorology, transported into the philosophical field, always, by destination, rediscover the same? The same *physis*, the same meaning . . . the same circle, the same fire of the same light revealing/concealing itself, the same turn of the sun? What *other* than this return of the same is to be found when one seeks metaphor? (266)

Joyce's concern with "the seim anew" (215.23) includes not only Vico's notion of cyclic history, which Vico endows with synecdochic connections throughout his discussion of it, but also the realization that cyclicity marks the individual's life as well as the relation between generations, where again synecdoche marks each aspect of relatedness, Issy, for instance, being the adolescent form of ALP. The Children's Games chapter offers such expressions of the theme as "for ancients link with presents as the human chain extends, have done, do and will again" (254.8–9) and "we are recurrently meeting em . . . in cycloannalism, from space to space, time after time" (254.26–27).

Heliotrope names the aspect of cyclicity that is the *Wake*'s concern in the Children's Games chapter, the sexuality of childhood. But heliotrope is also one of a series of synecdoches that figure sexuality at different stages in the cycle of life: sexuality as heliotrope as guessing game for children, sexuality as solution of geometry problem as theoretical knowledge for adolescents, sexuality as bed of fulfilled pleasure for lovers (Tristan and Iseult), sexuality as bed of incomplete coitus for the middle aged (Mr. and Mrs. Porter), sexuality as voyeurism for the elderly (The Four).

But what is the relation of sexuality to cyclicity? One possibility is that sexuality and cyclicity are both components of a larger chain;

another is that sexuality is synecdochic for cyclicity. As sexuality is consistently coupled with cyclicity throughout the *Wake* in synecdochic figures, I propose that synecdoche designates the relation between the two, rather than each be seen as components of an even larger whole. But if this is so, then it appears that Joyce's *Wake* challenges Derrida's project because at the heart of Joyce's operation is not *différance* but instead a cyclicity that goes beyond the linguistic, in the sense that the operation of sexuality-cyclicity precedes the operation of *différance*. From this perspective, in his insistence upon the possibility of unity Joyce is closer to Bruno than to Derrida, with the important difference that for Bruno such unity is grounded in the infinite unity of Being whereas for Joyce the grounds for unity lie in the capacity of synecdoche to enclose everything that is.

Beyond the fact that for both Derrida and Joyce the return of the same is an important notion and structure in their writing, perhaps even more significant is that both interpret it—that is to say, disseminate it—in comparable and yet radically dissimilar ways. For Derrida the return of the same that occurs in seeking metaphor, which is to say in seeking knowledge, places one in the contingent world of the absence of fixity as it indicates the impossibility of attaining to a condition of absolute presence. This contingent world is also the human world, but a world that defines humans in terms of linguistic operations. For Joyce, the "seim anew" places one in a different human world, a secular world where theology indicates human aspiration toward the infinite but recognizes that it is measured by finitude. The Children's Games chapter concludes in prayer, but prayer that recognizes not *theos* but the arts as offering such salvation as is available to humans: "Loud, heap miseries upon us yet entwine our arts with laughters low!" (259.7–8).

Heliotrope as return of the same, as the "seim anew," then, is both a major point in common and a significant point of division for Derrida and Joyce. But let us remind ourselves of what is perhaps the outstanding difference between them. We noted earlier that Derrida makes *heliotrope* as metaphor self-destruct, either by movement toward an unwarranted meaning as the presence involved in totalized monosemy or toward dissemination as the absence resulting from unlimited polysemy. Joyce does not force *heliotrope* as synecdoche in that direction. Such a construct would have been "natural" to work with since the sexual—like metaphor—cannot be what it is except through involving itself in a cyclic pattern of self-creation and destruction through desire, satisfaction of desire, renewal of desire. But Joyce does not work with satisfied desire in the *Wake*, but only with its absence, which is to say, desire as presence. And yet the fact that desire never fulfills itself in the text does not indicate a negativity about desire. Instead, we have a desire that in itself forms a positive rather than a negative condition. The desire at work in *Finnegans Wake* is thus closer to the notion that Gilles Deleuze and Felix Guattari advance, that desire is production, not lack. This connection will be explored in chapter 10. The point to be made here is that desire as presence explains why Joyce's *heliotrope* cannot be other, can be only itself. It also explains why, though polysemic, Joyce's *heliotrope* cannot be *relève* and why Derrida's can exist only on the condition that "the heliotrope can always be *relève*" (271).

Let us consider Joyce's *heliotrope* in the Children's Games chapter functioning as synecdoche and Derrida's *heliotrope* in "White Mythology" functioning as metaphor. Though Derrida operates with *heliotrope* as metaphor in his essay, he urges a metonymic reading of it, calling for adjacent multiplicity rather than selective substitution, as witnessed by his reminders to readers that heliotrope is flower and stone besides being sensory sun and metaphoric sun, divided and composite metaphor besides noncomposite and unitary nonmetaphor.

Though Joyce operates with *heliotrope* in his chapter as synecdoche, he implies a metaphoric hermeneutics, suggesting childhood sexuality as substitutive for *heliotrope* rather than opening the term to a multiplicity of readings. To note this is not to suggest that Derrida's *heliotrope* should have operated metonymically and Joyce's metaphorically. We have, here, two instances of Paul de Man's observation that the grammatical mode of a text undercuts or deconstructs its rhetorical mode: "A literary text simultaneously asserts and denies the authority of its own rhetorical mode."[9] But if Joyce operates with heliotrope as synecdoche while implying a metaphoric hermeneutics and Derrida operates with heliotrope as metaphor while implying a metonymic hermeneutics, what we also have is an additional source for the production of the incoherence that marks *Finnegans Wake*, tropes and tropism.

NOTES

1. For another perspective on how *heliotrope* functions in the Children's Games chapter, see Patrick McCarthy, chap. 6, "Whose Hue: Izod's Heliotrope Riddle," *The Riddle of Finnegans Wake* (Rutherford, N.J.: Associated University Presses, 1980), 136–52. In her essay, "Joyce's Heliotrope" (*Coping with Joyce: Essays from the Copenhagen Symposium,* ed. Morris Beja and Shari Benstock [Columbus: Ohio State University Press, 1989]), Margot Norris explores heliotrope in the context of Joyce's oeuvre. She maintains that heliotrope "is an overdetermined figure, a word that means many things at once and yet points to only one thing: desire. . . . heliotrope functions as a trope, a metaphor or figure of the movement of longing, reaching, turning, communicating, and dancing that signifies desire (3)."

2. See Grace Eckley's *Children's Lore in Finnegans Wake* (Syracuse: Syracuse University Press, 1985) for an elaboration of this notion, especially 130–45.

3. McCarthy, *Riddles,* 141–42, argues convincingly that more than the impotence of childhood sexuality is involved in Glugg's failure.

4. Christopher Norris, *Deconstruction: Theory and Practice* (London: Methuen, 1982), 46.

5. This is not the case for Derrida's more recent works such as *Glas* (1974), *La Vérité en peinture* (1978), and *La carte postale* (1980), all of which are much denser in their tropic structure than "White Mythology," and engage in more complex elaborations of the trace, spacing and, especially, dissemination.

6. In private correspondence Patrick McCarthy has observed that the middle anagram, "Ethiaop lore," contains an extra letter, *a,* so that the anagram is not perfect. A number of possibilities come to mind to "account" for this "imperfection": the *a* may have originated as an error and been allowed to remain; the *a* occurs near the middle (fifteenth letter) of the thirty-one-letter sequence and so signifies the "beginning" embedded in all creation; the *a* models *différance* in action; it illustrates Joyce's practice in the *Wake* that the "seim anew" is not perfectly identical with what preceded it, that similarity always already involves difference; the *a* offers another instance of any pattern in the *Wake* being broken at some point, perhaps in recognition that the human world is imperfect; the play of omega (the beginning *o*) and alpha (buried in the middle) is at work.

Concerning the possibility of the *a* as a mistake, a "typographical error," a definite answer cannot be ascertained. The anagram sentence seems to be a late addition to II.1. Joyce added the sentence at the galley proof stage dated by the printer 19 and 29 January 1938. Joyce's handwritten addition appears on page 399 of *The James Joyce Archive, Finnegans Wake, Book II, Chapter I.* Joyce appears to have spelled the word as "Ethiop." But in the page proofs for the manuscript of 20 and 23 September 1938, the word appears as "Ethiaop." Whether Joyce himself added this *a* or it was introduced by mistake and he let it go or he was unaware of it is impossible to tell from the archival material.

7. This word is Derrida's translation into French of Hegel's *Aufhebung.*

Alan Bass explains what Derrida accomplishes in rendering *Aufhebung* as *la reléve:*

> [Derrida] has proposed a new translation of [*Aufhebung*] that does take into account the effect of *différance* in its double meaning. Derrida's translation is *la relève.* The word comes from the verb *relever,* which means to lift up, as does *Aufhebung.* But *relever* also means to relay, to relieve, as when one soldier on duty relieves another. Thus the conserving-and-negating lift has become *la relève,* a "lift" in which is inscribed an effect of substitution and difference, the effect of substitution and difference inscribed in the double meaning of *Aufhebung.*

See Jacques Derrida, *"Différance," Margins of Philosophy,* trans. Alan Bass (Chicago: University of Chicago Press, 1982), 23 n. 1.

8. Jacques Derrida, "White Mythology: Metaphor in the Text of Philosophy," *Margins of Philosophy,* 241. For the remainder of the chapter, page numbers referring to this essay will be given in parentheses in the text.

9. Paul de Man, "Semiology and Rhetoric," *Allegories of Reading* (New Haven: Yale University Press, 1979), 17.

Chapter 6

Postal Systems:
Letter and Card

In writing *penny post* I had also foretold in my memory that *Jean le facteur* (Shaun, John, *the postman*) was not very far off. Another fraternal couple in pp making war on itself, *the penman and the postman*. The writer, Shem, is the heir of H.C.E., *Here Comes Everybody*, which I translate in my idiom as "Here comes whoever will have in body loved me." So I looked for the *penny post* for two hours, and here it is, at least here is one that one day you might bind to an all-powerful *"he war"* . . . while passing through *"his penisolate war"* and the *"sosie sesthers"* of the first page. Here then, from page 307 of *Finnegans Wake*: "Visit to Guinness' Brewery, Clubs, Advantages of the Penny Post, When is a Pun not a Pun?" Facing this, in the margin in italics, the names, you know. Here: "Noah. Plato. Horace. Isaac. Tiresias." On the preceding page, I'm sampling only this, for later: "A Place for Everything and Everything in its Place, Is the Pen mightier than the Sword?" which pulls the following string for example (p. 211): "a sunless map of the month, including the sword and stamps, for Shemus O'Shaun the Post . . ." Reread what follows in the vicinities of "Elle-trouve-tout" and of "Where-is-he?; whatever you like . . . " etc. Look at them, Sword/Pen.

I just called you, it was impossible, you understood clearly, one has to be naked on the telephone. But at the same time it suffices that you undress for me to see myself naked. Our story is also a twin progeniture, a procession of Sosie/sosie, Atreus/Thyestes, Shem/Shaun, S/p, p/p (*penman/postman*).

—Jacques Derrida, *The Post Card*

In the previous chapter we looked at how *heliotrope* functions for Joyce in the Children's Games chapter relative to Derrida's use of the word in "White Mythology," where, by his own definition, Derrida has a book rather than a text.[1] What relation obtains between Joyce's and Derrida's use of words, though, when both operate with texts? As text, *The Post Card* folds *Finnegans Wake* into itself, reads itself in relation to the *Wake*. With what interest? To what effect? Our interest will focus on "Envois," the first half of *The Post Card*, which Derrida calls "the preface to a book that I have not written" that "would have treated that which proceeds from the *postes, postes* of every genre, to psychoanalysis."[2] On the face of it, that statement gives little suggestion of the continuous, pervasive, and multifaceted bonds linking *The Post Card* to *Finnegans Wake*.[3] We will explore those bonds in terms of four notions, the first two of which are pairs that operate as "nonsynomic substitutions" for each other: message and sending, writing and reading, sequential order, and tropes.

As message *Finnegans Wake* links with *The Post Card* in at least three areas: message as dissemination, as cycle, and as performance. Both texts develop what their writers consider a new "language" that must work "differently" than did that of predecessors. Joyce's night book constructs the mind in sleep for which an appropriate language must be developed since, as quoted previously, "One great part of every human existence is passed in a state which cannot be rendered sensible by the use of wideawake language, cutanddry grammar and goahead plot" (*Letters* 3:146). In continuing to deconstruct what Derrida perceives as the tradition of Western philosophy, *The Post Card* cannot use that language traditionally since to do so would be to allow cooptation by it. Instead, the text's "I" writes, "I do not use the language of everyone, the language of knowledge, in order to bedeck myself or to establish my mastery, only in order to erase all the traits, neutralize all the codes" (80). That language of knowledge arose with Socrates and continues into Freud and Heidegger, but the tradition it traces is ending: "It's the end of an epoch" (190). The epoch's technology "is marked by paper, pen, the envelope, the individual subject addressee," and its literature is "essentially detective or epistolary" (191), whence the postcard format of Derrida's text. But the new epoch's technology is marked differently, by computer, modem, electronic mail, and, rather than "the individual subject addressee," everyone on the same LISTSERVER.

Parallel with that changed technology is a changed "message." Gregory Ulmer writes that "'Envois' may be read as an attempt to define a paradigm of thinking based on analogy and metaphor, denoting the necessary metaphoricity of philosophy and science in the process of presenting the object of research."[4] Although the focus of *Finnegans Wake* differs from that of *The Post Card*, the paradigm of its thinking is certainly "based on analogy and metaphor." While *sciencium* may involve "what's what" (415.16), *science* is named as "pundit-the-next-best-king" (505.27–28). But both formulations undercut science as objective formulation of existing reality. Brendan O Hehir and John Dillon place an asterisk before *sciencium* in their lexicon, indicating that "the word is not actually attested in the surviving corpus of Greek and Latin" (*scientia* is the neuter plural and the feminine singular, which O Hehir and Dillon define as "knowledge, skill, expertness, science").[5] If *sciencium* is Joyce's construct, a fiction,[6] and if he has defined that word as a knowing of "what's what," then the knowing of "what's what" also becomes a construct, a fiction. And if science is "pundit-the-next-best-king," the metaphor suggests that while science has professed itself as authority, it plays "second fiddle" to another, equally fictive "authority." Knowing, then, becomes a construct of fictions.

Concerning *The Post Card*, Ulmer comments that "ever since his first book, Derrida has been trying to alter the academic attitude toward fact, to begin to question the 'exemplariness' of fact, to encounter fact in its wild singularity" (52). This statement resonates strongly with one in *Finnegans Wake:* "Thus the unfacts, did we possess them, are too imprecisely few to warrant our certitude" (57.16–17). When Ulmer writes that Derrida in *The Post Card* "proposes a writing oriented towards thought rather than information" (45), we could assert that *Finnegans Wake* models such a writing. Here, in fact, is what Derrida has to say about Joyce and his *Wake:* "One asks oneself what [Joyce] wound up doing, that one, and what made him run. After him, no more starting over, draw the veil and let everything come to pass behind the curtains of language at the end of its rope" (240).

The notion of babel is significant for the *Wake* and *Post Card*. On pages 240 and 241, for instance, Derrida refers to at least nine passages in the *Wake* that deal with babeling. For both writers, babel measures not only the multiplicity in language but also its "illegibility," its "gaps." The postcards that "Derrida"[7] writes are marked by aporias: "Whatever their original length, the passages that have disappeared are indicated, at the very place of their incineration, by a blank of 52 signs" (4). Oxidation slower than fire has destroyed parts of the *Wake*'s letter—its tenure in the midden, Biddy Doran's beak—and its continuity, too, has been disrupted.

Concerning message as cyclic, both *Finnegans Wake* and *The Post Card* are four-part structures that recycle their ends for reuse as their beginnings. The words ending the *Wake* circle back to its opening words, "A way a lone a last a loved a long the," connecting with "riverrun, past Eve and Adam's, from swerve of shore to bend of bay." The "postcard" dated 17 November 1979 that appears on the back cover of *The Post Card* comes after the fourth part of that text and circles back to the opening of "Envois," the "letter" from Derrida dated 7 September 1979 that precedes the first postcard, dated 3 June 1977 (this inverting of sequence is a major theme of *The Post Card* and will be explored in the third section of this chapter).

The four parts of *The Post Card* move from the longest to the shortest: "Envois," "To Speculate—On 'Freud,'" "Le Facteur de la Vérité, and "Du Tout." Like book I of *Finnegans Wake*, "Envois" lays out themes that play throughout the text: the relation between writer and reader,[8] past and present, sending and receiving, Socrates and Plato, Socrates and Freud, Freud and Derrida, the pleasure principle and the postal principle. "To Speculate—on 'Freud'" reads Freud's *Beyond the Pleasure Principle* deconstructively: "If it is to assure its mastery, the principle *of* pleasure therefore first must do so *over* pleasure and at the expense *of* pleasure" (400); "the motif of power is more originary and more general than the PP [pleasure principle], is independent of it, is its beyond" (405); and "proceeding from a drive for power, and borrowing all its descriptive traits from this drive," the death drive "overflows power" (405).

Book III of *Finnegans Wake* may be called "The Book of Shaun." Interestingly, and probably not coincidentally, the title of part 3 of *The Post Card* is "Le Facteur de la Vérité, which may be translated "The Postman of Truth" as well as "The Factor of Truth" since *facteur* signifies both postman and factor. By this title, as Alan Bass indicates, Derrida points to "the question of the delivery of truth in psychoanalysis" (413 n. 1). "Le Facteur de la Vérité" reads Lacan's "Seminar on the Purloined Letter," adding a fourth player, that of narrator, to the triangle of glances Lacan had identified as determining the movement of the signifier (seeing nothing [the king's and then the prefect's position], seeing something [the queen's and then the minister's position], seeing the "complete" picture [Dupin's position]). Derrida suggests that Lacan's "forgetting" the role of narrator mirrors the tendency of psychoanalysis to claim it reaches (and delivers) truth, independent of the narrator/analysand, the analyst-as-Dupin "seeing" the "truth." In "correcting" Lacan, Derrida questions Lacan's claim that the letter/signifier always arrives; for Derrida the letter never arrives because it continually disseminates itself.

"Du Tout," the fourth part of *The Post Card*, explores the invagination by deconstruction of psychoanalysis-as-institution as both "du tout" and as "une tranche." Derrida characterizes psychoanalysis as institution by the following phrase, which he indicates is to be read "without any punctuation for the moment as if there were a dash of equal length between each word" (502):

CE–N'EST–PAS–DU–TOUT–UNE–TRANCHE.[9] (503)

A masterpiece of deconstruction, the phrase requires quoting Alan Bass's entire note about it:

> This sentence plays on lexical and syntactic undecidability. *Une tranche* is the usual French word for a slice, as in a slice of cake, from the verb *trancher*, to slice. In French psychoanalytic slang, *une tranche* is also the period of time one spends with a given analyst. There is no equivalent English expression. Further, the expression "du tout" can mean either "of the whole" or "at all." Thus, the sentence can mean "This is not a 'slice' [a piece, in the analytic sense or not] of the whole," or "This is not at all a 'slice' [in any sense]." The verb *trancher* can also mean to decide on a question or to resolve it in a clear-*cut* way; the English "trenchant" has a similar sense. Throughout this interview, the senses of *tranche* and "trench" beckon toward each other, finally coming together in the concluding discussion of schisms and seisms (earthquakes, cracking ground). (503)

Derrida concludes "Du Tout" with the following, which cycles the text on to the "final" postcard on the back cover of *The Post Card*, which in turn circles back to the text's beginning:

> Who will pay whom for Freud's *tranche*?
> Or, if you prefer, the thing already having been broached, who has it paid to whom?
> The bidding has been opened—for some time.
> Let us say that what I write or what makes me write (for example, since there are not only the texts, this time I mean the publications) would represent in this respect only one offer.
> An offer on the scene in which the attempts to occupy the

place of the *Sa* (that is, of the *Savoir absolu* stenographed in *Glas*) are multiplying, that is, simultaneously all the places, those of the seller, the buyer, and the auctioneer. (520–21)

As *Glas* tolls the bell for the bands, bonds, and bans of absolute knowledge, so has *The Post Card* done for the particular province of psychoanalysis-as-institution, using it as paradigm for the broader movement of deconstructing the possibility of absolute knowledge in the tradition of Western philosophy. If *Ulysses* tolls the bell for the "verities" of tradition in novel and epic, *Finnegans Wake* continues this process, extending it from the deconstruction of unifying style to include that of unifying narration, character, setting, plot, and so forth. Whatever "whole" we make of the text, it, as well as psycho-analysis, may be characterized by Derrida's phrase:

CE–N'EST–PAS–DU–TOUT–UNE–TRANCHE.

"What happens," "Derrida" inquires coyly, "when acts or performances (discourse or writing, analysis or description, etc.) are part of the objects they designate?" (391). His immediate context for the inquiry is Freud's *Beyond the Pleasure Principle,* in which Freud embeds the incident of his grandson's throwing the spool and pulling it towards him, symbolically controlling the *fort* and *da* he experiences but cannot control when his mother (Freud's daughter Sophie) leaves and later returns to him. That incident becomes paradigmatic of the pleasure principle itself. As Derrida notes, "One takes pleasure only to lose it—and to keep it *comes back, amounts* to the same" (397). Derrida himself embeds *Beyond the Pleasure Principle* in *The Post Card* in such a way as to make its act or performance "part of the object[s] [it] designate[s]." In other words, he makes the postal principle the *beyond* of the pleasure principle.

Now this is also Joyce's movement in *Finnegans Wake*, to make of his text an act or performance that is part of the object it desig-nates. As Samuel Beckett observed, perhaps at Joyce's instigation,

Here form *is* content, content *is* form. [Joyce's] writing is not *about* something; *it is that something itself.* . . . When the sense is sleep, the words go to sleep. (See the end of 'Anna Livia'). When the sense is dancing, the words dance. Take the passage at the end of Shaun's pastoral . . . .[10]

Both Joyce and Derrida situate their texts within the traditions they see as coming to an end, where their texts formulate that ending by the kind of *doing* each performs. Ulmer's claim that "the theme of *The Post Card* is precisely 'tradition,' into whose continuity Derrida insinuates himself" (47) may also be made about *Finnegans Wake* and Joyce. The tradition that concerns Derrida is that of Western philosophy in its dream that absolute knowledge was attainable. Where Freud believed that his research and writing constituted objective science, Derrida demonstrates it was permeated with autobiography. Although this implies absolute knowledge is not possible, at the same time it models the possibility of relational thought where, relative to writer rather than absolute in reference to "what is," the thoughts of one writer relate to and feed those of another, the chain growing and disseminating in uncontrollable ways. The tradition that concerns Joyce is the tradition that separates history from fiction, one culture from another. Working with the myths, religions, and languages of hundreds of ethnicities, Joyce weaves the monomyth of life, the family, embedding its dynamics in the mind of a sleeper or sleepers, thereby laying the claim that below the thousands of differences that separate one person from another, one culture from another, is the monomyth of psychic and cultural identity. The import of Joyce's message differs radically from that of Derrida's, since Joyce's text implies a "one" underlying the "many," whereas Derrida's announces the "many" underlying the illusion of "one." Derrida writes, for instance, "When one sends oneself post cards (or the dialogues of Plato) in order to communicate on the subject of post cards, the collection becomes impossible, one can no longer totalize, one no longer encircles" (207). And Joyce writes, "All the world's in want and is writing a letters. A letters from a person to a place about a thing. And all the world's on wish to be carrying a letters" (278.13–16). But though the message differs, both *Finnegans Wake* and *The Post Card* are acts, performances, in which, as Derrida writes, "What counts and is counted then, is what we do while speaking, what we do to each other, how we again touch each other by mixing our voices" (56).

What about the message in the *Wake*'s Letter, though? In book IV is the Letter about to be delivered? And what about *The Post Card*'s postcard that did not get delivered? Although it is no longer trapped in the dead-letter station, "Derrida" is not about to forward it once again to his correspondent. Why? Ulmer locates the card's possibility for not being delivered as an indication of the "discontinuity disruptive of tradition" (50). "Derrida" offers another possibility:

> There is no destination, my sweet destiny [fifty-two "blank" spaces occur at this point, indicative of the "incineration" that has destroyed parts of the correspondence] you understand, within every sign already, every mark or every trait, there is distancing, the post, what there has to be so that it is legible for another, another than you or me, and everything is messed up in advance, cards on the table. The condition for it to arrive is that it ends up and even that it begins by not arriving. (29)

He later comments on the notion of legibility as illegibility:

> The mischance (the mis-address) of this chance is that in order *to be able* not to arrive, it must bear within itself a force and a structure, a straying of the destination, such that it *must* also not arrive in any way. Even in arriving (always to some "subject"), the letter takes itself away *from the arrival at arrival.* It arrives elsewhere, always several times. (123)

The message cannot arrive, although the card may be delivered. The message as sign has no destination since within every sign there is distancing, which Derrida shows metaphorically as the postal process. This distancing from sender is what allows the possibility for another to receive it. But this very distancing means that the message is no longer what it was and so cannot arrive, although its form-as-card may be delivered. Every sign has within it, then, a self-inhering deconstruction that necessarily prevents it from arriving. Although the card may be delivered, the sign "always already" has gone on to another "subject" than that it was intended for. This is the motion of dissemination.

It is a different story with the *Wake*'s Letter, which may arrive, is expected to arrive. Which letter? That of ALP justifying and defending HCE? That of Issy addressing and inviting her love? That which Shaun claims he has tried to deliver and found all the addresses no longer current? That which Shem is said to have helped his mother write? It doesn't matter. All letters are one, the expression of a want. As Joyce wrote, "All the world's in want and is writing a letters." The nature of wants or desires is that, to be present, they must not be fulfilled; thus the Letter may be delivered and, again, it may not. In either case the want/desire will continue, in its present or modified form. With Joyce, the capacity for the Letter to arrive or not has to do neither with the "discontinuity disruptive of tradition" nor the deconstructive, disseminating quality of the sign but rather with the nature of desire, which concern we will consider more carefully in chapter 10.

The preceding two paragraphs have moved us from concern with the message as a certain kind of act or performance, a certain kind of cyclic structure, a certain kind of disseminating language, into a concern with message as that which must be sent through some system to some receiver. In *Finnegans Wake* that receiver is everyone, each of us. "All the world's on wish to be carrying a letters" because all the world's people have needs, and the letter, if it arrived, would deliver those needs. Meanwhile there is hope for and expectation of arrival. In *The Post Card*, too, the receiver is multiple but does not have the same identity, as is the case in the *Wake*. The writer, the future, the lover, the relative, these are some metaphoric identities by which Derrida indicates the receiver. In writing, the writer writes to her or his self, but because that self is never there to receive it, the message "always remains to be continued, to be forwarded" (149) into the future where eventually it will be rescued from the dead-letter files by some lover or relative, who will forward the message once again into the future, not the "same" message that issued from the first writer, but a "different" one. When "something" arrives for "someone," the sending of a message is a sending of seed, but the "ejaculation" may be "premature" or the receiver not receptive: "the old lady has remained impenetrable, virgin, impassive, somewhat amused, all-powerful" (184).

Borrowing from *Finnegans Wake*, Derrida uses Shem and Shaun as metaphors for the message/sending process: "the writing of the proper name, that of the *penman* Shem, sees itself interminably given over to the detours and wanderings of Shaun the *postman*, his brother" (165). Shaun is the post, the *facteur* both mailman and factor who uses tradition as the postage stamp that carries the message:

> This is a stamp. They have signed *our* I.O.U. and we can no longer not acknowledge it. Any more than our own children. This is what tradition is, the heritage that drives you crazy. (100)

As carrier of tradition, Joyce's Shaun too is stamped before journeying:

> And next thing was he gummalicked the stickyback side and stamped the oval badge of belief to this agnelows brow with a genuine dash of irrepressible piety. (470.29–32)

But where Joyce's Shaun is the post, the delivery system, Derrida's Shaun is multiple. The post is any delivery system: "technology, position, 'metaphysics'"; and the word is plural, not singular: "There is not even the post or the *envoi*, there are *posts* and *envois*" (66). But the plurality of *posts* affects the sending of messages. The post in the age of metaphysics assumed a single, individual addressee; that in the age of electronic mail assumes collective, undifferentiated receivers.

Writing and reading are intimately related to messages and delivery systems. In Derrida's terminology borrowed from *différance* and its relation to spacing, supplementarity, trace, and so on, we could say that writing and messages, reading and the postal system are "nonsynonymic substitutions" of each other. And just as the trace, supplementarity and spacing each elaborate an aspect of *différance*, so writing elaborates an aspect of message; reading, of the post. For both Joyce and Derrida, sexuality and fragmentation are metaphors for the writing/reading relationship. Derrida, for instance, figures writing as an act of sexual appropriation. "Derrida," the writer reading the Matthew Paris illustration of Plato and Socrates appearing on the front cover of *The Post Card* as well as on a plate inside the text, figures his relation to "Socrates" in this way:

> I no longer know to whom, imprudently, irrepressibly, I wrote this: that Socrates' back is the back of the post card (a curved and beautiful, beautiful surface, I am always tempted to walk with

him, to stroll around while slipping my hand into his revolver-pocket) and when he arrives at his depths, having probed them with his tongue, he is afraid, he invents platonism, he gives him a child in the back. (233)

"Derrida" figures Plato as writer appropriating Socrates thus:

I tell you that I see *Plato* getting an erection in *Socrates'* back and see the insane hubris of his prick, an interminable, dispropor-tionate erection traversing Paris's head like a single idea and then the copyist's chair, before slowly sliding, still warm, under *Socrates'* right leg, in harmony or symphony with the movement of this phallus sheaf, the points, plumes, pens, fingers, nails and *grattoirs*, the very pencil boxes which address themselves in the same direction. (18)

Shaun/Jaun reads Issy, delivering his sermon to her in sexual terms. Joyce writes,

(you gypseyeyed baggage, do you hear what I'm praying?) or, Gash, without butthering my head to assortail whose stroke forced or which struck backly, I'll be all over you myselx horizon-tally. (444.16–19)

In her soliloquy that ends *Finnegans Wake*, ALP reads/remembers HCE. Joyce writes,

Draw back your glave. Hot and hairy, hugon, is your hand! Here's where the falskin begins. Smoos as an infams. (621.24–26)

Derrida's sexualizing of writing/reading involves the act as a sending forth/embedding of seed, sometimes through artificial insemination: "*Plato* wants to emit. Seed, artificially, technically. That devil of a *Socrates* holds the syringe. To sow the entire earth, to send the same fertile card to *everyone*" (28). For Joyce the sexualizing of writing/reading is one aspect of desire, which he figures in sexual tropes. In the lines from ALP's soliloquy considered above, ALP desires that HCE rejoin her; Joyce images that desire as her drawing him to her, taking his hand/penis in the act of coming together again. In the

Shaun/Jaun sermon, Shaun "delivers" or "reads" the writing/message, desiring to join his labors as postman to the jouissance Issy offers but withholds or, more accurately, bears within herself and cannot "give" away.

The ambiguity about whether "Derrida's" correspondent is male or female has to do with how Derrida figures the reception/reading of messages/writing. The following are representative of how "Derrida" images the gender of his correspondent:

> I owe it to you to have discovered homosexuality, and ours is indestructible. I owe you everything and I owe you nothing at all. We are of the same sex, and this is as true as two and two are four or that S is P. Q.E.D. (53)

> to reach the conclusion from the fact that I say "it's nice that you are back" that I am certainly writing to a woman. (79)

> It is its address that makes it into a post card that multiplies, to the point of a crowd, my addressee, female. And by the same token, of course, my addressee, male. (112)

> I only wanted to say that all women would be you (but I only know one of them), when they are beautiful for having said "yes"—and you are a man. (176)

This ambiguity exists in part because "Derrida," and "behind" him, Derrida, is writing to the future, whose readers will be both male and female. In part it exists through what Derrida suggests is the "polymorphous perversity" of writing/reading, the necessity that writing is reading and reading is writing. And since the process is figured as sexual, then male is female and female is male.

Sexual ambiguity in *Finnegans Wake* has other dynamics. The only character whose identity is both male and female is The Four in their aspect as elders in book II, chapter 4. In that situation, the ambiguity of their sexuality is more the "remainder" of what age has subtracted from maleness than androgyny itself. The narrator says of them, "Truly they were four dear old heladies" (386.14–15); "they were all summarily divorced, four years before, or so they say, by their dear poor shehusbands" (390.19–20); the narrator speaks of

Matt as "the old perigrime matriarch" and "a queenly man" (392.19–20).

A second dynamics behind the feminizing of The Four has to do with one of the notions structuring II.4, that of the balance of opposites. Besides the balancing of male and female, other balanced oppositions include old and young, land and sea, self and otherness, past and present. But rather than maintain a "separate but equal" status, Joyce images these oppositions as interpenetrating and defining each other, in Derrida's language, becoming the supplement of each other. Thus, Matt's female qualities induced through aging define his maleness; his memories of his past interpenetrate and define his present, as his present modifies his memories of his past.

Besides writing/reading as sexual act, fragmentation in the sense of being caught up in an "uncontrollable" activity is a second pervasive metaphor of that reciprocal process. If what one reads are postcards, although these may be addressed to single addressees, as the cards travel through the postal system they are "open" to being read by anyone who works on the same circuit, which circumstance gives to the cards the near certainty of being misunderstood. Thus, Derrida implies, with the circuit of writer to understood or intended audience: the text is an "open" card that may be read, and misunderstood, by anyone. Not only may the misunderstanding arise because the card has been received by an audience other than that the writer "thought" s/he was writing for; but also, the social/historical process of transmitting the writing involves an inescapable effect of "blanking out" that Derrida images as incineration (5). Certain passages become unreadable. They have become blanks in the text. This fragmented uncertainty means that as readers we are always "beginning" to read somewhere in the "middle" of the text, a situation Derrida images through the fifty-two blank spaces that disrupt "Derrida's" cards periodically. In a passage strongly reminiscent of the *Wake*, "Derrida" writes, "You will say that 'to write' is indeed to scratch, no, he is scratching in order to erase" (49). Joyce, we remember, has the hen Biddy Doran "scratching" at the Boston "transhipt" and in so doing, "erasing" some of its passages as her claws "punctuate" it.

For "Derrida," the postcards he and his "correspondent" write are

the last letters, "retro" letters, love letters on a bellépoque poster, but also simply the last letters. We are taking the last *correspondance*. Soon there will be no more of them. Eschatology, apocalypse, and teleology of epistles themselves. (62)

This passage "addresses" Derrida's belief that the logocentric era has come to an end during the past hundred years.[11] Ulmer notes that for Derrida, "The logocentric epoch is a post card" (54). This is so, Ulmer writes, because "the feature that makes the letter exemplary of the logocentric era (a synonym for 'postal era') is that it is addressed and signed, directed or destined" (41). In logocentrism, Derrida argues, thinkers believed their ideas conveyed the truth about matters and that their words carried this truth to a chosen audience, who understood it as the speaker had intended. Transmission was direct, accurate, and truth bearing. But this was never the case: "I no longer know whom I wrote this to one day, letters are always post cards: neither legible nor illegible, open and radically unintelligible (unless one has faith in 'linguistic,' that is grammatical, criteria . . .)" (79). Not the attaining to truth through connection with absolute Being located outside and beyond language, but language itself is the basis of what and how we know. Thus, the postal system(s) is not simply a metaphor for the transmission of writing but "the 'proper' possibility of every possible rhetoric" (65).

Rather than travel directly from writer to reader, the postcard traces a path "determined" by what Derrida calls "switch points":

Afterward, on the lawn where the discussion continued, wandered along according to switch points as unforeseeable as they are inevitable. (15)

and

In several places I will leave all kinds of references, names of persons and of places, authentifiable dates, identifiable events, they will rush in with eyes closed, finally believing to be there and to find us there when by means of a switch point I will send them elsewhere to see if we are there, with a stroke of the pen or the *grattoir* I will make everything derail. (177)

Many of Derrida's notions about the fragmentation of writing/reading are modeled in *Finnegans Wake*. Fragmentation occupies a place of such importance in the *Wake*, in fact, that chapter 9 is devoted to exploring how it operates in Joyce's text. But our concern here is the extent to which fragmentation as Derrida writes it coincides with the fragmentation practiced by Joyce. Fragmentation as switch points is a major mode of operation in the *Wake*, functioning at the level of word, sentence, paragraph, section, chapter, book, and text. However, for Derrida the switch points lead to *différance*, where for Joyce they lead to the "seim anew," the "seim" being always both new and renewed. *Finnegans Wake* has received much attention as modeling "reality" as language based rather than as existing outside language's shaping power. That is, Joyce models individual words as well as longer units of writing as if they were clay, indefinitely malleable to the shape he as writer and we as readers make of them. But this malleability points to the relatedness of change rather than the disruptiveness of change.[12] And concerning the end of an era, *Finnegans Wake* is constructed of such ends, but they don't stay "ended"; they give birth to a new era that eventually grows old, again to give birth to the new. Although Derrida's *The Post Card* has a cyclic design, Derrida's model for the shape and movement of time appears to be switch points rather than the circle which turns on itself and returns to its beginnings again and again.

The Post Card and *Finnegans Wake* agree, however, that writing is rewriting; reading is rereading. Joyce rewrites himself, the Bible, the Koran, the Book of Kells, the lyrics of Thomas Moore, the tale of Dermot and Grania, tales his father told him; the list is capable of nearly indefinite expansion. And Derrida rewrites Plato, Dante, Voltaire, Nietzsche, Freud, Kafka, Heidegger. Also, both the *Wake* and *The Post Card* provide their readers with "directions" about how to read them. *The Post Card* describes reading as rereading:

Another way of saying that you had reread it, no?, which is *what one begins by doing* when one reads, even for the first time (59–60)

warns the reader not to be in a hurry to determine the text:

Because I still like him, I can foresee the impatience of the *bad* reader: this is the way I name or accuse the fearful reader, the reader in a hurry to be determined, decided upon deciding (4) reassures the reader that it uses words "differently" than the reader has come to expect:

> I do not use the language of everyone, the language of knowledge, in order to bedeck myself or to establish my mastery, only in order to erase all the traits, neutralize all the codes (80)

and explains the interdependence of reader and writer:

> Got nothing from you this morning. I am without strength for anything, even for writing you. . . . I want to recall you to my aid. . . . there it is you who are speaking in me. You recognize your discourse. You love me only when I am there. (113–14)

For its part, *Finnegans Wake* explains to its readers that they must expect that

> every word will be bound over to carry three score and ten toptypsical readings throughout the book of Doublends Jined. (20.14–15)

Further, if Shem/Glugg read "off his fleshskin" and wrote "with his quillbone" (229.30), so too does the reader need to read/write the *Wake* through the body:

> here keen again and begin again to make soundsense and sensesound kin again. (121.14–16)

Reading is a "Tobecontinued's tale that while blubles blows there'll still be sealskers" (626.18–19). The "ideal reader suffering from an ideal insomnia" (120.13–14) must

> look at this prepronominal *funferal*, engraved and retouched and edgewiped and puddenpadded, very like a whale's egg farced with pemmican, as were it sentenced to be nuzzled over a full trillion times for ever and a night. (120.9–13)

To this point in the chapter we have been examining the bonds linking *The Post Card* to *Finnegans Wake* in terms of two pairs of

"nonsynonymic substitutions," message/sending and writing/read-
ing. A third notion of significant linkage between Joyce's and Derrida's texts is that of order as a certain kind of sequence. Both texts
destabilize the paradigm of linear unilateral movement from past into
present. In his introduction to *The Post Card*, Alan Bass writes,

> One of the major concerns of *The Post Card* is the possible subver-
> sion of what is usually taken as a fixed sequence—e.g. Socrates
> before Plato, the passing of an inheritance from a prior genera-
> tion to a succeeding one, the death of the old before the young.
> What if the usual and seemingly fixed sequence were reversible?
> What if each term of the sequence contained within itself the
> principle that subverts the usual progression? What could there
> be between each term and itself that would operate this subver-
> sion? (ix)

Several pages later Bass extends the idea, drawing on Derrida's interest in "the overlap between Heidegger and Freud on the topics of
sending and destiny":

> If Being is sent, then there must be a system that sorts, routes,
> and delivers it. What if this system necessarily contained a kink,
> so that despite the absolute authority of its usual sequences (like
> the absolute authority of alphabetical order), somewhere it con-
> tained the subversion and reversal of its own progression (L
> before K)? (xii)

We can begin to explore this notion of a "principle" internal to
sequence such that it subverts and reverses the expected order by
looking at a sentence of "Derrida's":

> Imagine the day, as I have already, that we will be able to send
> sperm by post card, without going through a check drawn on
> some sperm bank, and that it remains living enough for the
> articial insemination to yield fecundation, and even desire. (24)

The expected order in this sequence is desire leading to insemination,
yielding fecundation. If we read sending sperm by postcard as the
direct sending of ideas and images by a writer to readers where the

writing is not itself derivative and secondary to speech as present and privileged, then what Derrida emphasizes is the germinating effects the writing can have, even if it predates its being read by a long time. The desire it yields, if fecundation occurs, is the reader's taking in the writing, during which process *différance* will make the writing *other* than it had been. The process itself has not changed, but the point at which we begin to observe has; rather than begin with the "first" writer's desire, we begin to observe the writing that the writer sent, the "sperm," after which we observe our response to it, whether or not insemination has taken place. If it has, that is, if some of the writer's writing lodges within us and begins to grow as a new object, "different" from what it had been when the prior writer sent it forth, then fecundation has occurred. After that, we will desire to send forth our own "sperm," at which time *différance* (for Joyce it would be a matter of cyclicity, the "seim anew") has begun its disseminating work.

Related to this inversion is the Socrates/Plato relation. "S. is P.," writes Derrida, "his father and his son, therefore the father of his father, his own grandfather and his own grandson" (47).[13] Plato "reads" Socrates, at some point "writing" him. In "reading" Socrates, Plato is in relation of son; in "writing" Socrates, Plato is in that of father. The two roles, however, do not remain separate, the one preceding and the other succeeding, but instead interact, producing a new generation of grandfather/grandson. But in "writing" Socrates, Plato sees him "only *from the back*. There is only the *back*, seen from the back, in what is written, such is the final word" (48). Perhaps if Plato could see Socrates from the *front*, absolute knowledge might be possible. But if Plato could see Socrates from the *front*, Socrates would then see only the *back* of Plato. The metaphor Derrida gives us does not allow for mutuality.

In another metaphor of inverted sequence, "Derrida" imagines "a secret correspondence between Socrates and Freud conversing with each other at the bottom of the post card, about the support, the message, the inheritance, telecommunications, the *envoie*" (175). Not only do "Socrates" and "Freud" define the "ends" of the logocentric era, but in imaging them corresponding with each other, Derrida emphasizes the extent to which each is the other's *différance*; "Socrates," that is, makes a "difference" in and for "Freud," who in coming at the "end" of the era, re-flects and re-presents Socrates differently than did Plato. Reproduction as re-producing an-other is the principle that subverts and inverts the "usual order." "Derrida" writes,

> Everything begins, like the post card, with reproduction. Sophie [Freud's daughter] and her followers, Ernst [Sophie's first son], Heinele [her second son], myself and company dictate to Freud who dictates to Plato, who dictates to Socrates who himself, reading the last one (for it is he who reads me, you see him here, you see what is written on his card in the place where he is scratching, it is for him that is written the very thing that he is soon going to sign) again will have forwarded. (63)

The present "reads" and thus "dictates" to the past, reproducing and necessarily changing it; the past, seen "differently" because re-produced, "forwards" its message again to the present, which in continuing to "read" it, and "dictate" to it, continues its *différance*. Although "Derrida" is the heir of "Socrates," "Socrates" is equally "Derrida's" "legatee" (93). And what Derrida leaves Socrates/Plato is a challenging of the absolutes they assumed:

> this old couple of bearded grandfathers, these inveterate counterfeiters who come to haunt our nights with their discourse on truth, on phantasmata and logoi, and pleasure and the beyond of pleasure, and politics, and tyranny, and the first and the second, and then Eros. (101)

But "they have never believed in it," their discourse, and with all "our" efforts to deconstruct it, "here we are at their command and on the program" (101).

For Joyce in *Finnegans Wake* the subverting and inverting of the usual order is also very important and exists at many different levels, from the treatment of single letters and words to the ordering of the *Wake*'s four Books. At the level of single letters we have F and its inversion, Ⅎ (266.22); at the level of single words, we have "the goddess Aruc-Ituc" (237.29), the inversion of Cuticura, a brand name of face cream. At the level of character, although we are "introduced" to The Four on page 13, we do not get a "description" of them until page 368, but this "description" does not "fit" that of The Four as the doddering elders they appear in the following chapter. At the level of chapter, Joyce writes of III.3 as "a description of a postman travelling backwards in the night through the events already narrated. It is written in the form of a *via crucis* of 14 stations but in reality it is only a barrel rolling down the river Liffey" (*Letters* 1:214). The relation between books I and III Joyce viewed as inverted and complementary images of each other:

> I had a rather strange dream the other night. I was looking at a Turk seated in a bazaar. He had a framework on his knees and on one side he had a jumble of all shades of red and yellow skeins and on the other a jumble of greens and blues of all shades. He was picking from right and left very calmly and weaving away. It is evidently a split rainbow and also Parts I and III. (*Letters* 1:261)

Thus, in terms of the Viconian life cycle, although book I is generally the book of birth, II that of marriage, III that of death, and IV that of rebirth, not only is each book "supplemented" by the orientation of the other three in such a way that each manifests all four processes, but the major orientations of books I and III are interchangeable with each other. That is, book III may be viewed as the book of birth; book I as that of death. Joyce, after all, viewed the relation between the two books/processes as that of tunnel, each of which end led to the other. To Harriet Shaw Weaver, Joyce wrote, "I think that at last I have solved one—the first—of the problems presented by my book. In other words one of the partitions between two of the tunneling parties seems to have given way" (*Letters* 3:110). Thus, the "births" of book I—the introduction of characters, motifs and themes, the new order of the "open door" instituted by Jarl van Hoother after the Prankquean's lessons, the discovery of the Letter—face the "deaths" of I: the falls of Finnegan and HCE; the battle and burial in Lough Neagh. And the "births" of III—Shaun as a figure of hope for others, the reconciliation of brothers in Jaun and Dave—face its "deaths": Shaun's journeying backwards in the river of time; Shaun as Yawn reviewing the fall of HCE; the unsuccessful coitus of ALP and HCE. And beyond this, Joyce has an inversion in the Vico cycle. Rather than read in the expected order of birth, marriage, death, *ricorso* or rebirth, we would begin with a dying that leads to marriage, out of which proceed births, from which develops rebirth. Book IV in the one case looks toward its beginning in book I as birth; in the other, as death. This makes of birth a kind of dying and of dying a kind of birthing. Joyce wrote the "ending" of the *Wake* so that it cycled round to the "beginning," which is really a middle: "The book really has no beginning or end. (Trade secret, registered at Stationers Hall.) It ends in the middle of a sentence and begins in the middle of the same sentence" (*Letters* 1:246). Although they use different tropes, then, both Joyce and Derrida invert the expected order. In *The Post Card* this inversion allows for the present to look back continually at the past, which is not a looking at the past itself but only at its back; and this involves rewriting that past as well as the present itself being written by it. In *Finnegans Wake*, what we have are cycles rather than epochs or eras. And one cycle is very much like another in its basic components: the human family, the human culture seen in its institutions of love, war, religion, arts. Where for Derrida *différance* is the operative word in the writings and rewritings of past and present, for Joyce the "seim anew" is the operative word in cyclicity.

We come, now, to the fourth and last notion in terms of which we are exploring the embedding of *Finnegans Wake* in *The Post Card*, tropes. Most of the tropes through which Derrida writes *The Post Card* are also those through which Joyce writes *Finnegans Wake*. Indeed, without exaggeration we might say that Derrida draws on *Finnegans Wake* as trope for the writing of "Envois." And "Derrida" as much as grants this, himself. In a complex tribute to Joyce via Nietzsche, "Derrida" writes, "James (the two, the three), Jacques, Giacomo Joyce—your *contrefacture* is a marvel, the counter part to the *invoice:* ' Envoy: love me love my umbrella' " (238). Tropic similarities include the following: anagrams, puns, other forms of word play, repeating motifs, phonic homonyms, ambiguous pronouns, nomination as metonymy, the identity of opposites, the identity of the comic and "sacred" tradition, Shem and Shaun as message/sending, the postcard/Letter as metaphor/synecdoche of a tradition of writing, number and sexuality as metaphor.

Several of Derrida's anagrams include *carte, ecart, trace* and *récit, écrit;* among Joyce's is "O theoperil! Ethiaop lore, the poor lie" (223.28). As is Joyce's, Derrida's punning is continual, including not only French but also multilingual puns: "the ayatollah telekom- meiny" (104)[14] and *fort,* in French meaning strong, a fort, and in

German, away or gone. Where Joyce played with words formed with the suffix *-ation* for designating the presence or influence of The Twelve in the text ("Your exagmination round his factification for incamination" [497.02]), Derrida plays with words formed with the suffix *-mission* to indicate the mission of the *envoi:* transmission, emission, remission, commission, omission (see 224). Derrida threads the repeating phrase *mais si, mais si* at least fourteen times through "Envois"; some of Joyce's repeating phrases—"repeated" nearly always with a difference that models his notion of the "seim anew"—include the Quinet flower passage and identifiable rhythms such as that of "beside the rivering waters of, hitherandthithering waters of. Night!" (216.4–5). As with punning, phonic homonyms are continual in each text. In *The Post Card*, Derrida works with *vert, verre, ver,* and *vers* (99) and *es, et,* and *hait* (22 and elsewhere) as homonyms or near-homonyms of each other. Through Bass's translation, Derrida gives us " 'connect, I cut,' " for Connecticut (113). Several of Joyce's include "seemetery" (17.36) for "cemetery" and "a place of seeming," and "raze a leader" (278.22), which suggests raising and destroying a leader as well as raising a ladder, ladder functioning both as sexual image and as part of the artist-as-builder motif, that is, Ibsen's Master Builder and Finnegan as hod carrier.

Where Joyce uses pronouns ambiguously so that we can't tell whether *he* refers to Earwicker, Hosty, or the Cad, or *she* refers to ALP or Kate, Derrida has a comparable maneuver with the second-person pronouns. *You* may refer to "my destiny" (45) and "my 'natural' state" (84–85), as well as to "Derrida's" correspondent, male lover, and female lover. For both writers, the capacity of pronouns for ambiguous reference is directly related to nomination as the play of metonymy. In *Finnegans Wake* this exists not only in the giant lists such as the 111 names of Anna Livia Plurabelle's "untitled mamafesta" and the fourteen pages of the names for "Finn MacCool" (126–39) but also in the condition that each of the *Wake*'s characters has multiple identities, as indicated by Adaline Glasheen's thirteen-page chart, "Who Is Who When Everybody Is Somebody Else."[15] It appears in a third form in the continual and shifting placement of the letters HCE and ALP to indicate the presence or influence at that point in the text of those characters. In a fourth form, nomination as metonymy appears in Joyce's plays with his own name as, for instance, "joyicity" (414.23) and "jimpjoyed" (68.02).

Of these four, Derrida uses all but the first. Concerning plays on his name, Derrida declares that he is signing the "postcards," his "envois," in "my proper name, Jacques Derrida," thus turning the signifier Derrida into the signifier "Derrida." He also calls attention to his name in such sequences as "James (the two, the three), Jacques, Giacomo Joyce" (238) and in any sequence involving the number seven, the number of letters in his first and last names. The multiple identities of the "you" has been mentioned above; a similar laying out of multiple identities for the "I" could also be made: as "Derrida," Derrida, the lover, the traveler to "Yale" and "Oxford," the writer, the challenger of philosophic tradition. But it is in the shifting placement of significant letters that Derrida is closest to Joyce concerning nomination as process. The *S* from "Socrates" and the *P* from Plato becomes the equivalent, in "Envois," to what Joyce does with ALP and HCE. As Ulmer writes,

> The proper names of Plato and Socrates are put in play as a monogram. Thus the S and P are combined to signify the abbreviations and terms relevant to the theme—"post script," "subject and predicate," "primary and secondary processes." (52)

Derrida has other plays in addition to those Ulmer names. For one, he highlights the *p/s* order in an extended passage, thus mirroring the inversion of order, Plato *before* Socrates: "a *psychoanalysis of* the *post*, a *philosophy of* the *post*, the *of* signifying belonging or provenance, psychoanalysis or philosophy operating *since, on the basis of* the posts" (176). When the initials *pp* occur, they signify various thematically related possibilities: the postal principle, the pleasure principle, primary process, penny post, picture postcard, penman/postman, parallel police, public/private. The inversion of *p* and *s*, postal system, gives *S.* and *P.*, which "Derrida" gives as *secret de Polichinelle* (255), which Bass explains as "the secret known to all" (xxvi), which, as we have noted above, is one way to look at the sending of postcards through the postal system.

Another trope *The Post Card* shares with *Finnegans Wake* is the identity of opposites. "Derrida," for instance, identifies being saved with being lost (32), writing with destroying (33), truth as fantasy (46), criminal with victim (67). For Derrida, however, these operations measure the play of *différance* rather than identity, each "opposite" actually containing in it its "other" and so always already being "other" than it "is" at any moment. When "Derrida" writes "if we do not destroy all the traces, we are saved, that is, lost" (32), behind those words is an operation that for Derrida goes something like this: the trace is what remains of experience rather than the fullness and presence of experience. In not destroying those traces we are saved in that they let us know where we have been previously. In that way, the trace saves us in the sense of preserving our sense of ourselves. But that is a deceptive sense, given the nature of the self. A more accurate estimate would reflect the extent to which, as "prisoners" in the house of language, we are lost not only in our traces but also in ourselves as constructs of language. And of course one of the traces behind being saved as being lost is the religious paradox of saving one's life by losing it, and losing it by saving it.[16]

For Joyce, however, the identity of opposites is not the play of *différance*. In joining the acts of rejoicing and grieving in the portmanteau word "laughtears" (15.9), Joyce points to the experience that laughter may become, and frequently involves, tears and vice versa. But after joining, the two separate again, just as Shem and Shaun come together momentarily, as in the Jaun/Dave reconciliation passage (462–68) and then separate into their polarities. Another example involves the phrase "boesen fiennd" (345.33), where we hear not only "bosom friend" and "bosom fiend," but the German *bosen Feind* or evil enemy and the Dutch *boezemvriend* or bosom friend (McHugh, *Annotations,* 345). The phrase occurs in one of the Butt/Taff interchanges, where each is acting out the skit of Buckley's shooting the Russian general. In this situation, the impulses toward seeing the other as friend (in shared human needs) and fiend (as desecrating the sacred) are both present. But the two impulses are separate; the one does not contain the other. They merge momentarily to separate.

The treatment of comic and sacred is another instance of the "identity" of opposites. "Derrida" writes:

> as for our Socratic novel, our infernal post card history, that I found it "comic" does not disaccord with the sublime. It is the sacred, for me, today still, but as such it also makes me laugh, it does leave us laughter, thank God. There, nothing is ever forbidden us. (176)

Here the comic is joined with sublimity and with the sacred, the sacred is joined with laughter, the sacred is linked with temporality ("today still") and with openness to all experience rather than the forbidding of some experience, each of which pairs merges terms usually at war with each other. Joyce, too, works with these same pairings, joining the sublime and the comic, the sacred and the temporal, the sacred and openness to experience. This linkage is a continual operation in *Finnegans Wake*, visible in the parodies of the Lord's Prayer and the Hail Mary as well as in parodies of material from the holy books of other religions besides the Christian. But we must remember that for Derrida the context for the "sublime" and the "sacred" is "our Socratic novel, our infernal post card history"; in other words, Western philosophic tradition. "God" is only a signifier in the phrase "thank God." Now while Joyce certainly treats dogma and icons as if they are signifiers, malleable and plastic as any words may be, there is also the sense that the sacred may be something in itself, the sense that the comic may be something in itself—and that when the two merge it is not only that neither is defined by emptiness, but that both have a kind of enormous fullness. Not that Joyce defines the sacred as an Ineffable One, but that *Finnegans Wake* implies it may be some thing—the capacity for momentary unity and union of all that is, the plasticity of language—rather than merely illusion and philosophic error.[17]

A final trope that the two works have in common is number. In the *Wake*, every character has at least one and sometimes several numbers associated with it. HCE, for example, has metaphoric identities in 1 and 7; ALP, with 0 and 111; in union, 10 is their number. Issy as a Rainbow Girl has a metaphoric identity with 29 (leap year); the pub customers, with 12; the old historians, with 4 and their 5th, the donkey. In *The Post Card*, 7 has metaphoric import as a generic number for the concept of a set: the number of letters in Derrida's first and last names, "seventh heaven" (55), seven tangoes ("Libertango, Meditango, Undertango, Adios Nonian, Violentango, Novitango, Amelitango, Tristango" [55]). An especially strong instance of this occurs in the following passage:

> and on the card's itinerary, short pause, you encounter Aristoteles: the male who begins to have sperm at twice 7 years, the

gestation of fish that corresponds to a period divisible by 7, the death of newborns before the 7th day and this is why they receive their name on the 7th, and the foetus that lives if it is expulsed at 7 months, and not at 8 months, etc., so only circumcision was missing from this history of animals. The first telephone number in El-Biar, the unforgettable one I had told you, 730 47: in the beginning was a seven, and at the end, and in the middle 3 + 4, and it turns around zero, the central. (254)

The number 52 is also significant, "a blank of 52 signs" (4), as the signifier that "Derrida" leaves to show the effect of "incineration" on the postcards. The passage quoted above, for instance, is preceded by "a blank of 52 signs" (one for each week in the year? one for each card in a deck?).

It seems plausible that Derrida models his two major metaphors of postcard and message/sending on the *Wake*'s Letter and Shem/Shaun. In earlier sections of this chapter we discussed Shem and Shaun as metaphors for the message/sending and writing/reading process. We also noted the metaphoric identity of the postcard with an entire tradition of philosophic writing and the Letter as synecdoche of *Finnegans Wake* as well as of writing itself. Another major borrowing from Joyce probably involves the often comic sexualizing of the writing/reading relation and of the message itself. Because these points have been examined in some detail earlier in the chapter, we need not reconsider them here except to draw attention to these areas of enormous tropic confluence between *The Post Card* and *Finnegans Wake*. By way of taking leave, let us call attention to one more instance of such confluence, the phrase which in the *Wake* occurs as "on the void of to be" (100.27) and in *The Post Card* as *en voie de l'être* (195). For Joyce, the phrase occurs as part of a metaphor for HCE, Everyman according to both Joyce's and Derrida's understandings:[18] "the prisoner of that sacred edifice . . . was at his best a onestone parable, a rude breathing on the void of to be." Derrida through Bass as translator precedes the French phrase with an English translation: "The letter . . . recalled to whoever, or on the way to being so, *en voie de l'être* . . . then can not arrive at its destination." But of course *en voie de l'être* is the phonic homonym of "envoy of the letter," which refers to "Envois" as "preface" to the book "Derrida" did not write as well as "envoy of being," which refers to Heidegger's concern with the sending of Being, in addition to translating into French the English phrase in Joyce's *Wake*, "on the void of to be."

We return, now, to the observation and question with which we opened this chapter: with what interest does *The Post Card* fold *Finnegans Wake* into itself? To what purpose and effect? At the heart of each work is a message troped as card or letter that has been sent but not received. Each work tropes the present looking back at, and at the back of, the past and rewriting as well as being written by it. In folding the *Wake* into itself, *The Post Card* tropes this activity itself, looking back at and at the back of its past in the *Wake* and rewriting the *Wake* in *The Post Card* as well as being written by it.

NOTES

1. See chapter 5. Because "White Mythology" proposes a "truth," that philosophy exists in and through metaphor and thus cannot address reality or attain to absolute knowledge, it cannot be a text, which disseminates itself endlessly, refusing summarizing statements.

2. Jacques Derrida, *The Post Card*, trans. Alan Bass (Chicago: University of Chicago Press, 1987), 3. Subsequent references will be cited by page number in the text.

3. In her essay "The Letter of the Law: *La Carte Postale* in *Finnegans Wake*" (*Modern Philology* 63 [1984]: 163–85, Shari Benstock examines these bonds thus:

In following the letter of the law in *Finnegans Wake*, this essay pursues *La Carte Postale*, a text that places the *Wake* in the general consideration of correspondence, emphasizing the transfer of letters through the postal system of desire, under the (letter of the) law of the unconscious. (163)

4. Gregory L. Ulmer, "The Post-Age," *Diacritics* 11, no. 3 (Fall 1981): 55. Further references will be given by page number in the text, in association with Ulmer's name to distinguish page numbers referring to *The Post Card*.

5. Brendan O Hehir and John Dillon, *A Classical Lexicon for Finnegans Wake* (Berkeley and Los Angeles: University of California Press, 1977), xxi, 365.

6. Joyce constructs "sciencium" as word play with *silentium*, one member of the Silences motif.

7. "Derrida" indicates the character "I" who writes the post cards to "you," as distinct from Derrida, who wrote *The Post Card*.

8. These words belong under erasure, as do many of those to follow. But since the orthographics of continually encountering quotation marks or striking out words is distracting, I am announcing here that any and all words describing or naming the movements Derrida makes concerning writing/reading are to be considered as under erasure.

9. In the background of Derrida's text may be René Magritte's painting, "The Treachery (or Perfidy) of Images," 1928–29, held in a private collection in New York. The image shows a pipe floating in space, below which Magritte has the caption, "Ceci n'est pas une pipe." For a reproduction, see among other sources H. H. Arnason, *History of Modern Art* (New York: Abrams, 1968), 295.

10. Samuel Beckett, "Dante . . . Bruno. Vico . . Joyce," in Beckett et al., *Our Exagmination Round His Factification for Incamination of Work in Progress* (Paris: Shakespeare & Co., 1929), 14.

11. Derrida coins logocentrism as the name of the era from Socrates to the work of Nietzsche, Heidegger, and himself, which privileged speech as truth and presence over writing as deception and absence. See *Of Grammatology*, trans. Gayatri Chakravorty Spivak (Baltimore: Johns Hopkins University Press, 1976), 43.

12. Strong confirmation of this may be seen "graphically" in the word maps that Umberto Eco and John Bishop draw. See Bishop's *Joyce's Book of the Dark*, 186–87 and 204–5 as well as Eco's *Aesthetics of Chaosmos*, 71.

13. "Behind" Derrida's words we may hear Joyce's in *Ulysses:*
When Rutlandbaconsouthamptonshakespeare or another poet of the same name in the comedy of errors wrote *Hamlet* he was not the father of his own son merely but, being no more a son, he was and felt himself the father of all his race, the father of his own grandfather, the father of his unborn grandson who, by the same token, never was born for nature.
(*Ulysses* [New York: Random House, 1961], 208)
And "behind" Joyce's words we may hear Wordsworth's, "The Child is father of the Man," in "My Heart Leaps Up."

14. Given the "telecommunicative" efforts of the late Ayatollah Ruhollah Khomeini during the 1970s and 1980s, this phrase has a currency Joyce would have enjoyed.

15. See Glasheen's *Third Census*.

16. For a Christian statement of this notion, see John 3:3–18.

17. In a 1953 interview with Richard Ellmann, Samuel Beckett remarked that for Joyce "reality was a paradigm, an illustration of a possibly unstatable rule" (*James Joyce*, 562). Because Ellmann reports Beckett's words as an indirect quote, it is difficult to assess the mix of Joyce's, Beckett's, and Ellmann's wording.

18. This chapter opens with Derrida's statement about HCE.

PART 2
Tropes and Incoherence in the *Wake*

Chapter 7

Troping the *Wake*

Chapters 1 through 6 have examined *Finnegans Wake* in terms of the incoherence readers experience, whether this is the massive incoherence that deluges readers new to the *Wake* or the incoherence undergone willingly by experienced readers, who know that in plunging into immersion without bearings, or bearings at first inadequate to account for the few familiar "seamarks," they open themselves to the possibility of discovery which will lead to an integration larger than hitherto existed. Our concern turns now to the relation between this incoherence and the *Wake*'s tropic language. All language is tropic, of course, and so the phrase "tropic language" is redundant. But whereas some texts foster the illusion that their language is mimetic, or serves mimetic ends, from its opening words through its closing words that circle back to the beginning, *Finnegans Wake* forces readers to confront and operate on its tropism. We can read Anne Tyler's *The Accidental Traveler*, for instance, and, though aware of that text's tropic language, experience it as a secondary effect of reading. But if we try to do that with the *Wake*, we distort it beyond recognition as an experience of reading the language Joyce wrote.

It is not the case that mimetic language differs in kind from tropic language; rather, each has different investments. Writing recognized as tropic emphasizes language as discovery and production; writing recognized as mimetic sees language as recovery and reproduction. Mimetic language is deeply tropic; but mimetic language has conventionalized tropism until it appears mimetic.[1] What is the relationship between the *Wake*'s tropism and its incoherence? What operations do each of the "four master tropes," to use Kenneth Burke's phrase, perform as they work with incoherence, or the appearance of it? In *Finnegans Wake*, tropes not only enact incoherence, I am claiming, but they also act upon that incoherence such that their productivity, their movement, suggests connexity that counters incoherence. For

Jacques Lacan and Roman Jakobson, two tropes, metaphor and metonymy, define linguistic processes. Following James Mellard and, behind him, Hayden White and Kenneth Burke, however, I find that synecdoche and irony are equally necessary with metonymy and metaphor for describing the *Wake*'s verbal movement.[2]

Metaphor comes into play in *Finnegans Wake* especially through its characters, who function metaphorically. ALP successively takes on all the female roles, that is, and HCE all the male roles, the precise role determined by the context of events. Thus, at moments when she is most "mythic," ALP becomes Anna Livia: we see her as the washerwomen describe her in I.8, pages 206–12, as Anna prepares for her journey and delivers gifts to her river children; we hear her voice in IV, pages 619–28, as she prepares to pass out to sea to undertake her cycle once again. When ALP is most "human," she appears as the hag Kate, relegated to bearing messages and cleaning rooms. When she exists as the potential for fruitful generation, she appears as Issy or one of Issy's forms. Similarly, HCE takes on the "mythic" role of Finn as he lies interred in the landscape, awaiting his next rebirth as hero, in which form ALP addresses him on pages 621–26. As representative of a culture's polar trends to both break away from tradition and create new forms as well as to establish tradition and compel adherence to it, HCE divides himself into his Shem and Shaun selves. As bearer of sexual guilt, HCE presents the fallen, human condition. When shattered by forces he cannot withstand, he becomes the Humpty Dumpty who, contrary to nursery-rhyme expectations, *will* be put together again to fall and rise again.

These metaphoric identifications of one character with another build upon similarity and act through substitution of the form x is y. But characters have the additional metaphoric function of naming processes. Where both HCE and ALP participate in the processes of fertile procreativeness and intimate partnership in the fall and rise of "sin," each also is metaphor for processes not found in the other, which complement and supplement the other. The HCE principle of committing sin, experiencing guilt, and continually attempting to explain away that guilt is counterbalanced by the ALP principle of tempting, pleasuring, and defending the guilt-ridden male principle. One of the most intriguing processes that ALP and HCE name lies in the domain of how words move. As river, Anna Livia's motion flows continually onward, eventually recycling itself as she moves from tiny stream to river Liffey to Irish Sea, is absorbed as water droplets to form clouds that in turn rain down upon and feed the stream to begin the cycle once again. This motion corresponds to the motion of words in the *Wake*, flowing continually onward, eventually recycling themselves as they move from the first encounter a reader has with a given word to recognition that the word is being encountered again and again, to the word's finding a "place" for itself within a tale, to the word's continuing to disseminate itself throughout the rest of the text until readers reach page 628 and find ourselves washed back to the first page to begin the cyclical flow of words once more. As mountain, land, and city, HCE's process embodies growth through accretion rather than onward movement. For that reason his motion is stasis in order that accretion may occur. This stasis corresponds to the text's periodic tendency to precipitate out from its powerful onward flow into its tales—the "ondt and gracehoper," Buckley and the Russian general, the ship's captain, and so forth. The ALP process names the text's flow and continuity, then, whereas the HCE process is a paradigm of its accretiveness.

By substituting for each other in the manner of Derrida's "nonsynonymic substitutions," the metaphoric nature of the *Wake*'s characters enacts the incoherence of identity: on the same page *she* can refer to ALP as well as Kate; *he*, to Hosty, the Cad, or HCE. But by the same operation as it enacts incoherence, metaphor also acts upon that incoherence, insisting on the tropic similarity of these characters. If one character names, substitutes for, and is similar to a number of other characters, then incoherence gives rise to coherence through the connexity of similarity; and coherence gives way to incoherence as the destabilizing of preconceptions, such as, for instance, the notion that a character has a unified—implying single—identity.

Where metaphor is the trope especially active in guiding readers to the relationship among characters, the trope of metonymy operates strongly at all structural levels: words, sentences, paragraphs, fragments, chapters, books, text. Metonymic networking, Hilary Clark shows, functions at the level of images as well as verbal chains. Referring to the *Wake*'s clusters of river, tree, and body images, Clark writes,

> Whether watery, woody or carnal then, networks inform our thinking about knowledge and about the writing and reading of

Finnegans Wake. Images of interbranching emphasize the idea
that every point of human knowledge, every pun and portmanteau word in the *Wake* is related to every other via a proliferating
and multidimensional network of connections. . . . Of course,
this network underpins any literary work; however, the *Wake*
foregrounds and reveals connections in the system by means of
its own verbal chains and nodes so that the *Wake* becomes a
miniature version of the network of semantic competence underlying *all* speech.[3]

Clark describes the process of verbal networking as beginning "by
tracing a chain of members of a general category. A word suggests a
category; then by association, a list consisting of members of this
category leads away from the initial word" (749). One such chaining
Clark offers as an example involves the insect and animal network
on 516.03–22; another, consisting of five separate but interwoven
chains, involves "Shaun's association with the Postal Service, the
Church, music, excessive eating, and . . . fine clothing" (see 404.27–
405.02) ("Networking," 750–51).

One of the hundreds of metonymically constructed portmanteau
words is "cellelleneteutoslavzendlatinsoundscript" (219.17), in which
we both hear the sequence of languages—Celtic, Hellenic, Teutonic,
Slavic, Zend, Latin, Sanskrit—and see the celluloid possibilities of the
soundscript that the Mime, as context for the word under consideration, offers as a "crowdblast" "wordloosed over seven seas" or, in
other words, as a wireless production broadcast over the oceans.

The same metonymy operates when the layerings of a word are
vertical rather than horizontal. Thus, "retempter" (154.6) as applied
to the Gripes suggests simultaneously the Latin *retemptor,* a redeemer
(which translates the Latin term), and a re-tempter. One type of
sentence that has its structure in metonymy may be seen in any of
the giant list sentences, such as the names of ALP's "untitled mamafesta," 104–7, or the description of Shem's house, 182–84. But the
more usual type may be seen in any of the sentences on the first page
of *Finnegans Wake.* The shortest is "Rot a peck of pa's malt had Jhem
or Shen brewed by arclight and rory end to the regginbrow was to
be seen ringsome on the aquaface." Here we move through the sequence of references to the popular song, "Willie Brewed a Peck o'
Malt," to Shem's and Shaun's imbibing of their father's liquor, to

Jameson whiskey, to the Guinness brewery, to the first two syllables of the Latin word *roridus*, whose meaning of "dewy" meshes with the generally "wet" images that populate the sentence, to Noah's drunkenness, to the Chinese word *shen*, meaning god or spirit, of which both whiskey and beer are examples, to the expectation that what one finds at the end of a rainbow is both dew and the color red, to the German words for "rainbow" and for "around," and to Genesis 1:1, whose words "And the spirit of God moved upon the face of the waters" are recalled at the end of the sentence.

Although all of the *Wake*'s chapters have a metonymic construction, I will work with II.2 to exemplify this. The spatial orientation of section 1, 260.01–263.30, articulates with the time orientation of section 2, 264.01–266.19, where readers see HCE, ALP, and the pub first in terms of their locations as places and bodies occupying physical space and then in terms of their historical development over time. The time of adulthood in section 2 is associated with the time of childhood in section 3, 266.20–275.02, as readers shift from HCE and ALP as adults into their younger forms as Issy and Shem/Shaun. Section 4, the original "Scribbledehobble" piece, incorporated into section 5, 275.03– 279.09, focuses a cause/effect relationship with this cyclic recurrence, recycling a number of the *Wake*'s major themes. The sexuality projected by Issy's footnote letter, which constitutes section 6, shows sequential progression with sections 4/5 as the means by which recurrence takes place. Issy's letter in section 7, 280.01–282.04, offers a part-to-part articulation with the letter of section 6, its "socially correct" form serving the same goals as does her "indiscreet" letter. Section 8, 282.05–304.04, offers metonymic renaming to these sexual concerns as the twins take their turn at adolescent knowledge of adult sexuality. All three children thus initiated into the condition of sexual knowledge, section 9 shows sequential progression with section 8 as the three prepare to take over their parents' place in time, having displayed their "knowledge" through a series of essay topics composing a sort of history that shows their readiness to "act" as well as to "know."

The structure of each of the four books of the *Wake* is also metonymic. In book I, for instance, the introduction of motifs and characters performed by chapter 1 has a part-to-part relationship with the background and general history of HCE offered by chapter 2. But as we learn in chapter 3, to know HCE's background is also to know (and hence to not know) his crime, which functions metonymically in chapter 4 as a name change for his death or disappearance. The Letter that chapter 5 presents offers readers a variety of readings for HCE or for any other "life" or history. An equivalent manner of "doing" history, the radio quiz program of chapter 6 parades us through another series of histories as one by one we visit the text's themes and characters. The "shaunish" orientation of chapter 6 finds its metonymic difference in that of chapter 7 as we meet Shem through "shaundished" eyes. A knower's recounting through a knowing that is inadequate to the condition to be known marks the metonymic difference and contiguity of chapters 7 and 8, where in the latter we meet the mythic stature of ALP through the diminishing vision of the washerwomen.

The trope of metonymy enacts incoherence through juxtaposing difference with difference; but in so doing, metonymy acts upon incoherence in such a way as to produce the connexity of part to part. If instead of the situation x is y we have the situation of x, y, then we must explore what in y is contiguous with x such that it can associate with x.

If the relation of character to character is metaphoric and the construction of discrete verbal units from the smallest through the largest is metonymic, synecdoche gives the relation of any one part to the larger cluster of which it is part. Robert Spoo declares that "the master trope of *Finnegans Wake* is synecdoche—the trope that permits of discoveries through either end of the telescope," which echoes Hazard Adams's claim that "synecdoche is the privileged trope of Viconian poetic history, as it is of *Finnegans Wake*."[4] While I claim none of the four tropes functions in a privileged or master relation to the others, just as no one character or tale or motif has a privileged or master position, the *Wake* does comment reflexively on its own synecdoche: "a part so ptee does duty for the holos" (19.01); "allforabit" (19.02); "a part of the whole as a port for a whale" (135.28); "the park is gracer than the hole" (512.28).

*Wake*an synecdoche operates chronologically as well as spatially, the part not merely standing for the whole, but actually being identical with the whole.[5] Thus the Letter not only stands for *Finnegans Wake* but is identical with *Finnegans Wake*; Irish history not only stands for the history of culture but *is* that history; Dublin not only stands for all cities but *is* everycity. Synecdoche that insists on part-whole identity rather than the part merely standing for the whole affirms paradox and oxymoron as its root. This synecdoche, which Joyce perhaps draws from Blake, places between the bounded and the infinite, between the open and the closed, the copula.[6] The bounded *is* the infinite; the infinite *is* the bounded.[7]

Such synecdoche by implication makes the *Wake*'s dreamer-reader-viewer both universal in everywoman-everyman and particular in each woman and each man. We are dealing here with the Viconian notion of the imaginative or poetic universal in relation to the concrete particular. But Vico believed the imaginative universal superior to the concrete particular in its capacity for attaining truth, the latter capable of reaching only certainty.[8] Thus, the whole that Vico's imaginative universal offered was greater than that of the concrete particular. Through *Finnegans Wake* Joyce denies this. If the concrete particular *is* the imaginative universal in addition to the imaginative universal's being the concrete particular, both are of equal magnitude, neither can be greater than the other, and each attains the same degree of truth and certainty, which in the *Wake* are constructed through competing perspectives rather than reconstructed from preexisting absolutes.

The *Wake* treats history and numbers as among the synecdochic processes showing the equivalence of imaginative universal and concrete particular. Imaginative universals in history, which is a metonym for myth, include the founding of a civilization by invasion, the history of a culture as the myriad entanglements of love and war, the pub as social institution, the battle for supremacy between old and new political-religious-social forces, and sexuality as the hub of both social and individual life.

Not only is Irish history a universal history and Dublin history that of all cities, but Napoleon and Wellington become any two opposing commanders; Parnell, any betrayed leader; Kitty O'Shea, the temptress behind any man; Mutt's and Jute's "dialogue," that between any conquered and conquering people; the Battle of Clontarf, any successful repulsion of invaders by the invaded; Brian Boru, any native hero; the dialogue between St. Patrick and the Archdruid, any conflictual encounter between an older and a newer religious order.

Each of the text's tales functions as an imaginative universal for history-myth, the tale of Jarl van Hoother and the Prankquean, for instance, offering the story of how negotiated settlements come about. The characters, too, function as imaginative universals, though not in the sense that—to use Vico's example—Homer's Ulysses gives the type for the clever man. Instead, each character is a set or collection of possibilities more diverse and/or more prototypical than any one concrete particular can exhibit. Thus, HCE is an imaginative universal possessing the potentialities and, at times, the actualities of Finn MacCool, Jarl van Hoother, Persse O'Reilly, the Russian general, the Norwegian captain, Parnell, King Mark, mountains, cities, and space. As imaginative universal, ALP comprehends the potentialities and, at times, the actualities, of mistress, wife, mother, daughter, hag, river, time, Penelope, Eve, the Prankquean, the hen. The relation of ALP and HCE to their concrete particulars is of course synecdochic.

The treatment of numbers as synecdochic process is equally important. As Glasheen and many other critics have pointed out, certain numbers are associated with particular characters.[9] But these numbers themselves have a synecdochic relation to the characters with whom they are associated. Thus, HCE is linked with the number 1 as synecdochic of several of his aspects: as the head or first man; as the erect penis. He has links with at least three other numbers. Seven names the number of articles of clothing he is consistently described as wearing and suggests his ties to the rainbow girls. Ten is his number when he is named in association with ALP, where its components of 1 and 0 represent HCE and ALP in their generative, reproductive capacities. 1132 breaks down into two components, each of which names a dichotomy within HCE: 11 as a number associated with renewal (10 as the number of a completed cycle, as in a decade, plus 1 to begin the next cycle) and 32 as a number associated with the Fall (objects fall to earth at the rate of 32 feet per second per second), which two aspects of renewal and Fall or guilt represent HCE's two primary impulses.

ALP is associated with at least three numbers: the zero, which functions as the sign of her vagina as well as the second digit of 10 which, like her, has neither beginning nor end but instead a perfect continuity; 40, which may be her age; and 111, the children she has produced considered as three ones, as well as the 111 tributaries that she has given birth to as river. Two is the number of the female principle, the two labial lips, two seen in Issy's double nature and the two females involved in the park incident; 3 is the number of the male principle, the penis and testicles, as indicated by the trios of male names such as Tom, Dick, and Harry as well as Shem, Ham, and Japheth, and also the three males involved in the park venture.

Four is the number associated with Mamalujo, whose most common name, in fact, is The Four: Matthew, Mark, Luke, John; Ulster, Munster, Leinster, Connaught; gold, silver, copper, iron; the four compass directions; the four annalists; the list of fours continues almost indefinitely. Six is the number of the twelve pub customers, often presented as two pairs of six. Seven is the number of the Flora girls. The numbers 283, 566, and 1132 function as generic names of years for "historic" events. Joyce thus demonstrates his conviction of the arbitrary connection between time and the events in history, as 566 is 283 × 2, and 1132 is formed by 283 × 4, 283 being, among other possibilities, the "year" of the death of Finn MacCool (McHugh, *Annotations*, 13).

The final synecdoche I want to consider involves the sexual act as synecdochic for all modes of founding: building a family, establishing a new social order, merging religious traditions, gaining knowledge. Common to all these acts of founding is the dynamics they share: the pattern of two or more formally separate perspectives coming together in some degree of involvement, leading to greater and greater integration of those perspectives, culminating in a climax, after which a separation of the two interests occurs, eventually leading to a beginning again of another mutual involvement, and so on. Stated most simply, this is the cyclic pattern of rise and fall, tumescence and detumescence, resurrection and dying. It is the cycle of desire: a period of mutually increasing desire, the satisfaction of that desire in some interpenetrating union, separation of the component parts leading to the possibility of renewed desire. Let us consider this cycle of desire as founding act as it moves through the Prankquean tale. The Prankquean "kidsnaps" the first jiminy, Tristopher, as part of her desire for vengeance against Jarl van Hoother for an insult, possibly his refusing to admit her willingly to his castle. When that action fails to fulfill her desire, she returns Tristopher and takes up the jiminy Hilary. When that, too, fails, she returns Hilary for a third attempt, but at this point the union leading to satisfaction of desire occurs: on her previous two attempts the Prankquean had engaged in "wetting" ("she made her witter before the wicked" [22.4–5] and "made her wittest in front of the arkway of trihump" [22.28]), which we should understand as both the act of micturating and fertilizing, as a prelude to asking the riddle of Jarl, "why do I am alook alike three poss of porter pease" (22.29–30). At those times Jarl could not respond to her, instead "laying cold hands on himself" at the top of his castle (21.10–11) or else "shaking warm hands with himself" in his cellar (21.35–36). But at the Prankquean's third approach, Jarl charges out to her "like the campbells acoming with a fork lance of lightning" (22.31) and "ordurd," which act calls forth a thunderword, the sound of his order to her which is simultaneously his ordure. This satisfaction of desire—he having opened his door and offered an act which balances hers of "wetting"—leads to the treaty that brings peace to their respective domains ("The prankquean was to hold her dummyship and the jimminies was to keep the peacewave and van Hoother was to git the wind up" [23.12–14]). Jarl van Hoother and the Prankquean now pursue their separate ends, which in time will lead to the renewal of desire and the beginning of the cycle once more in the next tale—the Mookse and the Gripes, Dolph and Kev's geometry lesson, Buckley and the Russian general, the tailor and the Norwegian ship's captain, Tristan and Iseult, and so on.

As do metaphor and metonymy, synecdoche both enacts chaos and acts upon it, transforming it. If metaphor tropes the identity of characters in the *Wake* and metonymy tropes the construction of words, paragraphs, chapters, and books, synecdoche tropes process in the *Wake*. The part contains the whole in terms of sharing its process and appearance; but similarly, the whole shares the part's process and appearance. And it is the latter part of the statement that fosters the reader's sense of experiencing chaos since, in *Finnegans Wake*, the whole of the text will share the part's appearance of disconnected fragmentation.[10] But in undergoing the possibility of fragmentation and disconnection, the reader begins to discover connexities within disconnectedness, shapes within the fragment. Through enacting chaos, then, the text acts on chaos so as to suggest its otherness—pattern and connection.

The remaining major trope, irony, accounts for much of the shape and tone of *Finnegans Wake*. As the trope of denial leading to dialectic, irony takes the form x is (not) y.[11] In both affirming that one thing is another thing and, simultaneously, is not that other thing, irony places the two things into dialectic relation with each other.

The beginning both is and is not the end; the rise both is and is not the fall, and so on. Irony thus contradicts the possibility for romance and tragedy and links comedy with satire. We see this operation toward the end of ALP's final monologue, where in her loneliness, isolation, and bitterness, she has the potential for assuming tragic dimensions. But just as this possibility asserts itself in our minds, she washes out to sea, to mingle her waters with those of her "cold mad feary father," where in losing her identity as self she creates the possibility for return in the cyclic process of synecdoche, which occurs, of course, as readers recycle back to the beginning to find her continuation. In the situation of Tristan and Iseult as young lovers in II.4, although we might expect the situation of romance, the text disallows that possibility by counterpointing their youth with the agedness of The Four and treating their lovemaking as soccer match, with orgasm a scoring of the goal. Northrop Frye identifies irony with cyclicity, which names the *Wake*'s shape,[12] Joyce suggesting, for example, that in *Finnegans Wake* he had squared the circle (*Letters* 3:161 n. 6; see also 186.12). As is appropriate for a text that splits and opposes itself in nearly every way possible, irony works in at least a double direction, both toward the ironic parodying of the sacred or the ironic sacralizing of the profane as well as toward the ironic masking of a vulnerable tenderness. The majority of religious references operate in the direction of ironic religious parody, as in the following passage:

> For hear Allhighest sprack for krischnians as for propagana fidies and his nuptial eagles sharped their beaks of prey: and every morphyl man of us, pome by pome, falls back into this terrine: as it was let it be, says he! And it is as though where Agni araflammed and mithra monished and Shiva slew as mayamutras the obluvial waters of our noarchic memory withdrew, windingly goharksome, to some hastyswasty timberman torchpriest, flamenfan, the ward of the wind that lightened the fire that lay in the wood that Jove bolt, at his rude word. (80.20–28)

"Krischnians" suggests both Christians and Hindu adherents of the god Krishna; to the Christian and Hindu religions are added several others with the references to both Jove and Mithra, the Persian god of light. The same Allhighest speaks equally for all four, though not for transcendent purposes but for such propaganda or missionary work as to require "his nuptial eagles" to sharp "their beaks of prey." The result is not passage into eternal life but another fall, this time "back into this terrine: as it was let it be, says he!" And regardless of the punitive or militaristic efforts of the gods Agni, Mithra, and Siva, human memory seeks solace in the magic words of a priesthood, whose words the narrator equates with the significance of "The House That Jack Built" through the rhythms of the last twelve or fifteen words.

The inverse of this profanation of the sacred is the sacralizing of the profane, seen, for instance, in Shem's making ink from his own excrement and urine. Irony of tone operates at a number of levels: in the nature of the situation itself, in the presentation of this act in High Church Latin (see 185), in the contrast between the abstract formality of the Latin and the "earthy" informality of the English parenthetical remarks ("highly prosy, crap in his hand, sorry!" "did a piss, says he was dejected, asks to be exonerated," "faked O'Ryan's, the indelible ink"), in declaring the similarity of this mission to that of "pious Eneas." But the sacralizing *is* present: whether interpreted literally or metaphorically as his decision to write autobiographically of the most "material" aspects of his life or to develop an original way of writing that will recognize the most "earthy" materials of life, its excrement, as just as deserving of a place in literature as the more exalted aspects—Shem's effort to create his own ink does result in the production of a sacred text, the *Wake,* sacred in the Viconian sense that the language the text creates shows forth its own divinity, which, in the *Wake* is its humanity. This is the founding of a new order, in a way entirely comparable with Eneas's founding of a new order.

The inverse in tone of both kinds of ironies so far examined is the use of irony as mask, behind which resides a vulnerable tenderness. We experience this, for instance, in some of the prayers the text offers and in some of the Anna Livia passages. The prayer that concludes II.2 reads:

> O Loud, hear the wee beseech of thees of each of these thy unlitten ones! Grant sleep in hour's time, O Loud!
> That they take no chill. That they do ming no merder. That they shall not gomeet madhowiatrees.

Loud, heap miseries upon us yet entwine our arts with laugh-
ters low!
Ha he hi ho hu.
Mummum.

Tenderness is masked by such ironies as reference to God as "O
Loud," which recalls Vico's belief that early humans conceived the
notion of god in the effort to interpret thunderclaps;[13] as the request
that no more than an hour's sleeplessness be endured; as the injunc-
tion that the beseechers "do ming no merder," which covers not only
the familiar commandment against killing, but also suggests the Latin
for urination as well as the French for excrement. But the tenderness
is present even more strongly: in the condition of the beseechers as
"these thy unlitten ones," "unlitten" suggesting those yet unborn or
unlittered, the condition of being unenlightened, and vulnerability
through being unlettered; in the requests for protection against
"chill," which can assume so many forms, and meeting "madhowia-
trees," which suggests the suffering of madness, howling, distress;
in the supplication for laughter as a counterbalance against misery;
in the prayer's final two syllables that suggest the rich possibilities
of *aum*, the holy syllable of the Upanishads, another variation of
amen, the German word for courage, *mumm*, and another of the text's
injunctions for silence.

Irony's tropic movement of both affirming and denying what it
asserts of course functions as rich seedbed of chaos in which the
reader may lie. But in being forced toward formulations such as *the
sacred is (not) the profane* and *the profane is (not) the sacred*, readers must
expand their notions of what they had considered sacred and profane. When this begins to happen, irony moves from enacting chaos
toward acting upon it so as to shape through dialectic a more compre-
hensive view or image than that which the reader had formerly held.

In exploring how each of the four tropes functions in *Finnegans
Wake*, I may have implied unintentionally that within a given unit
of the text one trope operates at a time. But instead the situation
obtains that in any given unit, whether word or paragraph, all four
function as supplements of each other. To show this, I want to consider four passages in which the *Wake* comments reflexively upon
itself. In doing so, I draw as a model on Hazard Adam's analysis of
how the four tropes constitute ALP:

ALP is the mother of Shem, Shaun, and Issy; she is also the mother of the letter. By metaphor she is all female figures. By metonymy she is the letter(s) she writes. By a synecdoche that contains this metonymy she is *Finnegans Wake*. Finally, by irony, which encloses the functioning of these tropes, she is, as Frye some years ago observed, a cyclical conception. She is the mover-movement of time and the text, never completed and always of the earth.[14]

We will follow a progression in these *mise en abymes*, from the Letter as words of a given appearance, to the Letter as words making a given impact, to the Letter as words issuing from a given writer, to the Letter as words composing a given kind of "totality." In the following passage we encounter the Letter's words as appearance:

One cannot help noticing that rather more than half of the lines run north-south in the Nemzes and Bukarahast directions while the others go west-east in search from Maliziies with Bulgarad. . . . But by writing thithaways end to end and turning, turning and end to end hithaways writing and with lines of litters slittering up and louds of latters slettering down . . . where in the waste is the wisdom? (114.2–5, 16–21)

In terms of metaphor, the Letter's words are a litter, a disorder, its "lines of litters slittering up and louds of latters slettering down." Metonymically, this is the sequential progression within which the words as appearance occur: we read what seem to be the words ALP has actually used in her letter (113.11–18); then we encounter the description quoted above (114.2–21); after which we read about the stains marking the letter (114.21–33). Reduced to the fewest words, this progression suggests that first we encounter "content," which we then observe as shaped in a certain way, after which we note how "life experiences" have "colored" this shape and content. As synecdoche, the appearance of the Letter's words form the microcosm to the macrocosm of the world: both are maps to be read, with lines of longitude and latitude (half its lines running "north-south," the other half, "west-east"); its "cardinal points"; the circular shape ("turning, turning and end to end"). As irony, the appearance of the Letter's words are (not) ordered and, simultaneously, are (not) disordered.

The words' "waste" is (not) "wisdom," and yet the "wisdom" is (not) "waste."

In this next passage we encounter the Letter's words as making a given impact:

> if a human being duly fatigued . . . , having plenxty off time on his gouty hands and vacants of space at his sleepish feet and as hapless behind the dreams of accuracy . . . were at this auctual futule preteriting unstant . . . accorded . . . an earsighted view of old hopeinhaven . . . could such a none . . . byhold at ones what is main and why tis twain, how one once meet melts in tother wants poignings . . . then *what* would that fargazer seem to seemself to seem seeming of, dimm it all:
> Answer: A collideorscape! (143.4–28)

As metaphor, the impact of interpreting the dreamer's dream is similar to the impact of reading *Finnegans Wake* is similar to the impact of "a collideorscape," understood as both the impact of looking at objects through a kaleidoscope and a dreamscape marked by collisions. As metonymy, question 9 and its answer quoted above lies between question 8, which inquires about the maggies, and question 10, which inquires into the nature of love and receives, as answer, Issy's "pepette" love letter. Placing the question about the impact of the Letter's words between Issy's temptress love letter and the maggies as metonymic temptresses who begin by "war loving" and, as signifier displaces signifier, end by "pick[ing] one man more," underlines the Letter as product of love and as female sponsored. Through synecdoche, the question of how to interpret the dream, which is the question of how to read *Finnegans Wake*, becomes the question of interpreting life in its broadest terms: to both find some unifying impulse and yet perceive the multiplicity continuously interacting with that unity ("byhold at ones what is main and why tis twain"). In terms of irony, the situation of x is (not) y resides in the components of the word "collideorscape," the answer to the question of what is the impact of the Letter's words. O Hehir and Dillon give as the definition of the Greek *kaloeidoskopos*, "beautiful-shape-watcher," and as the definition of the Latin *collido*, "to clash, beat or press together; to bring into conflict."[15] The definition of *kaloeidoskopos* is (not) that of *collido*.

In the third of the reflexive passages we encounter words as issuing from a given writer:

> this Esuan Menschavik and the first till last alshemist wrote over every square inch of the only foolscap available, his own body, till by its corrosive sublimation one continuous present tense integument slowly unfolded all marryvoising moodmoulded cyclewheeling history (thereby, he said, reflecting from his own individual person life unlivable, transaccidentated through the slow fires of consciousness into a dividual chaos, perilous, potent, common to allflesh, human only, mortal) but with each word that would not pass away the squidself which he had squirtscreened from the crystalline world waned chagreenold and doriangrayer in its dudhud. (185.34–186.8)

These words issue from a writer who is an "alshemist," thereby making the words, through metaphor, a matter of alchemy, transmuting the "dung" ("bedung" [185.32]) of life into words "that would not pass away." Through metonymy, Shem's body is his writing, as cause to effect. Through synecdoche, Shem is all writers, people who embody their writing in the writing of their bodies. And through irony, the text is "human only" and "mortal," but the words which constitute it will "not pass away." And, through another irony, that writing is "one continuous present tense integument," but it is composed of past, present, future, the Vico cycle of "unfold[ing]" at birth, "marry[ing]" into union with otherness, "mould"[ing] upon death, to be re-"cycle"ed into "history."

In the final reflexive passage we are considering, we encounter the Letter's words as constituting a given "totality":

> Our wholemole millwheeling vicociclometer, a tetradomational gazebocroticon . . . autokinatonetically preprovided with a clappercoupling smeltingworks exprogressive process . . . receives through a portal vein the dialytically separated elements of precedent decomposition for the verypetpurpose of subsequent recombination so that the heroticisms, catastrophes and eccentricities transmitted by the ancient legacy of the past, type by tope, letter from litter, word at ward . . . in fact, the sameold gamebold adomic structure of our Finnius the old One, as highly

charged with electrons as hophazards can effective it, may be there for you, Cockalooralooraloomenos, when cup, platter and pot come piping hot, as sure as herself pits hen to paper and there's scribings scrawled on eggs. (614.27–615.10)

Metaphorically, the words constitute the Letter as a Vico-cyclometer, a "totality" we experience as cyclic in the manner of Vico, coming into being, maturing, dying, being reborn—historically, culturally, linguistically; as a "cycle" that we must make turn through our readerly efforts; as a measure or "meter" of cyclicity. As metonymy the "vicociclometer" passage is cause to the effect of ALP's final monologue, the text tells us:

> as sure as herself pits hen to paper and there's scribings scrawled on eggs.
> Of cause, so! And in effect, as?
> Dear. And we go on to Dirtdump. Reverend. May we add majesty? (615.10–13)

Through synecdoche the Letter as "vicocyclometer" is microcosm to the macrocosm of *Finnegans Wake*, which in turn is microcosm to the world as litter or letter (O Hehir lists the Irish *liter*, meaning "letter," for the word *litter*).[16] Through irony, the Letter may arrive in the morning mail, and, again, it may not (the vicociclometer "may be there for you . . . when cup, platter and pot come piping hot"), but *may* is conditional. This is another instance of irony's x is (not) y, since the expectation that the Letter will arrive is enough to guarantee the continuation of the life process, "precedent decomposition for the verypetpurpose of subsequent recombination."

The tropism of *Finnegans Wake* is pervasive. The large-scale processes constituting books and text are identical with the small-scale processes that constitute words, sentences, and motifs: the similarity between related things that allows one to substitute for or replace another; the articulation of one thing to another, their contiguity acting to create associations; the interchangeability of one thing as part to another as whole, which in turn becomes part to a larger whole; the simultaneous affirmation and denial of two things as (not) forms of each other. But if the *Wake*'s language tropes everything it touches, then the notion of a literal level itself undergoes tropism and must be written about, instead, as "literal." As Stephen Heath observes, *Finnegans Wake*

> deconstructs the fundamental (contextual) distinction between the literal and the figurative: according to what criteria are any particular elements to be identified as metaphors in a text in which every element refers to another, perpetually deferring meaning.[17]

As examples of the text's "literal" level, consider the following statements:

> *Finnegans Wake* is set in Chapelizod. . . . The date of *Finnegans Wake* is Monday, the twenty-first of March, 1938, and the early morning of Tuesday the twenty-second. . . . Physically, HCE is a fat fifty-six year old man in terrible condition, white-haired, red-nosed, toothless, purblind and be-spectacled, once tall and straight, now stooped—he leans on a cane—and gross.[18]

John Gordon's descriptions, as parts, are not inaccurate; indeed, Gordon establishes textual bases for virtually all of his statements. But they are incomplete. Each needs to be supplemented by metaphoric substitution, metonymic association, synecdochic part-whole relatedness, and ironic denial-affirmation. Thus, while *Finnegans Wake* is set in Chapelizod, it is simultaneously set in the mind of a dreamer, in Ireland as a whole, in the world as a whole; its setting is as much nowhere as it is everywhere and somewhere. But the necessity for such processes problematizes the notion of representation. As N. Katherine Hayles writes,

> The proposition that we are always already within the theater of representation assumes at the outset that no unambiguous or necessary connection can be forged between reality and our representations. Whatever reality is, it remains unknowable by the finite subject. . . . The difference between a representation that is consistent with reality and one that depicts reality is the difference between a metaphor and a description. (*Chaos Bound*, 223)

Hayles's statement reverberates with Samuel Beckett's comment that for Joyce "reality was a paradigm, an illustration of a possibly unstatable rule" (Ellmann, *James Joyce*, 562). If reality is a "paradigm" and an "illustration," reality (always) already operates within the realm of trope. And if what reality illustrates is "possibly unstatable," then reality tropes something which is (always) already trope. Further, if that troping of a trope tropes a "rule," then the rule, too, is trope. Rewording, then, through substitution, reality, for Joyce, was a trope, a trope of a troped trope. Which brings us back, by "a commodius vicus of recirculation" (3.02), to our linking of the tropic nature of the *Wake*'s language to the reader's experiencing it as incoherence that approaches chaos. The context of Hayles's statement is her examination of the links among the new area of science called chaos theory, poststructuralism, and contemporary fiction. While in terms of its date of publication *Finnegans Wake* does not qualify as contemporary fiction, its constitution as text bears poststructuralist marks, such as indeterminacy, unreadability, resistance to paraphrase, and nonlinearity. In the second half of this century, Hayles observes, a variety of sciences as well as mathematics and literary studies had become "interested in exploring the possibilities of disorder," including nonlinear dynamics, fluid mechanics, quantum electrodynamics, fractal geometry, thermodynamic irreversible systems, biological systems theory, meteorology, epidemiology, and poststructuralism (*Chaos Bound*, xii–xiii). The link among these areas involves "the way chaos is seen; the crucial turn comes when chaos is envisioned not as an absence or void but as a positive force in its own right" (3), which is made possible by "the separation of information from meaning" (6). Within science two branches of chaos theory have arisen: the "strange-attractor branch," which focuses on "the orderly descent into chaos," and the "order-out-of-chaos" branch, which focuses on "the organized structures that emerge from chaos" (10). The "attractor" in the former branch is "simply any point within an orbit that seems to attract the system to it" (147). Interesting parallels exist between that notion and the use of "attractor" sets of terms within paragraphs or blocks of paragraphs that give focus and direction for how readers should relate that unit to other parts of the *Wake*. The sets of animal and insect "attractors" in III.3, for instance, focus readers' attention on HCE, under interrogation throughout the chapter, who as Earwicker is associated with "earwig" and as master builder of civilizations, with "cock."[19]

Other descriptions of chaos theory seem to apply to *Finnegans Wake* as well. Twentieth-century connotations of chaos involve "maximum information, dissipative reorganization, and deeply encoded structure" (19). About the *Wake*'s five major characters, readers receive nearly endless information—remembering that information, in chaos theory, is separate from meaning; that the text's organization is the reorganization of materials from Joyce's earlier writing as well as from the world's cultures; and that the more scholars study *Finnegans Wake*, the more they discover "deeply encoded structure," whether this is the structure of the *Wake* as text written by and of the sleeping body or as alchemical number system.[20] Hayles writes that while literary theorists "like chaos because they see it as opposed to order," scientists of chaos theory "value chaos as the engine that drives a system toward a more complex kind of order. They like chaos because it makes order possible" (22–23). The chaos of *Finnegans Wake* is more like that of scientific chaos theory than that of the literary theorists Hayles posits since rather than find that the text's chaos opposes order, what readers experience as chaos virtually without exception forces them to reconceive the structure of chaos such that it moves "toward a more complex kind of order." Hayles observes that

> the importance of chaos theory does not derive . . . solely from the new theories and techniques it offers. Rather, part of its importance comes from its re-visioning of the world as dynamic and nonlinear, yet predictable in its very unpredictability. (143)

Joyce hoped that by composing *Finnegans Wake* in discrete units related to each other in multiple kinds of ways, he was creating a dynamic, and nonlinear, system. Concerning the Patrick and Berkeley unit (609–13), Joyce wrote that "these are not fragments but active elements and when they are more and a little older they will begin to fuse of themselves" (*Letters* 1:205). Chaos theory looks in new ways at what appears to be chaos. This involves seeing the "recursive symmetry" in repeating processes such that rather than being stymied by the differences in the "particularities of a given function," one focuses instead on "universality in the way large-scale features relate[d] to small details" (154). Hayles exemplifies recursive symmetry through the following thought experiment:

> Imagine two paintings, each showing an open door through which is revealed another open door, through which is another and another. . . . One way to think about the doors in these two paintings is to focus on the particularities of the repeated forms. Suppose the doors of the first painting are ornately carved rectangles, whereas the second painting shows doors that are unadorned arches. If we attend only to shapes, the paintings may seem very different. But suppose we focus instead on the recursive repetition and discover that in both paintings, the doors become smaller at a constant rate. Through this shift in focus we have found a way of looking at the paintings that reveals their similarity to each other and to any other painting constructed in this way. The key is recursive symmetry. (154)

The notion of recursive symmetry is significant for understanding the dynamics of a number of *Wake*an metaphoric processes. Take, for example, the triangulation among sexual desire, theology, and humor. Each of these is a door opening on an unknown; what *Finnegans Wake* does is to align these doors so that when one opens the door of sexual desire, behind its productive desiring is desire for merging with the infinite. But when one looks out that theological door, behind its productive desiring is the desire for merging with humor, its desire for amalgamation with the other—often at the other's expense—producing a merging between the infinite and finite unknown at least on a local level.

In chaos theory, the notion of recursive symmetry operates in tandem with the notion that the results of measurement are dependent on the scale used for measuring rather than claiming scale invariance for its results. The results of measurement depend not only on the relative units of the scale used but indeed on the type of scale itself. Thus, humor as the scale for measuring one's desire for merging with the other gives a different measurement than do the scales of theology or sexual desire. But all three processes measure the dynamics of merger.

One of the ironies of chaos theory is that unpredictability does not oppose pattern. Referring to the results of several groups of scientists, Hayles notes that "'chaos' connotes a *patterned* unpredictable trajectory" (216), commenting that "even Mandelbrot (1983), though his rhetoric celebrates disorder, looks for the symmetry groups that will allow chaos to be understood as iterative extensions of regular forms" (216). In *Finnegans Wake,* such symmetry groups include the Cad, Hosty, and HCE; Jarl van Hoother, the Norwegian ship's captain, the Russian general; Iseult, Issy, and Esther van Homrigh; the Prankquean, ALP, and the hen, Biddy Doran. Readers see evidence of *"patterned* unpredictable trajectory" in both small and large units. A number of details on pages 119 to 124 that might otherwise offer only "information" take on "pattern" as well when readers can extrapolate from Joyce's words to *The Book of Kells* and see that the latter text patterns the *Wake.* Thus the following words describe the *Kells's* manuscript style as well as that of the Letter:

> For, with that farmfrow's foul flair for that flayfell foxfetor . . . who that scrutinising marvels at those indignant whiplooplashes; those so prudently bolted or blocked rounds; the touching reminiscence of an incompletet trail or dropped final; a round thousand whirligig glorioles. (119.10–15)

A final parallel between chaos theory and *Finnegans Wake* involves the relation between "local" and "global." In chaos theory, according to Hayles,

> The local designates the site within the global at which the self-similarities characteristic of the system are reproduced. Conceived as images of each other, local and global are related as microcosm is to macrocosm, although each level also contains areas so complex that they are effectively chaotic. (219)

This, of course, is the iterative process by which, for instance, ALP comprehends all stages of female life, the global form of the local Issy, Anna Livia, and Kate; and HCE, all stages of male life, the global form of Dolph and Kev, Shem and Shaun, St. Patrick and the archdruid. It is as well the process by which Joyce writes universal history/myth as the recursive symmetry of alternating between global lovemaking and global war making, using "local" love affairs such as that of Dermot and Grania and "local" wars as the Battle of the Boyne.

Iterativeness, recursive symmetry, scale variance, patterned unpredictability, and local-global mirroring: these processes that define chaos theory also describe *Wake*an processes. That they do so testifies to the powerful dissemination of ideas and models between the European and American cultures in the first three or four decades of this century. Although chaos theory as a science has arisen since the 1960s, the ideas behind it grew out of relativity and quantum mechanics, the rubrics of which occasioned much concern in Joyce's Europe. Chaos theory, of course, describes a field of science; *Finnegans Wake* names a work of literature. That makes chaos theory at most a metaphor for talking about the *Wake*'s language; and once we have undercut that metaphoricity with the metonymy of other metaphor systems—that, for instance, of Derrida and Kristeva, with the synecdoche of the complex history of Western notions of order and disorder, with the irony that literature is (not) science—we have remaining only the small space which *Finnegans Wake* shares with chaos theory. But it is the space of tropes, and that, after all, has been the focus of this chapter.

NOTES

1. I am grateful to Patrick O'Donnell, Department of English, Purdue University, whose comments helped clarify my thinking about tropic versus mimetic language.

2. See Jacques Lacan, "The Agency of the Letter in the Unconscious or Reason since Freud," *Ecrits*, trans. Alan Sheridan (New York: W. W. Norton, 1977), 146–78 (subsequent references are given in the text); and Roman Jakobson, "The Metaphoric and Metonymic Poles," *Critical Theory since Plato*, ed. Hazard Adams (New York: Harcourt Brace Jovanovich, 1971), 1113–16. See also Hayden White, *Metahistory* (Baltimore: Johns Hopkins University Press, 1973), 31–38, and *Tropics of Discourse* (Baltimore: Johns Hopkins University Press, 1978), 1–25; Kenneth Burke, *A Grammar of Motives* (New York: Prentice-Hall, 1945), 503–17; and James Mellard, *Doing Tropology* (Urbana: University of Illinois Press, 1987), 1–12.

3. Hilary Clark, "Networking in *Finnegans Wake*," *James Joyce Quarterly* 27 (1990): 746. Subsequent references are given in the text.

4. Robert Spoo, "Preparatory to Anything Else . . . ," *James Joyce Quarterly* 27 (1990): 721; Hazard Adams, *Antithetical Essays in Literary Criticism and Liberal Education* (Tallahassee: Florida State University Press, 1990), 162.

5. Adams, *Antithetical Essays*, 23.

6. In "The Supplement of Copula: Philosophy before Linguistics" (*Margins of Philosophy*), Derrida offers a history of the copula as "remainder." Quoting Benveniste, Derrida writes that the Greek language gave the verb *to be* " 'a logical function, that of the copula (Aristotle himself had remarked earlier that in that function the verb did not actually signify anything, that it operated simply as a synthesis' " (196). But the verb for *to be* did not always "not actually signify anything." Derrida, through Benveniste, notes that the range of inflections of *to be* derives from three different stems: the Sanskrit *es*, " 'that which from out of itself stands and which moves and rests in itself' "; the Indo-European *bhu*, "to emerge, to be powerful"; and the Germanic *wes*, "to dwell, to sojourn" (204). The copula as supplement is thus the remainder of what is left out of a much greater lexical fullness, the copula viewed "as a process of falling, an abstraction, degradation, or emptying of the semantic plenitude of the lexeme 'to be' " (203). Derrida asks, "What remains in a supplement of copula?" (205).

7. Adams, *Antithetical Essays*, 28.

8. See Giambattista Vico, *The New Science*, trans. Thomas Goddard Bergin and Max Harold Fisch (Ithaca, N.Y.: Cornell University Press, 1968), 75–76.

9. See, for instance, the entries under "Seven," "Three," and so forth, in Glasheen's *Third Census*.

10. Chapter 9 explores the nature of the *Wake*'s fragmentation, so I will defer discussion until then.

11. Burke, *Grammar of Motives*, 503.

12. Northrop Frye, *Anatomy of Criticism* (Princeton: Princeton University Press, 1957), 214 and elsewhere.

13. Vico, *New Science*, 117–18.

14. Adams, *Antithetical Essays*, 164–65.

15. O Hehir and Dillon, *Classical Lexicon*, 105.

16. Brendan O Hehir, *A Gaelic Lexicon for Finnegans Wake* (Berkeley and Los Angeles: University of California Press, 1967), 77.

17. Stephen Heath, "Ambiviolences: Notes for Reading Joyce," in *Post-Structuralist Joyce*, ed. Derek Attridge and Daniel Ferrer (Cambridge: Cambridge University Press, 1984), 41.

18. John Gordon, *Finnegans Wake: A Plot Summary* (Syracuse: Syracuse University Press, 1986), 8, 37, 45.

19. See Clark, "Networking," 749–53, for further examples.

20. See, for instance, Bishop's *Joyce's Book of the Dark*; and Barbard Di Bernard's "Alchemical Number Symbolism in *Finnegans Wake*," *James Joyce Quarterly* 16 (1979): 433–46.

Chapter 8

Waking the Tropes: A "Methodology" for Reading *Finnegans Wake*

From examining the *Wake*'s tropic language, we move now to examine the act of reading the text, the four major tropes naming processes that readers perform in reading *Finnegans Wake*. As the similarity between things allowing one to substitute for another, metaphor not only gives the relation among the text's characters, "times," and "places," but also directs readers to note its other "nonsynonymic substitutions." As the articulation of one thing to another such that the contiguity of each to the other creates associations, metonymy not only gives the mode of construction for all the text's verbal units from smallest to largest, but also directs readers to perform metonymic acts of relatedness. As part-whole interchangeability, synecdoche not only names the process by which Letter becomes *Wake* becomes world and sexual act becomes religious longing becomes the comedy of fusing separate and opposed dynamics, but also moves readers between part and whole. And as the simultaneous affirmation and denial that two things are (not) forms of each other, irony not only recognizes that the fused refuse fusion and then, separated, move toward it again, directing ends back to their beginnings and masking vulnerability with humor, but also asks readers to make parallel motions of simultaneous affirmation and denial.

These four tropic movements call upon readers to become acrobats of *Finnegans Wake*, reading horizontally, vertically, circularly—as simultaneously as possible. Any given passage in the *Wake* functions through all four verbal operations, each of which I designate a logic, in order to emphasize that each marks a principle by which readers make connections among textual elements and thus discover the *Wake*'s coherence evolving from what may have seemed its chaos.

But none of these four logics is Aristotelian. Of the three laws characterizing Aristotle's logic, not one applies to the *Wake,* which in fact subverts each of them. The law of identity declares that a thing is what it is and is not something else; the law of contradiction claims that the same attribute cannot both belong and not belong to the same subject at the same time and in the same respect; the law of the excluded middle holds that an attribute either does or does not belong to a subject, thereby excluding any middle ground between truth and falsity.[1]

But in the *Wake*'s logic it is precisely these laws which do not hold. Nothing is what it is, and everything is something else, whether we are speaking of a "year" such as 432, the character of ALP, or a "place," the Hill of Howth. Similarly, the same attribute both does and does not belong to the same subject at the same time and in the same respect: Shaun simultaneously has no legs and is two-legged; Izod is both attracted to Glugg and rejects him; ALP's river gifts to her 111 children are both plague and blessing. And since the *Wake* rejects the polarities of truth and falsity, opting instead for Bruno's law of the mutual attraction of opposites, the law of the excluded middle loses its capacity to operate.

Rather than through Aristotle's linear logic, *Finnegans Wake* proceeds through the four tropic logics operating simultaneously in any given passage. One of these is the logic of metaphor. Forming the basis of the *Wake*'s treatment of times, places, and characters, the logic of metaphor allows Dublin, Georgia, to substitute for Dublin, Ireland, as well as to form the link that allows Sir Tristram to shift his base from "North Armorica" to "Europe Minor" (3.5, 6). Substitution allows the progression in Shaun's advertisement of Shaun = John = butcher = Wyndham Lewis = spatial orientation (172) and in Shem's advertisement of Shem = Jymes = commandment breaker = Hamlet = concerns with time (181). The necessary conjunction of sun and rain to produce a rainbow accounts for the triad of sun god Shaun, rain in the potential form of Issy as Nuvoletta and in the actual form of Issy's tears, and the Rainbow Girls as a result of the interaction of Issy/rain and Shaun/sun. To carry further just one of these strands, the sun = Shaun = the son = the Son = Jesus Christ = the Light = the light = the sun = Helios = Apollo as sun god. But these strands do not remain separated. For example, Apollo as god of poetry = Shem = darkness = the devil = Old Nick = St. Nicholas = Santa Claus = giver of gifts = ALP = the Letter.

Another logic is that of metonymy, which works in at least three ways. One of its aspects, which I designate metonymic clustering, involves the principle that a section of the *Wake* proceeds with a cluster of related words that reflects its mood, provides a counter-point to overt themes, or in other ways suggests to readers how the passage might be read. The Ondt and Gracehoper fable, for instance, is packed with several hundred words relating to insects—their scien-tific and common names, the stages of their development, their be-havior, their mythic and historical associations. Since both the ondt and gracehoper belong to the phylum of insects in at least one sense of their identities, the connection between characters of the fragment and the word clusters relating to insects is clear. Similarly, when Joyce packs at least 350 river names into book I, chapter 8 (Ellmann, *James Joyce*, 610), the connection between them and Anna Livia as the river Liffey is again clear.

Sometimes, however, the relation of the word clusters to the passage's characters is puzzling. In their dialogue, for instance, Archdruid Balkelly speaks in pidgin Chinese and St. Patrick in pidgin Japanese. Why Chinese for the archdruid and Japanese for the saint? And why pidgin, in any case? The pidgin language connects with those passages in the *Wake* where other dialects are presented in a similar manner, but why, for instance, do Balkelly and Patrick speak pidgin Chinese and Japanese rather than, for instance, Muta and Juva in the preceding section? Part of the answer lies in readers recognizing Chinese and Japanese as the languages of historically hostile cultures, with Japan as the invader/aggressor—hence Patrick as Japanese and Balkelly as an invaded Chinese; another, in recalling that pidgining in language occurs as an effect of the process of blend-ing cultures, as invaded people adopt features of the invaders' lan-guage and vice versa—hence pidgining as another name for the over-all process of "the seim anew." Further, the association of British Patrick and Irish archdruid with Japan and China links West and Orient in the universality of the conflict between an older and a newer social/religious order.

Some passages show the influence of two or more groups of word clusters. Many of the words in Johnny MacDougall's commentary in book II, chapter 4, for instance, can be clustered under two categories, horses and Irish myth/history. Here, the horses associate Johnny with his province of Connaught, an area which by tradition has been especially interested in horses; the myth/history cluster links Johnny to his role as one of the four historians.

Each passage, then, proceeds with a metonymic clustering appropriate to its "subject," generating a series of words that suggest ways the reader may view that subject. In addition each passage proceeds on the basis of another metonymic operation, the direction of its movement as linear or recursive. Two opposing directions work simultaneously in any passage, a narrative forward movement and a motivic circular movement, one or the other usually prevailing. Readers might expect that in the *Wake*'s tales, the narrative forward movement would prevail and that in other passages the motivic circular movement would dominate, but this is not so. While narrativity dominates movement in the Prankquean/Jarl van Hoother tale, for example, it does not in the tale of how Buckley shot the Russian general or the tale of Kersse the tailor and the Norwegian ship's captain. Although the geometry lesson contains much narrative material, long subsections of it are so heavily motivic that they defy efforts to narratize them.

To see how the direction of movement within a passage affects readers' perceptions of its logic, let us compare the two Mutt and Jute dialogues, 15.29 through 18.16 and 609.24 through 610.32. The narrative content of the earlier subsection may be quickly summarized: a Dane named Jute and a Celt named Mutt attempt conversation but cannot progress beyond speaking at cross purposes to each other. The motivic content, however, is rich. Motifs may be grouped into four categories: those dealing with Irish history, those associated with the characters of *Finnegans Wake*, those related to Irish culture, and those focusing on *Wake*an notions and images, as, for example, the Fall.

When we examine the latter Mutt and Jute passage, however, motivic development plays an insignificant role; what impels the reader through the lines is not recognition of familiar motifs but of the narrative sequence, which does not manifest itself clearly upon the first reading. In keeping with the rebirth theme present in all subsections of book IV, Mutt has become Muta, the Latin form of "I change," and Jute has become Juva, suggesting the Latin *juvenilis*.

The narrative that develops may be summarized thus: Muta and Juva observe smoke coming from the old Head of Kettle (Kinsale), the smoke from St. Patrick's paschal fire. They watch St. Patrick arrive with his retinue and see Archdruid Balkelly awaiting him.[2] King Leary has bet half his crown on each man, so that no matter which one loses, Leary will be associated with the winner. Juva declares he's betting ten to one on the outsider, St. Patrick. Muta responds by stating a cyclic theory of social interaction: that once unification has been attained, it gives way to diversity, which leads to combat, which results in appeasement, which returns the cycle to unification once again. They enact this cycle as Muta asks to borrow Juva's "hordwanderbaffle," which suggests not only hot water bottle but also that Muta is asking the use of Juva's language (in Danish, *ord* means "word"). The cycle will be reenacted a second time in the dialogue to follow between archdruid and saint.

A third kind of metonymic logic operates from one thought to the next. Here, neither clusters of related words nor narrative connexity nor recursive motifs helps the reader to move from one sentence to the next. What the reader must do is recognize the nature of the associations that connect sentence with sentence or group of sentences with another group. One example of associative logic is the long transition between the end of the Prankquean/Jarl van Hoother tale and the beginning of the fragment in which Finnegan wakens at his wake, 23.12 through 24.15. What we are asking, in other words, is how Joyce moves from the tale into the wake. The tale itself concludes with a sentence that wraps it up and brings it to an "official" end: "the prankquean was to hold her dummyship . . . and van Hoother was to git the wind up" (23.12–14). This sentence is followed by a statement of the tale's "moral": "Thus the hearsomeness of the burger felicitates the whole of the polis" (23.14–15). Within the statement, sounding the Dublin city motto motif functions to broaden the concerns from the private relationship between the Prankquean and Jarl to their role as members of the community. This broader perspective provides the framework for the long midsection of the transition, 23.16 through 24.2. Here the Jarl takes on a succession of identities as community leader, with the Prankquean as his cohort. We see the Jarl become the old Norse warrior Norronesen, which identifies him with Homfrie as invading Dane, future leader of his people, and makes of him an Adam, the male member of the originating pair. The

Prankquean becomes Irenean, born in Ireland and identified with peace, which associates her with Livia, as she is named in this sequence. The female member of this originating pair, Livia/Eve attempts to get a message to her mate, but he can't hear. After this failure, she disappears from the rest of the transition. Left alone, Norronesen becomes "that mighty liberator, Unfru-Chikda-Uru-Wukra," recognizable as Humphrey Chimpden Earwicker. In this role he provides his followers with laws ("louse") and delivers them "to boll weevils" (which echoes the conclusion of the Catholic version of the Lord's Prayer—"and deliver us from evil, amen"—but subverts it since the lawgiver delivers his followers *to* evil), works hard, and dies (24.3– 11). But like any fallen leader, he is prepared to rise again, given the opportunity. This condition of course identifies him with the fallen Finnegan who now awakens, asking whether proper provisions have been made for his wedding/wake, calling for the water of life, *"Usqueadbaugham!"* and enraged that he has been considered dead (24.12–15). With that, we arrive at the fragment that completes the chapter, Finnegan and his friends at the wake.

The transition has been a series of metonymies, modulations in identity, from the private individual van Hoother to the community burger to the warrior Norronesen to the great leader Unfru-Chikda-Uru-Wukra to the fallen Finnegan and his potential for rebirth as the risen Finn. Looked at in this way, the modulations mark a progress from less inclusive to more inclusive identity, or from a nearly totally private to a nearly totally public identity.

Generally speaking, any passage whose movement cannot be accounted for by related word clusters, narrative concerns, or recurring motivic material will probably be explicable through examining its metonymic associations. Besides the above passage, other fragments whose movement may be clarified by analysis of associative linkages include the long parenthetical "half time" in book II, chapter 2, during which Shem and Shaun change sides (287–92) and the introduction to book II, chapter 3, which precedes the tale of Kersse the tailor and the Norwegian ship's captain (309–11).

A third logic, that of synecdoche, operates broadly throughout the *Wake*, one part or one individual not simply standing for but actually identical with a larger entity or a class. In the previous chapter, for instance, we observed that a "year" such as 432 or 566 or 1132 is identical to the whole of time viewed as the chronology in which events occur. An event such as the fall of Finnegan is not only inter-changeable with an equivalent event such as HCE's crime in the park, but both are identical to the fall of humans from perfection and the resultant humanizing of an imperfect world. Places as well as times are treated synecdochically: Ireland is identical with all countries, Dublin with all cities, HCE's pub with all social gathering spots. Characters, too, are synecdochic, HCE identical with all mature males, Shem and Shaun with all younger rival males, Issy to all adolescent females, ALP to all mature females.

Besides these general uses of synecdoche, the *Wake* offers innu-merable specific instances of the same principle. Margot Norris de-clares that

> the most notable example of synecdoche in *Finnegans Wake* is found in the initials of HCE embedded in the three-word se-quences. They may indicate a repression of the thought of HCE by substituting another, less disturbing thought in its place, with only the initials to show that HCE ever occupied the thought at all. Conversely, certain word groups may unconsciously recall HCE. For example, when Shaun is accused of "homosexual catheis of empathy" (522.30) . . .[3]

The number two indicating female involvement and the number three indicating male involvement in HCE's crime in the park consti-tutes a synecdoche that plays hundreds of times throughout the text, from a passage as "explicit" as the "duo of druidesses . . . and the tryonforit of Oxthievious, Lapidous and Malthouse Anthemy" (271.4) to a passage as "abstract" as "you too and me three" (161.30). Sexual-ity is synecdochic for half of life; war, for the other half; thus the continuous veering back and forth between embattled natives and lovemaking invaders. "Wetting the tea" is synecdochic of sexual or-gasm; "heliotrope" functions synecdochically as immature, unful-filled sexuality. Shaun as post and Shem as pen are synecdochic of the roles of transmitter of culture and creator of culture, as are the tree and the stone synecdochic of two forms of life formulatable as a number of polarities such as present/past and growing/fixed. "Half a tall hat" is synecdochic of The Four, as is a white hat of Finn himself. Synecdoche occurs on even so small a scale as the single word, "Loud" being identical to "Lord," where the loud voice of the Lord, heard in the thunderclap, identifies the Lord. These formal synecdoches form small patterns that in turn reflect larger and larger parts/ whole identities, until finally every part reflects every whole or, as Blake writes, we see the world in a grain of sand.

Synecdoche thus gives the pattern by which readers discover the connectedness among separated passages as well as the forms that particular words and phrases take. As one of the text's logics, however, synecdoche does not account for the *Wake*'s consistent undercutting of metaphoric similarity, metonymic progression, and synecdochic part-whole identity. Let us consider how the fourth trope, irony, performs this function under the aegis of a pervasive fictiveness. Stephen Heath offers this account of such a logic:

> One of the key stresses of Nietzsche's work may be summarized by the following: "Because we have to be stable in our beliefs if we are to prosper, we have made the 'real' world a world not of change and becoming, but one of being." The apparatus of a vraisemblable, the given series of beliefs defining the "'wahre' Welt," functions as a self-perpetuating stabilization, converting the world into a realm of essence (whether theological or the fixed "Reality" of mechanistic materialism). It is this stability that is shattered by the writing of Joyce's texts in their definition of a logic of fictions, not of truths; their attention to what is called in *Finnegans Wake* "the fictionable world" (345.36). *Finnegans Wake*, transforming the "real Matter-of-Fact" of realist writing into a "matter of fict" or "mere matter of ficfect" (532.29), is the negation of any vraisemblable.[4]

If by fiction we understand a set of invented circumstances in which belief or disbelief is irrelevant, we might define one aspect of the logic of the ironic fictive as that which obtains when words operate on other words not out of belief but out of the attitude, "what if..." Considering Hans Vaihinger's notions about fictions, Hazard Adams writes that for Vaihinger, ideational constructs are fictions, "means that the mind constructs for attaining certain purposes."[5] Adams clarifies a statement by Vaihinger, explaining that

> what he means is that fictions posit statements that have all the appearance of violating our concept of the factual or logical. For

a fiction to be a fiction, there must be awareness that the fiction is such a deviation [from reality], and the fiction must be a means to a definite end. (189–90)

We can combine these ideas to obtain a more complete understanding of fictions, of their ironic structure as x is (not) y: their logic operating from a base in play rather than in truth or belief, their status as ideational constructs for attaining certain ends, their apparent violation of the reader's concept of the traditionally factual or logical.

We see fictive logic most clearly in those chapters and tales governed either by a relatively specifiable overall design or by a relatively high rate of narrative connexity. The Children's Games chapter, for instance, with its pantomime format and the three attempts Glugg makes to guess the color of Izod's drawers at once violates the reader's concept of children's language at play even as it confirms the reader's sense of the material underlying much of children's play. The chapter's ideational construct is expressed as the immature, unconsummated nature of sexuality in childhood. Similarly, while suggesting its relatedness to Aesop's fable of the ant and grasshopper, the fable of the Ondt and the Gracehoper violates the logic of the earlier version's moral precept by undermining the ondt's behavioral superiority and maintaining a balance between the ondt's spatial and the gracehoper's time orientation. Again, the fable's ideational construct supports its structure, establishing reciprocity between rival male siblings.

The logic of ironic fiction may be helpful in combating some confusions about *Finnegans Wake*. A number of critics, for example, have claimed that book I, chapter 7, the Shem chapter, shows inadequately transformed autobiographical material from Joyce's life and is hence an aesthetic failure.[6] Though we recognize the narrator's shaunish bias against Shem and see that he bypasses no opportunity to derogate Shem, we should also observe that the narrator declares the chapter's modus operandi in its opening paragraph when he announces that he will put "truth and untruth together" to obtain his portrait of Shem. That free combination of truth and untruth, fact and "ficfect," addresses the chapter's basis in play rather than in any "truths" about Joyce's life.

Shaun or his narrator, for instance, writes that

he even ran away with hunself and became a farsoonerite, saying
he would far sooner muddle through the hash of lentils in
Europe than meddle with Irrland's split little pea. Once when
among those rebels in a state of hopelessly helpless intoxication
the piscivore strove to lift a czitround peel to either nostril, hic-
cupping, apparently impromptued by the hibat he had with his
glottal stop, that he kukkakould flowrish for ever by the smell,
as the czitr, as the kcedron, like a scedar, of the founts, on
mountains, with limon on, of Lebanon. O! the lowness of him
was beneath all up to that sunk to! (171.4–13)

The passage suggests certain events in Shem's life that have well-
known counterparts in Joyce's: Joyce's self-exile from Ireland, his
choosing to live on the European continent. But more significant than
these for the reader's experience with the passage is the degree of
play that, in these lines as well as others, interacts so strongly with
any autobiographical material as to reorient that material as "ficfect"
rather than as fact. Shem runs away with "hunself," where "hun"
quadruply names the Danish word for "she," a member of Attila's
invading party, a German soldier of World War I, and a savage or
destructive person in general.

In thus associating the peace-loving and war-avoiding Shem
with the same sorts of people he had tried to escape, the narrator
helps undercut the very picture of Shem he has been attempting to
build. In the same way, the example the narrator gives of Shem's
lowness—his attempting to sniff a citron peel while hiccuping a
speech that associates him with his father through the stammering
common to both—denies that same lowness and suggests instead the
insipid love of nature that HCE sometimes affects when trying to
deny his guilt. Not only is ironic fiction present in this passage
through the narrator's undercutting his own efforts, but it also offers
itself even in the words' verbal surface. We encounter this heptad of
prepositional phrases: "as the czitr, as the kcedron, like a scedar, of
the founts, on mountains, with limon on, of Lebanon." We hear, too,
the near-equivalence of "with limon on" and "of Lebanon."

That same situation of ironic fiction obtains in other "autobiographical" sections of the chapter: Shem/Joyce's "cowardice" in the
face of war, his absurd pride in his writing, the condition of his home,
the autobiographical basis of his writing. In each case, irony so un-

dercuts "fact" with "ficfect" that not only does it become impossible to sort out "truth" from "untruth," but it is irrelevant as well since what the reader encounters can be recognized only as the text's verbal surface, never as referentiality. Materials that may have their counterparts in the world of time and space enter *Finnegans Wake* but, because of the degree of irony, they quickly lose their discreteness as specifiable references to that world.

We will continue to think about the Shem chapter as we explore two other characteristics of the logic of ironic fiction, its status as ideational construct existing to attain certain ends, and its apparent violation of the reader's concept of the traditionally factual or logical. One way of expressing the ideational construct is to recognize that the dominant fiction at work in book I, chapter 7 is that the writer's personality, work, and life-style are at variance with those accepted by a society—represented in this chapter by Shaun or his narrator—as its norms. The end or purpose attained by such a construct allows Joyce to carry on his theme of the rival brothers, this time extending it to the polarity suggested by the subtitle of C. H. Peake's text on Joyce, *The Citizen and the Artist.* If readers have survived the first six chapters of *Finnegans Wake,* by the time they reach the Shem chapter they realize the extent to which the text violates traditional expectations about the roles of fact and logic in a work of imaginative literature. *Finnegans Wake,* however, does not violate principles of fiction; rather, it doggedly carries them to their logical extremes.

Violations more specific to this chapter involve reader expectations about the nature of biography, which is, after all, the literary mode operating in book I, chapter 7. We expect, for instance, that biographers or their narrators will be sympathetic to or at least "objective" about the lives of their subjects; that they will not allow another mode to intrude upon their biographies; that a certain order will govern the arrangement of their subjects' lives, and so on.

Given the *Wake's* nature, though, readers expect these expectations to be violated, as indeed they are. Neither chronology nor any other specifiable order determines the arrangement of the events of Shem's life about which Shaun chooses to tell us. We learn, for instance, of Shem's role as tenor after we read of Shem's finding himself facing a gun, but the reverse order would work as well. Not just one literary mode but three intrude on Shaun's biography: the football match ballad (175), two advertisements (172 and 181), and an unincorporated dialogue complete with change of characters' names (187–95). And finally, as we have already noted, Shaun or his narrator not only fails to show "objectivity" or "sympathy" for his subject, but loses no opportunity to disparage and demean him. Thus, reading the *Wake* in terms of the logic of fiction helps us remember that any aspect of the text undercuts its own enunciation.

This examination of how the four tropes operate as logics governing acts the reader must perform shows the necessity of reading *Finnegans Wake* in multiple directions, not one at a time, but as simultaneously as the reader can manage. Some of the logics, that is, require a horizontal reading; others, a vertical reading; and still others, a circular reading. The logics of ironic fiction, of metonymic association, and of metonymic narrative forward movement, for example, ask the reader to link one sentence or paragraph to the passage that follows. On the other hand, the logics of synecdochic part-whole identity, metaphoric substitution, and metonymic motivic recursiveness require that the reader link separated passages. The logic of metonymic clustering asks yet a third direction, the vertical, as readers discover linked word caches within a passage. What these multiple reading directions require is that the reader approach the *Wake* in the manner in which an orchestral score is read: horizontally for the diachronous elements, vertically for the synchronous elements, and recursively for the varied repetition of elements previously introduced.

A reading of any passage from the *Wake* should consider each of these logics. Often, however, a reader will focus on one of them, excluding other ways the text moves or giving the privileged operation such prominence as to negate the influence of others. Clive Hart, for instance, declares that "the brief qualifying and elaborating phrases have become Joyce's fundamental units, and in the long run they are usually more important for the sense than is the skeletal meaning of the sentence to which they were annexed" (*Structure and Motif*, 41). Danis Rose and John O'Hanlon simplify reading *Finnegans Wake* to an even greater extent:

there are two basic levels to every sentence in the *Wake*: the first is the *sense*, what it is that the sentence is trying to say; the second is a *complex of allusions* to external data chosen to counterpoint, comment on, provide an alternative example for, or even in some cases to flatly contradict the sense. In the main part of this study, we endeavour to summarise the first level, to present what we call the *narrative*. That this first level is somehow the more important may easily be deduced from the fact that, deprived of their association with the narrative, the allusions together form an incoherence; they are discrete, discontinuous.[7]

Where Hart sees the sense of a passage as the sum of "brief qualifying and elaborating phrases" plus "the skeletal meaning of the sentence to which they were annexed," Rose and O'Hanlon oppose the sense of a passage to its other components which, for them, consist of its allusions. Understandably, different readings of the *Wake* obtain from viewing the text as proposed by Rose and O'Hanlon, by Hart, and by me. To show these differences, we will work with one passage, the interchange between the archdruid and St. Patrick, reading it in turn by each of the three modes. Rose and O'Hanlon suggest that readers begin by recognizing the narrative level, for them more important than that of allusions. Because the early drafts typically contain fewer details than does the published text, some critics such as Hart claim that the narrative line is easier to follow in them. Let us read the archruid/St. Patrick interchange as it appears in David Hayman's *A First-Draft Version of Finnegans Wake;* we will notice that the "skeletal meaning" of sentences Hart mentions is notably lacking.

The archdruid then explained the illusion of the colourful world, its furniture, animal, vegetable and mineral, appearing to fallen men under but one reflected of the several iridal gradations of solar light, that one which it had been unable to absorb while for the seer beholding reality the thing as in itself it is, all objects showed themselves in their true colours, resplendent with sextuple glory of the light actually contained within them. To eyes so unsealed King Leary's fiery locks appeared of the colour of sorrel green, His Majesty's saffron kilt of the hue of brewed spinach, the royal golden breasttorc of the tint of curly cabbage, the verdant mantle of the monarch as of the green of laurel boughs, the commanding azure eyes of a thyme and parsely aspect, the enamelled gem of the ruler's ring as a rich

lentil, the violet contusions of the prince's features tinged uni-
formly as with an infusion of sennacassia.

Bigseer, refrects the petty padre, by thiswise apatstrophied as
he appropinquisher to his gnosegates a handcaughsheaf of
shammyrag as the sound sense sympol of the fire that the sun
in his halo cast.

Good safe firelamp! hailed the heliots. Goldselforelump! alled
they. Awed. Where theron the skyfold high trampatrampatramp. Adie.

'Tis gone in farover. So fore now, dayleash. And let every
crisscouple be so crosscomplimentary little eggons, youlk and
meek in a farbiger pancosmos. With a hottyhammyum all round.
Gudstruce!

Yet is no body present which was not there before. Only is the
order other. Nought is nulled. *Fiutfiat.*![8]

We might paraphrase the narrative level of this passage as follows: "The archdruid, who is also Berkeley, declares that the material
world is an illusion, the objects of which appear to the eyes of unenlightened persons as the outer appearance of the color reflected by
the object rather than the color absorbed. The archdruid himself and
other seers, however, behold reality itself, 'the thing as in itself it is.'
If seen as it is in reality, the object shows itself through the light it
absorbs; in other words, in its inner reality. To such eyes, King
Leary's red hair looks green, his orange kilt looks green, his yellow
breastwork looks green, his green mantle looks green, his blue eyes
look green, his indigo ring looks green, the violet bruises of his features look green. Patrick does not reply to being thus addressed.
'Bigseer,' he thinks, and wipes his nose on a clump of shamrocks,
making this triply orbed leaf the symbol of the holy trinity, the
Father, the Son, the Holy Ghost. The observers to this meeting of
saint and sage cheer Ireland, the trinity, and St. Patrick. They are
awed. Day comes on. Night has vanished, and day holds reign for
now. No new elements have been introduced into life by this interchange, and nothing has been taken away, but the order of life has
been changed."

When we compare this first-draft version with that of the published text, 611.4–613.14, we see that Joyce added few narrative elements. We shall concern ourselves later with these and other addi-

tions he did make, but for now let us examine the adequacy of this narrative account of the passage. A basic deficiency is that it cannot deal with the considerable indeterminacy present in Joyce's first-draft version. For example, when Patrick thinks of the archdruid as "Bigseer," is he being sarcastic? If so, that tone affects a reading of the sentence. On the other hand, perhaps he is identifying the archdruid with the *sight* half of the sight/sound polarity while he himself identifies with the *sound* half. Patrick, after all, makes the shamrock the "sound sense sympol" of the holy trinity by blowing his nose on it. Or, again, perhaps he is using "Bigseer" as "God!," an expletive. If the sight/sound polarity is involved, then the fragment is not self contained but instead links with other fragments in which a split in the sight/sound polarity occurs, which is generally the case whenever Shem and Shaun appear. Another sequence within the passage also calls into question the adequacy of treating it as a self-contained narrative. With the declaration that night has vanished and day now reigns, we have the polarity of dark/light before us. Readers meet that polarity not only in the Shem/Shaun fragments, but in others as well, so that the archdruid/St. Patrick passage begins to radiate far beyond the confines of the words that compose it.

Still another indeterminacy lies in interpreting the archdruid's seeing everything as shades of green. One possibility is that we are to realize the archdruid has contradicted himself: he sees every object as green, denying the uniqueness of the object's internal reality that obtains from the particular tone in which the absorbed colors blend together. Inner reality's being monochromatic from one object to another thus denies the claim that the inner reality of a thing provides insight into the nature of that thing. Another possibility for interpretation, however, is that the archdruid sees the continuity of reality from one object to another and realizes that it is only their surfaces that differ. If their internal natures are the same, then it is natural all would be seen as shades of green. But this continuity from one object to another is precisely the nighttime reality of the *Wake*, which makes continuous claim to the capacity for identity and identification of one thing with another. From this interpretation, we might identify the archdruid's reality with the nighttime dream continuity of all things and St. Patrick's reality with the daytime distinction between things. St. Patrick's reality is that in which one looks for adequate and effica- cious action, such as Patrick's making the shamrock a palpable symbol of the Trinity; the archdruid's is that in which one sees the unity of all that is, as the archdruid indeed demonstrates through his "color analysis" of King Leary. A third possibility involves the implication, derived from the continual "harping" on green, that everything is Irish, which is indeed the case through synecdochic logic. But there is also a joke here about a certain kind of Irish patriotism.

This brings us to the final indeterminacy we shall consider. St. Patrick's association with the coming of daylight is usually interpreted as a signal victory for him over the archdruid, as though the order he represents will be the order that shall endure in Ireland for ages, perhaps for eternity. But through his associating Patrick with day and the archdruid with night, Joyce indicates that Patrick's victory is merely temporary since with the return of darkness, the archdruid's mystic, intuitive, and subjective vision will again resume command. In any case, the alternation between day and night, between inner subjective vision and efficacious action, is a natural rhythm which moves independently of human desire and influence.

As we have seen, reading this passage only as narrative distorts it because indeterminacies must be "determined" in order that the narrative may proceed. Such treatment implies not only that the passage is self-contained and independent of other passages, but also that only one event occurs at a time as well as that an event can be given a single adequate reading. But as examination of even the first-draft version of the St. Patrick/archdruid interchange shows, a single event requires multiple considerations: a number of events may occur simultaneously, and the passage, rather than being self-contained, has ties to other passages that bear on the import of its narrativity. If this is so in Joyce's earliest available treatment of a passage, it is even more strongly the case in the published version.

Let us approach the Patrick/archdruid passage next from the position advocated by Clive Hart: that the key to the *Wake*'s sense is the text's "brief qualifying and elaborating phrases" rather than "the skeletal meaning of the sentence to which they were annexed." Although such "qualifying and elaborating phrases" exist even in the first-draft version, it was primarily this kind of addition Joyce made as he continued to work on a passage. What we require is a single sentence from this section, rich enough in such phrases to invite examination, yet brief enough to allow a reasonably thorough reading. That requirement is difficult to attain, given the average sentence length of twenty-one lines in the two paragraphs that dominate pages 611 and 612. Our recourse will be to limit ourselves to the following lines of one sentence:

> Bymeby, bullocky vampas tappany bobs topside joss pidgin fella Balkelly, archdruid of islish chinchinjoss in the his heptachroma-tic sevenhued septicoloured roranyellgreenlindigan mantle fin-ish he show along the his mister guest Patholic with alb belon-gahim the whose throat hum with of sametime all the his cassock groaner fellas of greysfriaryfamily he fast all time what time all him monkafellas with Same Patholic, quoniam, speeching, yeh not speeching noh man liberty is. (611.4–11)

What we find upon examining the "brief qualifying and elaborating phrases" Hart designates as important is that their "sense" repeats information stated or implied elsewhere in the passage. Hart's decla-ration that "in the long run they are usually more important for the sense than is the skeletal meaning of the sentence to which they were annexed" is simply inaccurate. The words in the lines quoted above fall into three clusters, all three of which show the match in "sense" between skeletal meaning and qualifying or elaborating phrases. The first two lines are marked by the presence of slang and pidgin terms: "topside" as Chinese pidgin for "bishop," "bobs" as slang for "shil-lings," "bymeby" as slang for "by and by," "joss" as pidgin for "God," "chinchinjoss" as Chinese pidgin for "religious worship." This use of slang and Chinese pidgin introduces the archdruid in the mode Joyce chooses to present him here, as a Chinese whose English contains numerous pidgin terms. The word "vampas," by the way, probably refers to the paschal fire Muta and Juva observe Patrick lighting on page 609. The third and fourth lines emphasize the notion of color, which dominates the fragment as a whole, symbolizing the differing perspectives of the two men: the notion of seven-hued color is associated with the archdruid and is presented four times, once each in Greek, English, and Latin, and then in terms of the seven rainbow colors; white is associated with Patrick. The remaining lines develop the two men's approaches to verbalization, Patrick along with the monks accompanying him preferring to chant rather than to speak (recall his deliberate silence later when he makes his gesture of the "sound sense sympol") and the archdruid beginning his rambling reflections that culminate in the notion of inner reality, with the claim that no man is free.

Hart's insistence on a divergence of "sense" between that contained in the skeletal meaning of a sentence and that implied by qualifying and elaborating phrases is inaccurate, then. As approaches to reading *Finnegans Wake*, neither Rose and O'Hanlon's position nor Hart's enables us to make the connections that *Finnegans Wake* offers. Let us attempt a third reading of the same passage based on tropic logics, beginning with the trio that operate primarily between this and other passages. Of the three, synecdochic logic offers the fewest insights into the Patrick/archdruid passage. Through the synecdoche of HCE's initials identifying his presence, we realize that we are to associate King Leary with HCE when Leary is referred to as *H*ighup *B*ig *C*ockywocky Sublissimim*e*. In case we have missed that reference, the words in the following sentence provide another synecdoche of the same kind: "Hump cumps Ebblybally" (612.15). Another synecdoche that operates both within the passage as well as between this and other passages is the use of color. The archdruid's seven-hued mantle and Patrick's white tunic are both synecdochic of the perspectives through which each views the world. In the Children's Games chapter, the color heliotrope is identical to the active sexuality Issy would like to initiate but cannot. Through synecdoche, too, the Rainbow Girls and the archdruid are linked. A synecdoche that operates only within the passage is the phrase "zoantholitic furniture, from mineral through vegetal to animal," "furniture of earth" being Bishop Berkeley's synecdoche for the totality of material objects in the world (McHugh, *Annotations*, 611).

Metaphoric logic provides a wealth of significant links between this and other passages. We noted earlier the presence of the sight/ sound and light/dark polarities that occur in numerous passages. Through metaphoric logic, we recognize that the acts of Kev's hitting Dolph and Buckley's shooting the Russian general are similar to and can substitute for the archdruid's "shuck[ing] his thumping fore features apt the hoyhop of His Ards" (612.34–35) as well as for Patrick's wiping his nose on the shamrock. Another pair of substitutable acts is the Russian general's violating Irish turf by using it to wipe his arse and Patrick's sacralizing that same turf by making a handful of shamrocks the symbol of the Trinity. It is not the first time in this text that Joyce has made violation and sacralizing two sides of the same coin.

Metaphoric logic also points out the similarity of the rival brothers seen elsewhere, for instance as the Dolph/Kev pair and here as arch-druid/Patrick. Finally, as noted above, King Leary in this passage becomes an HCE figure, bearing the power of the father but lacking both the energy and the vision of the sons who vie for his kingdom.

The logic of ironic fiction provides the structure in which the passage's narrative rests. The basis in play may be seen in the manner in which Leary's bet is couched, such that no matter whether saint or sage is victor, Leary's money rests with the winner. And of course turning conflict between two religious systems into competition whose result can be betted upon is perhaps the passage's most pervasive ironic fiction. Play is seen, too, in the archdruid's aggressive anger towards Leary, thrusting his fingers up the latter's arse, which when read in context manifests neither anger nor aggression but instead suggests a sexual act that calls to mind the buggery that HCE may or may not be guilty of through his crime in the park. The fictive end attained in the fragment is the establishment of the dynamics of social change, where change in the social order is viewed as natural, inevitable, and rhythmic or cyclic. The side that can create an image symbolizing unlimited power in such a way as to be comprehensible to the masses will predominate until such a time as the side that can generate a sense of the power of invisible mystery resumes control of those same masses. In the end, Joyce implies the equivalence of both sides. The apparent violation of traditional logic that marks the fictive may be observed in the fragment's dense wordplay as well as in its languages of pidgin Chinese for the Irish-born archdruid and pidgin Japanese for Patrick, the transplant to Ireland.

Let us move to the trio of metonymic logics operating primarily within the fragment. Not at all coincidentally, those same three groupings of words with which we earlier analyzed an eight-line sequence—those words relating to pidgin Chinese/Japanese, those relating to the nature of color, and those depicting the tension between verbalization and action—can be used to cluster nearly all the words in the remaining lines of the two-page fragment (611.4–613.14). The only one we would add is references to Irish culture, including religious phrases and lines from songs and poems. These four groups constitute the logic of metonymic clustering under which the passage's various words and phrases may be organized.

The logic of metonymic association is not helpful in understanding this passage, perhaps because the Patrick/archdruid interchange is dominated by narrative concerns and verbal play but virtually uninfluenced by the capacity of one word, phrase, or sentence to generate another solely through associational links. The Patrick/archdruid passage is powered equally by both forms of the metonymic logic of direction, forward narrative movement and recursive motivic movement. Joyce did not delete any of the original elements of the narrative as he continued to work on this passage, but he added elements as well as greatly enriched its wordplay. What follows is one possible narrative account of the pages as published in *Finnegans Wake:*

"Then. By and by, the bullocky, flaming, twopenny-shilling bishop/god Chinese-pigeon speaking fellow Balkelly, archdruid of Irish religious worship, wearing his seven-hued mantle, finished his ruminations. He spoke to his guest, Catholic Patrick, who, wearing his priest's white tunic, was chanting along with the gray friars accompanying him, all of them fasting. He said to them, 'No man is free. The visible world and its play of forms—the world of Lord God—is veiled with illusions. Nothing we see, whether animal, vegetable, or mineral, appears to ordinary humans except as one color out of the many gradations of light, the one color it cannot absorb. However, for one skilled in vision and having knowledge of the being of beings, such a person knows that reality is within, is inward and inner, rather than external. Such reality, things as they are in themselves, shows itself to seers in the sextuple glory of the light the object-in-itself contains inside itself.'

"The Roman Catholic, stereotypically, didn't understand what the archdruid had said to him. Anyway, tomorrow would not recover the thing-in-itself, contrary to the archdruid's maintaining that it would be recoverable in the future. By and by, the bullocky, flaming, twopenny-shilling bishop/god Bilkilly-Belkelly tried again to explain to Patrick, verbigerating from a low murmur but moving to a hurried, loud, singsong voice. Patrick listened but understood less and less. High King Leary's red head, the archdruid explained, looked green; his saffron kilt was green; Patrick did not comprehend that Leary's golden breastplate was green; his green raincoat was green; his blue eyes were green; the blue gem on his forefinger was green; the violet contusions on the face of HCE/Leary were green. Now did Patrick understand, the archdruid wondered? Then it was Patrick's turn.

"Punctuation. New paragraph. Patrick reflects ironically that the archdruid is indeed a bigseer, whacking his words out in a tottering manner, tritely calling things up and pronouncing on them in an absolute, black or white manner. But Patrick's own empirical views have been atrophied and paralyzed by the archdruid's false logic. Heaven-blessed due to the principles of God's promise in the biblical rainbow, for the time being those watching Patrick are completely open-minded in their neutrality between the possible verity/greenness of the sage and the probably conquering capacity/redness of the saint. Patrick then brings a handkerchief of shamrocks up to his face to wipe his nose. He genuflects once, twice, thrice, to the rainbow, a second powerful symbol in addition to that of the shamrock of the Holy Trinity of Father, Son, and Holy Ghost. As he kneels, praying, the sun begins to rise.

"Everyone else is highly impressed by this action. But Bilkilly-Belkelly-Balkally, who would like to shut out the symbols Patrick is introducing, shoves his thumb and four fingers up the High King's arse. The watching Irish masses, now openly converted to Patrick's side, proclaim 'Good safe firelamp'/God save Ireland! They watch, awed, as the sun and day take over the sky." (From here to the end of the passage, the text shows very few differences from the first-draft version. Note, however, that *fiutfiat* has become *fuitfiat*.)

While this narrative provides the reader with a sense of the passage's forward-moving connexity, it does not account for more than half the words in the passage. Many of the other half are involved in wordplay that results in the reader's having to make connections among elements of the passage in order to understand what Joyce is doing with these words. One of the wordplays involves Joyce's use of the "three-times-is-a charm" motif, which Margaret Solomon observes marks the three-part structure of many of the *Wake*'s tales.[9] In this passage, however, three designates the number of times a word or phrase will appear, sometimes moving from the descriptive to the comparative to the superlative degrees as it repeats. Examples of the latter kind of triple repetition include the references to the archdruid as first "Balkelly," then as "Bilkilly-Belkelly," and finally as "Bilkilly-Belkelly-Balkally" and the rainbow as first "Balenoarch" (*arcobaleno* is the Italian for "rainbow;" Joyce's anagram allows him to suggest, among other possibilities, Noah and the flood, against the repeating of which act comes the rainbow as God's promise), next as "Great Balenoarch," and third as "Greatest Great Balenoarch." Other triple references include the earlier-mentioned "heptachromatic," "seven-hued," and "septicoloured" mantle of the archdruid, the world's "zoantholitic furniture" as the triple "animal," "vegetal," and "mineral," the structure of "trampatrampatramp" and "the firethere the sun in his halo cast" (the Father, the Son, the Holy Ghost).

Besides the wordplay of triple namings, Joyce engages in the play that pidgining of English allows, seen, for instance, in such "pidginisms" as "tsinglontseng," "untisintus," and "patfella," in addition to the slang and pidgin Chinese noted earlier. A third form of verbal play is the "formal" openings and closings of the passage's paragraphs. The first paragraph opens with "Tunc," which parallels the second paragraph's opening with "Punc." The first paragraph closes with the formulaic "Hump cumps Ebblybally!" and "Sukkot" gives a phonetic equivalent of the other name by which Patrick was known, *Sochet*.[10] The question mark in "Sukkot?" invites Patrick to speak. (By the logic of metonymy, the British Sochet or Sukkot is associated with the Egyptian *Sekhet*, the first term of the phrase designating the Egyptian name for the Elysian fields, *Sekhet hetep*.[11] And that in turn has another link through metonymic logic. But to return to the matter at hand:) The second paragraph closes with the equally formulaic "Onmen," a variation of the hundreds of *Amens* that close paragraphs periodically throughout the text. Nor are these two the only paragraphs to be so treated. The top paragraph on page 613 ends with the phonetic equivalent of the Latin closing of a prayer, "per jucundum Dominum nostrum Jesum Christum Filium Tuum" ("through our dear Lord Jesus Christ Thy Son"), and the paragraph that concludes the passage ends with another Latin phrase Joyce uses frequently throughout the text to close a section, "Fuit fiat," "as it was, let it be."

Still another kind of verbal play occurs in phonetic equivalences or anagrammatic variations between metonyms. Examples include "seecut" and "Sukkot" (612.14, 15), "Good safe firelamp" and "Goldselforelump" (613.1), "hueful panepiphanal world," "zoantholitic furniture," "furnit of heupanepi world," "fur of huepanwor," "panepiwor," and "obs of epiwo," (611.13, 14, 18, 19, 22, 24), "aposterioprismically apatstrophied" and "paralogically periparolysed" (612.19–20), and "bygotter," "bogcotton," and "begad" (612.31–32). These four kinds of play do not exhaust the passage's verbal complexities, but they indicate the extent to which the passage slows down apprehension of the forward-moving narrative by forcing readers into vertical and recursive directions.

This analysis shows, I hope, that reading the Patrick/archdruid passage through the text's four tropic logics enables readers to discover many more of the intricate connections that compose the *Wake* than do readings that focus on its "sense" or "narrative level," plus or minus its allusions. Because these multiple processes operate simultaneously, any attempt to fix upon one or even several of them and claim that they form the *Wake*'s core violates the variety of processes constituting a full reading of the text. It is not the case that the *Wake* consists of a central core of images or ideas—such as the tales, the Viconian structures, the Brunonian oppositions—about which erupt massive digressions. Indeed as Derek Attridge points out, recalling Derrida, the notion of digression only reinforces the notion of center or centrality, a digression being perceived only insofar as it departs from a center recognizable as such.[12] Rather than proceeding on the basis of specifiable central concerns, the *Wake* moves instead through its tropic language that, by remaining always in process—substituting itself, associating itself with its other, identifying part and whole, simultaneously affirming and denying all the preceding operations—defies formulation of what it is "about." This is not to say that passages cannot be given a narrative accounting. It is rather that such an accounting cannot address all or even the majority of the kinds of movement occurring in the text at that point. At every instant, the text is definable as the acts its words perform—its logics—and since these performances never settle into specifiable "sense" but are structured as dynamic process, the text's "sense" is constructed through the reader's performing its verbal acts, troping its motions.

NOTES

An earlier version of part of this chapter appeared in *Twentieth Century Literature* vol. 35, no. 2 (Summer 1989): 195–203.

1. Aristotle's words are quoted in Reuben Abel, *Man Is the Measure* (New York: Free Press, 1976), 51.

2. Although the traditional interpretation of Patrick's relation to Ireland is that he converted the country to Christianity, Joyce maintained that Ireland had converted Patrick to its own ends. In a note to Harriet Shaw Weaver,

he wrote, "I send you this as promised—a piece describing the conversion of S. Patrick by Ireland. You may keep the other rough drafts." The note, in Joyce's handwriting, appears in *The James Joyce Archive, A Facsimile of Drafts, Typescripts, and Proofs for Finnegans Wake, Book IV*, arranged by Danis Rose with the assistance of John O'Hanlon (New York: Garland Publishing, 1977), 146e. It is also published in Joyce's *Letters* 3:79.

3. Margot Norris, *The Decentered Universe of Finnegans Wake* (Baltimore: Johns Hopkins University Press, 1976), 107.

4. Heath, "Ambiviolences," 39.

5. Hazard Adams, *Philosophy of the Literary Symbolic* (Tallahassee: Florida State University Press, 1983), 188.

6. Clive Hart, for instance, writes of the "often unstable duality of art-for-art's sake and personal confession in *Finnegans Wake*." He further declares that "this personal—often uncomfortably personal—art was the only kind Joyce could create or understand" (*Structure and Motif*, 24–25). David Hayman evaluates Joyce's use of autobiographical material differently. See especially chap. 6 of *"Wake" in Transit.* Hayman concludes that "though the *Wake* cannot be read as a Joyce family melodrama, it is useful to recall that Joyce always tapped his own biography, preferably his most intimate and disturbing life, for its aesthetic potential. This raw stuff he ultimately sublimated" (94). Hayman claims further that through Joyce's use of his own dream material, he achieved some of the emotional intensity he needed to make *Finnegans Wake* "an intensely personal, if rigorously controlled, portrait of the nocturnal male psyche haunted by actions and urges, a portrait only half submerged in a sea of vibrant dream language" (154).

7. Danis Rose and John O'Hanlon, *Understanding Finnegans Wake* (New York: Garland Publishing, Inc., 1982), x.

8. David Hayman, ed., *A First-Draft Version of Finnegans Wake* (Austin: University of Texas Press, 1963), 279–80.

9. See part 1 of Margaret C. Solomon's *Eternal Geomater* (Carbondale: Southern Illinois University Press, 1969).

10. *St. Patrick: His Writings and Muirchu's Life,* ed. and trans. A. B. E. Hood (London: Phillimore and Co., 1978), 83.

11. Atherton, *Books at the Wake*, 196.

12. Derek Attridge, "The Backbone of *Finnegans Wake*: Narrative, Digression, and Deconstruction," *Genre* 17 (1984): 375–400.

Chapter 9

The Limon in the
Orangepeel: Fragment
as Trope

While the reader may experience *Finnegans Wake* initially as an irreducible chaos, gradually its incoherence metamorphoses into an exhilarating turbulence that the reader is not only caught up in but also, to some extent, generates. As tropes, fragment and desire maintain especially close links to the *Wake*'s "hordwanderbaffle" (610.30), the Letter that, we have observed previously, serves as synecdoche for the text itself. We read that the hen, the dump's "limon," "unexpectedly . . . threw up a few spontaneous fragments of orangepeel, the last remains of an outdoor meal by some unknown sunseeker or placehider *illico* way back in his mistridden past" (110.28–31). And again, we read that the hen, now "Mrs Hahn," "pokes her beak into the matter with Owen K. after her, to see whawa smutter after, will this kiribus pouch filled with litterish fragments lurk dormant in the paunch of that halpbrother of a herm, a pillarbox" (66.23–27). In both instances, what the hen finds are fragments, each of which is linked to the Letter as well as to desire.

The two passages quoted above describe the fragments scratched up by the hen as "litterish" and "spontaneous." "Litterish" indicates not only waste or garbage but also, through *liter*, as O Hehir tells us, the Irish for *letter*. The fragments of the previous passage are described as "spontaneous," a word close to the way Joyce hoped the *Wake*'s components would relate to each other. But he denied these components were "fragments," answering Harriet Shaw Weaver's charge that the early Patrick and Berkeley section he had sent her were incoherent by explaining that its components "are not fragments but active elements and when they are more and a little older they will begin to fuse of themselves" (*Letters* 1:205). While recognizing that Joyce's response is at least partially a game designed to draw Weaver's reservations about his new work into collaboration in producing it, we may yet ask what the reader's role is if these "active elements" "fuse of themselves."

The notion of fragment suggests at least three possibilities: a part broken off from the whole, a part that is incomplete because isolated or detached from the rest of itself, and an unfinished part. But none of these applies to the components of *Finnegans Wake:* Joyce believed he had finished writing the *Wake;* and in reading it, although we know when we come to page 628 that our next page is 3, we believe that in one sense we have "finished" reading the *Wake.* Further, no part is isolated or detached from the rest of itself; instead, each part is overdetermined in its ties with all other parts. Finally, no part is broken off from the "whole." As a matter of fact, Joyce was notorious for expanding the "whole" in ways that questioned what sort of "whole" the *Wake* could achieve if virtually anything could be incorporated into it. He had written to Weaver, for instance,

> that you might "order" a piece and I would do it. The gentlemen of the brush and hammer seem to have worked that way. Dear Sir. I should like to have an oil painting of Mr Tristan carving raw pork for Cornish countrymen or anicebust of Herr Ham contemplating his cold shoulder. (*Letters* 1:245)[1]

The *Wake*'s components are not fragments defined by passive inertness, but active elements defined by their spontaneous activity. They are elements in the sense of being basic, irreducible parts of which larger components are built, as molecules are composed of atoms, compounds composed of molecules, and so on. The elements, which had not been fragments "by nature" but fragments only in the sense of being as yet separate, blend by a kind of mixing; they join, through metonymy, metaphor, synecdoche, and irony.

Nevertheless, it is "fragments," not "active elements," that the hen in the *Wake*an passages quoted above finds. By the trope of irony, "fragments" are (not) "active elements." As I write *fragment*, then, I keep in mind the notion of *active element*, but I also remember that fragment connotes the possibility of incoherence through unrelatedness, where active element does not. The reader has no trouble with active elements that fuse. Incoherence arises for readers from fragments that do not become active elements and thus do no fusing.

In the sense of containing the potentiality for fusion through mutually active elements, fragments are the units of which *Finnegans Wake* is composed, ranging in size from a single word through several paragraphs of a chapter. They also vary in kind. In addition to the fragment we identify as composed of patterned word sequences, we can identify voice fragments and rhythm fragments. Learning to read the *Wake* involves learning to connect the mutually active elements of rhythm, voice, and word sequence. This chapter will focus on relatively short fragments of voice, rhythm, and word sequence. But before looking at these, I want to place *Wake*an fragments in relation to those of some other works in which the fragment is also significant.

Ernst Behler offers five reasons why a literary work may exhibit fragmentariness, all of which consider the condition to result from incompleteness: the text was mutilated during the process of historical transmission; the author died before being able to complete the work; the author ceased work on it because of a shift in or lack of interest; the work is intentionally fragmentary because its author considers it aesthetically pleasing in that form; the text is intentionally fragmentary because the author wishes to show something about the nature of completeness using the shape of the fragment.[2]

Because the *Wake* is not incomplete, the nature of its fragments differs from the fragmentariness considered by Behler. Of the reasons he offers, only the final one is applicable to *Finnegans Wake*, and that in only a limited sense. Though the *Wake* is composed of fragmentary sections, its shape cannot be considered fragmentary since by the "end" of the text all its cycles are ready to begin again. As the narrator who concludes book II, chapter 3 tells us, "All's set for restart after the silence" (382.14). Considered in relation to each other, the *Wake*'s interactive fragments suggest that wholeness and completion are human constructions rather than inherent properties of an experience.

In a typology of the fragment, another possibility exists besides incompletion. A fragment may be complete, synecdoche functioning as the principle by which "the fragment implies the whole while still being a part."[3] Because the two previous chapters explore this aspect of the fragment, I will not do so here, except to reiterate that this part-whole relationship is very much the nature of the *Wake*an fragment.

A third kind of fragment is that written by some Romantic writers. Thomas McFarland characterizes Romanticism as dominated by the sense of "incompleteness, fragmentation, and ruin" because of the Romantics' "pervasive longing . . . for an absent reality."[4] While recognizing that the emotion arising from one's sense of being surrounded by ruins and ruination is shared by all ages, McFarland believes the Romantics experienced this emotion especially strongly, finding "in fragments and torn forms deeper meanings and presentiments than in completions" (14). He differentiates between classic and Romantic awareness on the basis of how each resolved problems of "temporality and its dissipations. The classic looks to the idea of perfection and completeness . . . the Romantic to infinity" (28). For Romantics, infinity was the only true whole, and it constituted a "transcendently constituted whole," one that could be achieved only in the epiphanies "of art or those of philosophy and love" (409). But the only wholes encountered in experience are fragments and at best "nominal wholes, contingent wholes, and wholes of faith" (409). This unbridgeable gap between the "true" whole of infinity and the "limited" whole of experience results in the Romantic melancholy which is "shorn of hope and therefore posits no otherness toward which to strive" (17). McFarland notes that the fragmentariness of some Romantic texts such as Byron's *Don Juan* and De Quincey's autobiography was based on their being "open forms" that "could be added to indefinitely" (20).

Clearly, the *Wake*'s fragments differ from those of Romantic works. Since Joyce invited friends such as Weaver to suggest "topics" he could write into the text, and since he himself continually added detail and incident, one might think that the *Wake* participates in that Romantic, indefinitely expansible, open form. But although *Finnegans Wake* is indefinitely expansible within the fragmentary sections of which it is composed, its four-part structure and its 8-4-4-1 ordering of chapters within the four books forms a completed, and closed, design. The text, in other words, offers internal openness rather than open-endedness. The capacity of the *Wake* to contain anything and everything addresses its status as microcosm of the macrocosm, its synecdochic part-whole identity. Its expansibility is the product of

Joyce's sense of completion as a human construct rather than of the Romantic sense of the melancholy inevitability of incompleteness.

Where Romantics gauged the inadequacy of contingent wholes offered by experience in terms of their distance from the transcendent whole, infinity, *Finnegans Wake* denies transcendence through irony, synecdoche, metonymy, and metaphor, maintaining a steady foothold in the humanly finite. The traditional sources of transcendence—God, patriotism, history, philosophy—measure instead the human capacity for survival and love, shown in this "nightbook" in their nighttime forms of anxiety, guilt, and illicit desire. In place of the infinite, the text commends acceptance of fragments for their possible networks of connectedness among the disconnected. But connectedness among fragments is a matter of creation and discovery—Joyce's and the readers'—rather than an inherent condition. The text strongly suggests that the only wholes are those of human making.

The Romantic melancholy that found expression in "fragments and torn forms" plays no role in the *Wake*. There, continuing is constructed as the process of piling up of piece on piece, fragment on fragment; and the text shows that such a process reels with humor, irreverence, and reiteration. Where the Romantics' sense of "incompleteness, fragmentation, and ruin" looks backward to an "absent reality," Joyce's *Wake* looks simultaneously toward past and future, finding that the present cannot be separated from either and that in any case, regardless of what else it may or may not be, "reality," like the notion of the "whole" and the "complete," is constructed through human perspectives and languages rather than a transcendent presence or absence.

Where the Romantic fragment testifies simultaneously to its incompleteness and to the absolute wholeness that contains it, Joyce's fragment—whether as word sequence, rhythm, or voice—declares its simultaneous status as self-defining entity and as link with virtually all other entities through tropic processes. This shift implies a vast difference in the relation between part and whole from that recognized by literary as well as other traditions prior to Nietzsche's thought. The sense of a whole has traditionally implied certain notions: an engulfing totality that either once existed or will exist at some future point; social and biological evolution that works to form harmonious wholes out of disparate parts; the whole as either an original totality from which its parts derive or else a totality derived from its parts. But the sense of the whole that Joyce's text implies involves a different agenda. If totality can be spoken of at all, it coexists with its parts as a new part in itself but neither totalizes nor unifies them. And the function of such a whole is to form networks for connections rather than to mark the presence or absence of transcendence.[5]

A fourth "type" of fragment occurs in some works that undertake to express a broad range of cultural concerns, for which works Northrop Frye suggests the term "encyclopedic form."[6] I have in mind such works as Burton's *The Anatomy of Melancholy*, Blake's *The Four Zoas*, Flaubert's *The Temptation of St. Antony*, and Rabelais's *Gargantua and Pantagruel*, with which *Finnegans Wake* maintains ties in that these texts, besides their encyclopedic quality, tend to share the qualities of being extravagant, carnivalesque, heavily intertextual, nonlinear, multiply dialogued, and fragmentary. Like the *Wake*, *The Anatomy of Melancholy* is a compendium of all sorts of information about the times in which Burton lived. Defying genre categories, *Anatomy* draws widely on other works and is concerned with the Fall, which it views as the root cause of melancholy. Another similarity includes the many different modes and genres that it inscripts— digression, poetry, lyric description, Latin passages, outline, treatise (on hunting), retelling of love stories. Unlike the *Wake*'s stance of irreverent humor, however, *Anatomy* declares that melancholy "is the character of Mortality."[7]

Another of these encyclopedic texts with which the *Wake* is closely related is *The Temptation of St. Antony*, which Michel Foucault credits with being its forerunner: "In writing *The Temptation*, Flaubert produced the first literary work whose exclusive domain is that of books: following Flaubert, Mallarmé is able to write *Le Livre* and modern literature is activated—Joyce, Roussel, Kafka, Pound, Borges.[8] Like the *Wake*, Flaubert's *Temptation* produces "the simultaneous existence of multiple meanings" and creates an ambiguous figure in St. Antony that is "simultaneously a form of duration and eternity, acting as conclusion and a fresh start" (Foucault, *Language*, 99, 101). As does the *Wake*, *Temptation* draws heavily on other texts, and its distinctiveness also lies in the way it organizes these other texts into "an extremely complex composition" (Foucault, *Language*, 104). Like both *Wake* and *Anatomy, Temptation* offers the encyclopedic learning of a culture.

The Four Zoas is another text with which *Finnegans Wake* forms significant ties.[9] Both are constructed around the notion of the Fall and the resurrection, Albion undergoing division when he can no longer maintain his faculties in proper relation to each other and finally regaining unity when he restores that relation. Both texts are constructed about the character of a male whose identity is a composite of that of all the other male figures in the text. Both proceed by way of a parataxis that makes extremely heavy demands on their readers, both espouse a "universal" mythology, and both operate in a space and time unconstrained by chronology and physical geography. Each text engages its narrators in nontraditional behavior, and both writers echo and parody their own as well as others' works. Each text is a "night book," and each presents a fluid interaction between past, present, and future. Also, in each the younger generation replaces the older after competing for control. Finally, a cyclic view of history operates between generations, historical periods, and entire cultures.

Gargantua and Pantagruel offers as many parallels with the *Wake* as does *The Four Zoas,* though the parallels are of a different sort. Both texts contain autobiographical elements but require judgment on the part of readers in considering the use each writer makes of that material. Both *Wake* and *Gargantua* exude immense energy; each delights in deliberate contradictions. Neither attributes dialogue to clearly identified speakers, and both overtly parody elements of Christian worship and practice. Both texts "construct" such words as they need; both revel in puns. In both, human bodies have openly sexual and excremental functions; in both, delight is taken in extravagant dress. The *Wake* and *Gargantua* each engage in extensive wordplay and take pleasure in the capacity of language for multiple significations. Both exhibit encyclopedic learning and refer frequently to other texts, often through parodying them. Finally, both make significant use of lists and inscript a variety of genres and modes of writing.

How can recognizing the relatedness of *Finnegans Wake* to texts such as *The Anatomy of Melancholy, The Temptation of St. Antony, The Four Zoas,* and *Gargantua and Pantagruel* enable us to better understand the nature of the fragments of which the *Wake* is composed?

All of these texts require readers to discover and/or create their coherence. All offer a wealth of particular detail that, considered in isolation, can appear incoherent. Such detail becomes coherent insofar as readers learn to relate it "to the entity to which [it] contribute[s]."[10] Michael Polanyi and Harry Prosch indicate that meaning (I prefer to use the term coherence) has a "from-to structure": one perceives *subsidiaries,* which mean something not in themselves but rather "something *to which* we attend *from them,*" that upon which they focus.[11] That is, readers of all these texts need to learn how to collect the myriad fragmentary details they encounter to construct larger textual entities of which these details can form parts. One difference between an initial reading of the *Wake* and a rereading is that at first readers see only the particular details that, piled next to, on top of, and crisscrossed with each other, suggest no pattern, no connection with other details. The details or fragments as such are incomprehensible. On a second reading, readers begin to sense how details repeat and create variations on each other through metaphor, form associations with each other through metonymy, negate and affirm each other through irony, and indicate part-whole identity through synecdoche.

For readers of most novels, the sense of connection, continuity, and wholeness is present before the act of reading even begins, both in the paradigms that the genre of novel has traditionally offered as well as in the relationship that the reader assumes to exist between that novel and the referential world. But *Finnegans Wake,* like its encyclopedic and fragmentary cohorts, maintains a tropic relationship with genres and referentiality that requires that the reader encounter it on its own terms rather than via paradigms by which it may be preprocessed. Those terms involve encountering a nearly infinite number of details in fragmentary contexts, discovering their relatedness and thus constructing patterns of interconnection, until the seemingly disparate fragments fuse—to return to Joyce's word—into a joint vision articulating itself through tropes of cyclic recurrence, the rhythm of desire for merger with and then separation from one's opposite, and the endless plasticity of all that exists through language.

The word as fragment has the potential for activation through the reader's activity, becoming an active element capable of fusing with other words, including forms of itself. Such activation operates in at least two modes: different words within the same sentence, and the "same" word in different sentences. Each operation makes its own demands on the reader. Words functioning within the same sentence create elaborate metonymies that move toward fusion if thus recognized; if not, the words remain as fragments. I will work with the following sentence as paradigmatic of the process of words fusing within the unit of sentence: "The house of Atreox is fallen indeedust (Ilyam, Ilyum! Maeromor Mournomates!) averging on blight like the mundibanks of Fennyana, but deeds bounds going arise again" (55.3–5). Even within the sentence, words function metonymically in at least two ways: within the structure of a single word, and between contiguous words. Between contiguous words in the sentence above, readers encounter the following metonymic associations: from Greek myth and tragedy, the house of Atreus, including its role in the Greek-Trojan war (Ilium as Troy) and its fall from power; from Russian folklore, Il'ya Muromets, the popular hero-warrior; from classical Latin, the word *maeror*, signifying mourning; from modern Italy, Miramar, a castle near Trieste; from Ireland, the Thomas Moore song "Avenging and Bright," the bogs of Ireland ("the mundibanks of Fennyana"), and the suggestion of Finn (in *fenny*); from Christianity, spiritual resurrection ("These Bones Gwine to Rise Again" as "deeds bounds going arise again").

Within a single word, metonymic associations abound. "Atreox" suggests at least three: the house of Atreus that represents the fall of all families and dynasties; a *tree*, as opposed to a stone, plus an *ox*, which recalls Apollo's oxen stolen by Hermes, which led to the curse on the house of Atreus—in other words, another "original" sin (Hermes, by the way, is represented by the stone, making him a Shaun figure through metaphor); and *atrox*, the Latin for gloomy or hideous. "Indeedust" also suggests at least three associations: the phrase "in the dust," the punning superlative of "indeed," and an emphasis upon the nature of the fall that has occurred, a fall *in deed*, the deed betokening HCE's fall into dust. "Ilyum" is not only a varied repetition of "Ilyam" but also has its own intentions: "Ilyam" suggesting the Latin accusative case for *Iliadem*, meaning "the Trojan woman," or Helen; "Ilyum" suggesting the Latin name for Troy, Ilium. What happens here is linkage between the sexual act and the fall.

"Maeromor Mournomates" suggests at least four metonymic associations: toward the Latin *maeror*; toward its English translation, mourning; toward the mourning of mates, which occurs in all wars and all falls; and toward Miramare, associated with the fall of both Maximilian and Napoleon III. "Mundibanks" offers at least three associations: it suggests the Latin *mundi*, meaning "of the world"; it points to "mountebanks"; and it names both the muddy banks lining the river Liffey and the rival brothers theme of *Finnegans Wake*. These interactive metonymies suggest the Fall as coextensive with the world, a matter of mountebank activity, and a muddying of otherwise clear and discrete issues. "Fennyana"'s associations move in three directions: Ireland as "fenny" or boggy; Finn and his Fenians; and Finn/HCE and Anna Livia.

Fusing the words of this sentence as active elements, we note some additional metonymic associations. Woman not only leads to the Fall (Ilyam) but also provides the motivation and matter for the rise (HCE and Anna Livia). The sentence opens with deeds having fallen but closes with possibility for deeds rising. The sentence thus establishes links through metaphor with all other sentences in *Finnegans Wake* that work with the themes of rise and fall, man and woman, sin and sex, love and war, being wronged and arighting oneself; with all sentences in which opposites meet, mate, die through temporary concurrence, and then rise again as opposites to repeat the cycle; with all other sentences of the text, in other words.

The "same" word in different sentences makes somewhat different demands on the reader if its isolation as fragment is to move toward fusion as active element. I will work with *sycamore* as paradigm of how the *same* word, including its variant forms, operates differently in different contexts or sentences, these differences adding up, over the distribution of the wordplays in the text, to a network of similarities through the trope of metaphor.

The context of *sycamore* in book I, chapter 1 involves Finnegan at his own wake at the point he has begun to resurrect himself. His friends encourage him to lie back down: "You're better off, sir . . . remembering your shapes and sizes on the pillow of your babycurls under your sycamore by the keld water" (24.31). Here the sycamore appears to be a tree, the phrasing recalling Joyce's description of *Finnegans Wake* as the dream of old Finn, as he lies beside the banks of the Liffey, remembering the history of Ireland and the world (Ellmann, *James Joyce*, 557). This passage links Finnegan with Finn and relates to the notion of resurrection. "Sycamore" next appears in book I, chapter 4, where The Four remember an early amorous adventure: "It was when I was in my farfather out at the west and she and myself, the redheaded girl, firstnighting down Sycomore Lane. Fine feelplay we had of it" (95.21). Here "Sycomore Lane" functions as an equivalent of Lovers' Lane, the spelling change from "sycamore" to "sycomore" possibly connoting the sophomoric nature of this love memory.

In book I, chapter 8 the context for the word's appearance involves the questioning washerwoman's asking the answering washerwoman to tell her about Anna Livia's first lover; the following is part of her response: "in the silence, of the sycomores, all listening . . . he plunged both of his newly anointed hands . . . in her singimari saffron strumans of hair" (203.21). Here "sycomores" suggests not only trees, but also The Four in their role as voyeurs of others' lovemaking. In book II, chapter 1 the word occurs in the context that, arising from the dead, HCE is spoken of: "he is as good as a mountain . . . what haver saw his bedshead farrer and nuver met his swigamore" (241.21). *Sycamore*, transformed to "Swigamore," suggests the Danish word for mother-in-law, *svigermore*, the Whiggamores, who were seventeenth-century Scottish insurgents, and also HCE's taking swigs from his customers' deserted half-full glasses. With *bedstefar* as the Danish for grandfather, part of the two-line sequence involves relatives; another part suggests HCE's sexual prowess. Both notions of love and resurrection come together here.

In book II, chapter 2 the word occurs in the paragraph following the Quinet passage written in French. Picking up on the flower themes of the Quinet lines, the paragraph opens with references to flowers, then follows with suggestions of names of characters from several of Shakespeare's plays. Into this context comes the following line: "Sickamoor's so woful sally" (281.20). The line names two trees, sycamore and sally, another term for willow, so that it continues the botanical line of the Quinet passage. In addition it identifies one of three *Othello* characters suggested in the paragraph: Othello is the Moor whose love (amour) has been sickened with the jealousy implanted by Iago, whose woe over Desdemona will cause him to be "so awfully sorry" when, after killing her, he learns of her innocence and Iago's treachery. The term "sally" also suggests Desdemona, who sings the willow song shortly before her death. In this context "sickamoor's" is associated with the notion of love in its fallen form, as opposed to its resurrecting possibilities.

In book II, chapter 4 *sycamores* appears in a context that focuses upon The Four. Here they are seabirds following the love boat in which Tristan and Isolde pursue their love: "and they kemin in so hattajocky . . . to the solans and the sycamores and the wild geese and the gannets and the migratories" (384.1). This is a peculiar list of birds. "Solan goose" is another name for gannet, so the gannet is named twice; and since "solan" consistently is associated with "goose," geese are named twice also. Twice two is four, The Four. But "sycamores" has no connection with these migratory seabirds. Perhaps the narrator is calling readers' attentions to The Four as alien to the seabirds with which they attempt to blend themselves. In any case, the presence of *sycamores* in this context asks readers to recall contexts in which the term has previously occurred. Because The Four have assumed this seabird identity to facilitate their voyeurism of Tristan's and Isolde's lovemaking, *sycamores* is associated with sexual love, love in its resurrecting capacity.

Four pages later in the same chapter, the word appears in the context of Tristan's and Isolde's lovemaking: "after that there he was . . . poghuing her scandalous and very wrong, the maid, in single combat, under the sycamores, amid the bludderings from the boom" (388.24). Although the conventional spelling of sycamore is used, the word applies not to trees, since we are afloat on the high seas, but to the eightfold gaze of The Four as they continue their voyeurism, still in search of resurrection. When the word appears again, its context is provided by the fact of The Four's now residing in a rest home for the aged; the passage details some of the problems the elderly face, including the condition that "they were all sycamore and by the world forgot" (397.23), "sycamore" indicating its near-phonetic equivalent of being "sick all the more" as one ages.

In book III, chapter 2 Issy writes a love letter to Jaun, responding to his previously declared love for her: "Everyday, precious . . . I will dream telepath posts dulcets on this isinglass stream . . . under the libans and the sickamours, the cyprissis and babilonias" (460.23). "Sickamours" here forms part of the series of trees named in these and nearby lines as well as defines Issy's condition as "lovesick," also recalling another lovesick character, Othello. The word thus plays into the two notions of love and trees, the latter of which forms a complex matrix of associations with related notions such as the development of the alphabet and literacy, all letters in the Irish alphabet having tree names.[12]

In book III, chapter 3, as The Four approach Yawn to begin interrogating him, the following lines mark the appearance of the word: "And a crack quatyouare of stenoggers they made of themselves, solons and psychomorers . . . with their hurts and daimons, spites and clops" (476.15). The context places The Four in one of their typical roles as investigators of history, marked here as elsewhere by polar qualities: both wisdom and madness ("solon" indicating a sage such as Solon, and "psychomorers" suggesting both that which relates to the soul and the condition of being mad), maturity and immaturity ("psychomorers" as well as "sophomores"), their association with the four card suits and their vulnerability to allowing their interpretation of "the facts" to be influenced by "their hurts and daimons, spites and clops." "Psychomorers" here carries the notion of polarity.

As HCE speaks in defense of himself, explaining his introduction of ALP to The Four, the motif appears again: "I introduced her . . . to our fourposter tunies . . . those whapping oldsteirs, with sycamode euphonium in either notation" (533.17). In context, "sycamode" forms part of the multiple references to music (modes, euphonium, and notation, plus others in nearby lines, as well as the "chamber music" one makes with a commode), in addition to which it identifies the presence of The Four. McHugh points out that "whapping oldsteirs" refers to Wapping Old Stairs, in East London, and that "wap" is cant for "copulate" (*Annotations*, 533). In this maze "sycamode" carries out the interweaving of a number of notions: sexuality, music, local place-names, the elderly.

The word also occurs in book III, chapter 4, where The Four have resumed their familiar places as voyeurs, this time as the four posts of the Porters' bed: "therenow they stood, the sycomores, all four of them, in their quartan agues" (555.08). Here "sycomores" identifies The Four with the illness of old age. The context associates the term with sexuality that, as the chapter proceeds, will be incapable of "wetting the tea" and will thus be "fallen" rather than "resurrecting."

That *sycamore* in both book I, chapter 1 and book II, chapter 1 is associated with the resurrection notion and in the final chapters of books I, II, and III with the voyeurism of The Four is one small evidence of the intricate patterning and connexity of *Finnegans Wake,* thus forming part of the falling and rising theme. This analysis of sycamore shows how the same word in different contexts tends to operate. Such a word develops dynamically through the reiteration and variation of its form, which is flexible, responding to the context in which it occurs. Although such a word tends to be associated especially closely with a particular character and notion, it connects with a range of notions and characters. With sycamore, for instance, although its closest association is with The Four in the theme of sexual love as resurrecting or fallen, it also touches Issy, Anna Livia, HCE, and Finnegan and develops the principles of polar opposition as well as the cyclicity of the life span, seen here in the phase of old age.

I have been working with the word as fragment that needs to become active element, both as different words within a sentence as well as the same word in a variety of sentences. In doing so, I have used at least one term that requires defining, and I need to introduce a substitution, as metaphor, for another. Beyond that, I want to show how these terms bring together the active elements that in fusing or connecting with each other, set the text's dynamics in motion.

I have used the word *theme* but not defined it. By theme I indicate those instances of cyclicity and transformation that play throughout *Finnegans Wake.*[13] As I read the text, its themes carry out two principles: Vico's notion of the cyclicity of history as it moves from one age to another and then circles back upon itself to begin the cycle again, and Bruno's notion of the mutual attraction of polarities for each other, which causes them to move toward each other, meet, take on each other's identity, and then diverge, eventually to repeat the process. Both Bruno's and Vico's ideas present processes of transformation through cyclicity. Some of the *Wake*'s major polar themes include rise and fall, love and war, birth and death, sacred and secular, guilt and innocence, time and space; two other major themes include the pervasive interpenetration and energizing effects of sexuality and culture, and the family in its various manifestations—the natural landscape; the nuclear family of father, mother, and children; the civil family of city, nation, and civilization; and the entire human family.

As *Finnegans Wake* is composed of interconnecting themes, each theme is composed of interconnecting motifs, which term I had replaced in the analysis of sycamore with *notion*, since I had not yet defined it. I use *motif* in Clive Hart's sense of "a short verbal construct, characterised by certain easily recognisable patterns of rhythm, sound, form and sometimes, sense" (*Structure and Motif*, 20). Motifs vary in length from a single word to a phrase to a sentence to a paragraph. Examples of one-word motifs include sycamore and Finn—which through metaphor is identical to fin, *fin*, finish, phoenix, phoenician. Examples of phrase motifs include many rhythmic motifs, such as "The House That Jack Built." An example of brief sentence-long motifs is the request for time; the Quinet flower passage exemplifies an extended sentence-long motif. But all motifs undergo expansion and contraction rather than remain at a fixed length as well as undergo variations in wording, rhythm, and context. A single motif tends to be associated especially strongly with one theme but usually contributes to others as well. As we saw with sycamore, for instance, that motif has especially close ties to the theme of rise and fall through its associations with sexual love as resurrecting or fallen; but sycamore also weaves into the theme of aging. Both themes relate to the more general principle of cyclicity.

For indicating the clustering of motifs to form themes, a third term is helpful, for which I prefer *networks* to Hart's "motif-agglomeration" or David Hayman's "nodal system." Two different sorts of networks occur: the networking of a motif as it plays over the range of the entire text, of which sycamore is an instance; and the networking of various motifs that connect with each other to compose a particular section of the *Wake*.[14]

Let us examine the way the request for time motif develops a variety of themes as it moves through different contexts. In book I, chapter 2 the motif is strongly associated with HCE and the guilt he feels for the crime or indiscretion he committed in the park. When the Cad "accosted" him "to ask could he tell him how much a clock it was" (35.18), HCE responds with a doubly inappropriate response: an abstract statement about the nature of universal time and a vigorous denial of guilt—about which the Cad had never asked. A chapter later, in a passage that deals generally with themes relating to the Fall, a variant of the Cad's request for time occurs: "Tal the tem of the tumulum" (56.23). Besides the strong evocation of HCE's guilt, this variant relates to the additional themes of death and creation through recalling Tem, the creator in the *Egyptian Book of the Dead* and the tumulus or burial mound, which itself offers strong ties to the midden mound, another sort of burial ground.

In book I, chapter 6 after the Mookse rails at and condemns the Gripes, the Gripes asks him, "By the watch, what is the time, pace?" (154.16). Here the motif develops the theme of rival brothers, the Gripes dealing well with time but not space, and the Mookse coping well with space but not time—clearly a parallel with Shem's poor sight but good hearing and Shaun's weak hearing but clear sight. In book I, chapter 8 the motif appears when the questioning washerwoman asks the answering washerwoman, "Fieluhr? Filou! What age is at?" (213.14). McHugh explains that "Fieluhr" is how a Frenchman would hear the German "Wie viel Uhr?" or "What's the time?" (*Annotations*, 213). In this context the motif relates neither to guilt nor to rival brothers but instead to change from one form to another as the washerwomen begin their transformations to tree and stone.

In book III, chapter 3 when HCE recounts his great deeds as founder of civilization, he concludes his oration with "Thus be hek. Verily! Verily! Time, place!" (546.23–24). The motif appears here as both the request for time and the space-time polarity. It thus suggests the rival brothers theme, with Shem as time and Shaun as space, in addition to time as the fluid medium in which civilizations rise—and fall. The motif appears three times in book IV. Into a passage in which various voices have called for dawn and resurrection comes the call for "Tim!" (598.27), which is at once a call for Tim Finnegan to arise from the dead as well as the familiar call for time. In this context, the motif responds to the theme of time as the cyclic return in which resurrection is possible. On the next page, in the same context, comes this call: "Time-o'-Thay!" (599.3). Here again Tim is called to rouse himself from death, and the time of day is requested, both of which bear upon time as cyclic recurrence; in addition, we hear the call for "tea time." Here, "Time, please" and "they all drank tea" function as two motifs for closure, signaling that time is running out and that the end of the narrative is near. The motif returns as Anna Livia speaks to her man of the hooths, encouraging him to arise from his sleep. She recalls their sons' tendency to change positions with each other and then adds, "I seen the likes in the twinngling of an aye. Som. So oft. Sim. Time after time. The sehm asnuh" (620.15). In this instance, the motif develops several of the time themes: time as age following age, in which the "sehm asnuh" recurs again and again; and time as the medium in which opposites move toward, merge with each other, and then diverge into opposition again.

This analysis, as does that for sycamore, indicates how motifs function: not only diction shifts, but so does the orientation of motifs as they appear in varying contexts which tie them to varying themes; though they may have especially close ties to one character—in this instance, HCE—they are associated with a number of other members in the *Wake*'s shifting cast; they develop a number of different themes, filling out the potential dimensions of any given theme so that it begins to interact with other themes, refusing containment.

These elements characterize the way motifs as fragments function, regardless of their length, but several additional elements compose the longer motifs, some of which result from the interaction of smaller units that consistently appear in conjunction with each other. The Quinet flower motif, for instance, grows out of three such units: the presence of flowers, the passage of time, and polar oppositions. In the passage 14.35–15.11, these flowers are named: cornflowers, duskrose, twolips, whitethorn, redthorn. Time spans the millennia between Heber and Heremon's founding of the Irish people and the present time of being on the brink of war: "Since the bouts of Hebear and Hairyman . . . these paxsealing buttonholes have quadrilled across the centuries and whiff now whafft to us, fresh and made-of-all-smiles as, on the eve of Killallwho" (14.35–15.11). Some of the oppositions include "laughtears" (15.9), peace and war ("pax" and "Killallwho"), and the antagonism between the legendary Irish colonizers known as the Fomorians and the Tuatha Dé Danaan as well as between the Viking ("Oxman" and "Danes") invaders and the natives of ninth-century Dublin.

In another of the full statements, 354.22–34, these flowers are named: "ivies," "idies," "iries," "muskat grove," "bright plinnyflowers in Calomella's cool bowers." Time is the fluid medium in which oppositions coexist peaceably: "When old the wormd was a gadden" can be both "when the old snake was a gadding" to tempt Eve and "when all the world was a garden." Some additional oppositions include "Anthea" (Aphrodite was a flower goddess) versus the "idies iries" (Dies Irae) versus "lancifer lucifug" (Lancelot and Lucifer), raven versus dove, and "gells" versus "buys" (female and male as well as selling and buying).

At 615.2–10, the Quinet flower passage appears in the context of The Four's vehicle as a metaphor for the dream itself and for the dreamer/reader's effort to understand the dream. These flowers are named: "Giacinta" (Italian for hyacinth), "Pervenche" (French for periwinkle), and "Marguerite" (French for daisy). Time operates as the medium in which the text has taken in "the dialytically separated elements" of "*h*eroticisms, *c*atastrophes and *e*ccentricities transmitted by the *a*ncient *l*egacy of the *p*ast" and recombined them so that "Finnius the old One . . . may be there for you." The text, in other words, has restored the possibility of unity of experience for those who can read it. Opposites in this context have been "anastomosically assimilated and preteridentified paraidiotically." Since "anastomosis" names the operation of connecting separate channels through which liquid flows, the text declares the manner by which a unity of experience can be restored: by showing the connections between what is separated.

These same three units compose even the partial appearances of the Quinet flower motif, as in 28.26–29:

> *Les Loves of Selskar et Pervenche*, freely adapted to *The Novvergin's Viv*. There'll be bluebells blowing in salty sepulchres the night she signs her final tear.

Two flowers are named, the "pervenche" (periwinkle) and the bluebell. Several oppositions include virgin and wife ("viv" is Danish for "wife") as well as life and death ("bluebells" and "salty sepulchres"). In this passage time is identified as "the night she signs her final tear"—a reference in other words, to the "end" of *Finnegans Wake*, which is also its "beginning"—so that time is here associated with cyclicity.

In 53.8–11, the motif takes the following form:

> And there oftafter, jauntyjogging, on an Irish visavis, insteadily with shoulder to shoulder Jehu will tell to Christianier, saint to sage, the humphriad of that fall and rise while daisy winks at her pinker sister among the tussocks and the copoll between the shafts mocks the couple on the car.

The flowers here are daisy and pinks. Opposites include Jews and Christian, saint and sage, rise and fall, the couple "between the shafts" (horses) versus the couple "on the car" (humans), and male versus female genitalia (the "copoll between the shafts" as the penis and testicles; "the couple on the car" as the vulval labia and clitoris). The time is that in which the story of Humphrey's rise and fall will be told, at a "jaunty" pace that recalls the jaunting cart of The Four, with an "Irish" perspective; time, in other words, is that required for reading *Finnegans Wake*. And because by synecdoche the *Wake* is microcosm to the macrocosm, time is also that required for reading the world, for reading life.

In addition to defining the concerns of the Quinet motif as those of cyclic growth and the functioning of polarities over time, the consistent conjunction of flowers, time, and oppositions becomes a means for identifying the presence in the text of the Quinet motif. In the same way, the conjunction of certain smaller units of sound announces the presence of other motifs, such as the riddle and the "rhythmic waters" motifs. Three units of sound, for instance, create the pattern by which readers identify the presence of the latter motif: alliteration, the dominance of dactyllic rhythm, and, when the motif appears in its complete form, an ending punctuated by an accented, one-syllable word, preceded by an unaccented, one-syllable preposition. The passage offering the most elaborate statement of this rhythm concludes book I. As the two washerwomen are transformed to tree and stone, the questioning woman continues her request for the answering woman to tell her tales of "stem or stone":

> And ho! Hey? What all men. Hot? His tittering daughters of. Whawk?
>   Can't hear with the waters of. The chittering waters of. Flittering bats, fieldmice bawk talk. Ho! Are you not gone ahome? What Thom Malone? Can't hear with bawk of bats, all thim liffeying waters of. Ho, talk save us! My foos won't moos. I feel as old as yonder elm. A tale told of Shaun or Shem? All Livia's daughtersons. Dark hawks hear us. Night! Night! My ho head halls. I feel as heavy as yonder stone. Tell me of John or Shaun? Who were Shem and Shaun the living sons or daughters of? Night now! Tell me, tell me, tell me, elm! Night night! Telmetale of stem or stone. Beside the rivering waters of, hitherandthithering waters of. Night! (215.29–216.5).

In addition to the three sound units described above, this passage is composed of others as well, but it works with the three extensively enough that readers' ears become attuned to the motif as pattern of sound, especially in its final two lines. Two variants precede this appearance: "they were all night wasching the walters of, the weltering walters off. Whyte" (64.20–21), and "and watch her waters of her sillying waters of" (76.29). The absence of the concluding, accented one-syllable word marks the latter variant as a partial rather than a full statement of the motif.

The nine appearances following the most complete statement testify to Joyce's rhythmic inventiveness:

And his dithering dathering waltzers of. Stright. (245.22)

arride the winnerful wonders off, the winnerful wonnerful wanders off (265.15–16)

to rout them rollicking rogues from, rule those racketeer romps from, rein their rockery rides from. Rambling (355.16)

The for eolders were aspolootly at their wetsend in the mailing waters, trying to. Hide! Seek! Hide! Seek! . . . and they were all trying to and baffling with the walters of, hoompsydoompsy walters of. High! Sink! High! Sink! (372.34–373.7)

the rashest of, the romping, jomping rushes of (441.03)

Amingst the living waters of, the living in giving waters of. Tight (462.4–5)

on the bibby bobby burns of.

————Quatsch! (520.26–27)

————Among the shivering sedges so? Weedy waving

————Besides the bubblye waters of, babblyebubblye waters of?

————Right (526.5, 9–10)

Cant ear! Her dorters ofe? Whofe? Her eskmeno daughters hope?
Whope? Ellme, elmme, elskmestoon! Soon! (572.16–17)

The final variant returns to material from the passage quoted above
as containing the most elaborate statement of this rhythmic motif,
echoing the lines "Tell me of John or Shaun? Who were Shem and
Shaun the living sons or daughters of? Night now! Tell me, tell me,
tell me, elm! Night Night!" In addition to its identity as recognizable
rhythmic units of sound, the "rhythmic waters" motif is marked by
characteristics discussed earlier: the motif's appearance being influenced by the context in which it occurs, its association with a multitude of characters, and its development of various themes.

Besides identifying motifs through rhythmic patterns and consistently recurring conjunctions of smaller word units, such as flowers,
time, and cyclicity for the Quinet motif, readers also learn to identify
the text's myriad and shifting voices. Such identification enables
readers to move from encountering the text as chaotic fragmentation
to experiencing it as the fusion of active elements. As an area for
analysis, however, the functioning of voice offers considerably more
difficulties than do those of rhythmic and verbal motifs. One reason
is that for the latter, significant analysis already exists. Clive Hart's
index of motifs and David Hayman's nodal framework for examining
them provide enormous help in identifying smaller verbal units of
motifs and in clustering them.[15] Books containing the music for songs
in the *Wake* help to identify rhythmic motifs.[16] Sustained work on
voice as sound, however, has yet to be undertaken, most studies
exploring voice as sense.[17]

Another reason for the difficulty in analyzing voice involves its
amorphousness in contrast to the more readily apparent motif. Our
eyes, that is, are more proficient at identifying variants on a verbal
pattern that usually has visually recognized elements than our ears
are at identifying the aurally recognized elements that identify a voice
unless, of course, the passage is identifiable by strongly rhythmic,
alliterative, or other aural qualities. Even so, such qualities are more
a function of motif than of voice since alliteration and rhythm in
themselves do not suggest the intonations of a particular voice.

Let us take sound as our point of entrance to voice and consider,
for their possible guidance, some of the narrators' comments on
sound:

Behove this sound of Irish sense. Really? Here English might be seen. Royally? One sovereign punned to petery pence. Regally? The silence speaks the scene. Fake! (12.36–13.03)

likeas equal to anequal in this sound seemetery which iz leebez luv (17.35–36)

(here keen again and begin again to make soundsense and sensesound kin again) (121.14–16)

In the buginning is the woid, in the muddle is the sound-dance and thereinofter you're in the unbewised again, vund vulsyvolsy. (378.29–30)

Can you not distinguish the sense, prain, from the sound, bray? (522.29–30)

Vouchsafe me more soundpicture! It gives furiously to think. (570.14–15)

Not a salutary sellable sound is since. (598.04)

These passages suggest a number of notions for readers: that we should listen for the distinction between the Irish and the English sounds and senses of words; that silence is a significant part of sound; that sound is a cemetery/"seemetery" in which we should not mistake the "seeming" for the sound; that one function of the text is to bring together sound and sense, sense perhaps having become abstracted from sound to the point that when we "hear," we "hear" only what we expect, whereas Joyce's text forces us to hear sound that, by counterpointing sense, deters us from listening in a "preprogrammed" way; that between the word as "buginning" and the interpretation or "end" as "unbewised"—both in the sense of "unproved" (*unbewiesen*) and not the product of conscious mind (*unbewusst*) (McHugh, *Annotations*, 378)—lies the "muddle" of sound; that sense and sound are not equivalents; that sound can be a starting place for discovering sense. Granted, the *Wake*'s sound is not the *Wake*'s voices. Nevertheless, those voices operate within the framework of the text's sound, and as we explore recognizing fragments of voice, we will do well to hold in mind some aspects of that framework.

Besides voice serving the text's role as link between sense and sound, voice serves another textual role as deconstructor of expectations. Readers may expect that voice in *Finnegans Wake* functions similarly to its functioning in most novels. But lacking stability and denying continuity, voice instead serves in the same manner as do the text's other fragmentary—and hence potentially incoherent—elements: as that for which connexity must be discovered/created.

If the *Wake*'s voices communicate with each other less than they perform at each other, interpreting this performance falls to readers, who become—in many senses—the conductors of the score Joyce offers them. What is the nature of that score? For *Finnegans Wake*, voice only partially reflects backward from the speaker's word to the individual and social parameters constituting that voice, since voice is less an ideology than a rhythm, less a sociology than a timbre, less a psychology than a pitch. This is not to say that psychology, sociology, and ideology are not present; rather, it is to observe that this text subordinates them to the word as semiotic and symphonic.

I suggest that we attempt to hear each voice as it sounds in a particular context, in terms of the physical components of that sound: its rhythm, tone, dialect, or vernacularity. Once such descriptions exist, we may compare how a voice's sound varies with context and which of its components remain relatively unchanged. Shaun's voice when operating in the context of his rivalry with Shem, as in book I, chapter 7, probably differs in some ways from his voice in the context of Shaun as the young form of HCE, as in book III, chapter 2. In the same way, the voice of The Four when interrogating Yawn probably differs in some ways from their voice as they announce the sexual activity of Mr. and Mrs. Porter. Also, The Four sometimes speak in four different voices rather than in one composite voice. As a focus for this suggestion, I will examine some characteristics of the sound of Anna Livia's voice as we hear it in her final monologue and then use these characteristics by which to determine whether it is her voice we hear in certain lines of book I, chapter 8 or that of the washerwomen.

Here is the sound of her voice as she begins the monologue:

Soft morning, city! Lsp! I am leafy speafing. Lpf! Folty and folty
all the nights have falled on to long my hair. Not a sound, falling.
Lispn! No wind no word. Only a leaf, just a leaf and then leaves.
The woods are fond always. As were we their babes in. And
robins in crews so. It is for me goolden wending. Unless? Away!
Rise up, man of the hooths, you have slept so long! (619.20–27)

What I hear in these lines is a slow, smooth flow of sound, induced
at least in part by the predominance of soft consonants such as *L, S,*
and *R,* a sound appropriate to a river's voice whose currents are calm
and steady.[18] The tone is personal, caressing, affectionate, marked
slightly by the effects of Irish on English diction and syntax.

And here is her voice toward the end of the monologue:

But I'm loothing them that's here and all I lothe. Loonely in me
loneness. For all their faults. I am passing out. O bitter ending!
I'll slip away before they're up. They'll never see. Nor know.
Nor miss me. And it's old and old it's sad and old it's sad and
weary I go back to you, my cold father, my cold mad father, my
cold mad feary father, till the near sight of the mere size of him,
the moyles and moyles of it, moananoaning makes me seasilt
saltsick and I rush, my only, into your arms. (627.33–628.04)

Again, I hear a smooth flow of sound, built at least in part on soft
consonants as well as on the repetition of words and phrases. Now,
though, the pace is somewhat quickened, as befits the seemingly
quickened pace of the river as it nears the sea into which it empties.
Although the words speak of anguish, their softened sound cushions
the impact so that the tone approximates acceptance rather than ag-
ony.

Let us compare these sounds of Anna Livia's voice with some
lines from book I, chapter 8, all of which are generally credited to the
two washerwomen. I would claim, however, that based on sound,
the middle section of the passage reproduced here should be identified as the voice of Anna Livia:

Are you meanam Tarpey and Lyons and Gregory? I meyne now,
thank all, the four of them, and the roar of them, that draves
that stray in the mist and old Johnny MacDougal along with

them. Is that the Poolbeg flasher beyant, pharphar, or a fireboat coasting nyar the Kishtna or a glow I behold within a hedge or my Garry come back from the Indes? Wait till the honeying of the lune, love! Die, eve, little eve, die! We see that wonder in your eye. We'll meet again, we'll part once more. The spot I'll seek if the hour you'll find. My chart shines high where the blue milk's upset. Forgivemequick, I'm going! Bubye! And you, pluck your watch, forgetmenot. Your evenlode. So save to jurna's end! My sights are swimming thicker on me by the shadows to this place. I sow home slowly now by own way, moyvalley way. Towy I too, rathmine.

Ah, but she was the queer old skeowsha anyhow, Anna Livia, trinkettoes! And sure he was the quare old buntz too, Dear Dirty Dumpling, foostherfather of fingalls and dotthergills. Gammer and gaffer we're all their gangsters. (214.33–215.15)

In this passage, I hear first the voice of the questioning washerwoman, followed by the answering washerwoman. Then the questioner asks a second question, but rather than the answerer responding to it, we hear the voice of Anna Livia, beginning with the words "Wait till the honeying of the lune, love!" and concluding with "Forgive me quick, I'm going! Bubye!" In the words that follow we hear the voices of both washerwomen, who remind each other of the work they are finishing up, name their home destinations (Moy Valley and Rathmines), and acknowledge their own and others' relatedness to ALP and HCE, everyone's first parents.

The sound of the voice that speaks in 215.3–7 differs from the voices that speak in 214.33–215.3 and 215.7–15. The Anna Livia voice is marked by the presence of the same sostenuto consonants as we observed in Anna Livia's final monolgoue, L, S, and M, whereas the washerwomen voices show more end-stopped and staccato consonants, such as T, D, and K. At least in part because of the different prevailing consonants, the tempos of the two sets of voices contrast with each other, the Anna Livia pace rather slow, as heard for instance in the sequence "Wait till the honeying of the lune, love!" The pace of the washerwomen is faster, heard in "Ah, but she was the queer old skeowsha anyhow, Anna Livia, trinkettoes!" The tones differ, too, the Anna Livia voice projecting a statelier, more personal quality than the gossiping, "fishwife" tones of the washerwomen.

Finally, the degree to which we hear the influence of Irish diction and syntax on English is less pronounced in the Anna Livia voice than in the washerwomen voices. While some differences exist between the voice of Anna Livia as it appears in 215.3–7 and as it exists in 627.33–628.04—such as the degree to which words and phrases undergo varied repetitions—so many significant similarities exist between the two as to convince me that it is Anna Livia's voice we hear in the former passage rather than an unbroken washerwomen exchange.

By discovering and/or creating connections, such as we have been doing in connecting the voice of Anna Livia in her final monologue with her voice within the washerwomen's exchange, we trope voice. In the passages examined above, voice is metaphoric in the identity of Anna Livia's voice between the final monologue and its presence within the washerwomen's exchange. But within that exchange, her voice is metonymic with that of the two washerwomen's voices surrounding hers. In its rhythms and tones, Anna Livia's voice is synecdochic of the river Liffey. And by irony Anna Livia's voice is (not) that of the washerwomen.

Whether troping voice or rhythm or verbal motifs of whatever length, we are working with fragments as active elements, seeing their connections with what is identical to, contiguous with, part of, and (not) themselves. Fragment, of whatever size and kind, is the *Wake*'s working unit. And if allowed as microcosm of the macrocosm, the *Wake* by synecdoche suggests the fragment is also the universe's working unit. But, by irony the text denies as well as affirms this possibility, the *is* of affirmation balancing the *not* of denial in the dynamic tension and balance characteristic of the text. Thus, voice fragment is rhythmic fragment is verbal motif; fragment, fragment, fragment, ad infinitum; fragment is *Wake* is universe; fragment is (not) text is (not) universe.

So where have we arrived? In the *Wake*'s words, "As we there are where are we are we there from tomtittot to teetootomtotalitarian. Tea tea too oo" (260.1–3). In other words, from alpha (*A*s) to omega (*oo*).[19] Fragment, text, universe. Is. Not.

NOTES

1. For details of Weaver's "commission" to Joyce that he incorporate material about the giant's grave, see *Letters* 3:144 n. 1; and Ellmann's *James Joyce*, 594–95.

2. Ernst Behler, "Das Fragment," in *Prosa kunst ohne Erzählen*, ed. Klaus Weissenberger (Tübingen: Niemeyer, 1985), 125–45.

3. Hazard Adams, "Must a Poem Be a Perfect Unity," *Antithetical Essays*.

4. Thomas McFarland, *Romanticism and the Forms of Ruin* (Princeton: Princeton University Press, 1981), 11. Further references to this work will be given in parentheses in the text.

5. Many of the ideas presented here about the shift in notions about wholes derive from Gilles Deleuze and Felix Guattari, *Anti-Oedipus: Capitalism and Schizophrenia*, trans. Robert Hurley, Mark Seem, and Helen R. Lane (New York: Viking Press, 1977), 42–44. Subsequent references are given in the text.

6. Frye, *Anatomy of Criticism*. See Frye's discussion of encyclopedic works, 54–58 and 315–26.

7. Robert Burton, *The Anatomy of Melancholy*, ed. Rev. A. R. Shilleto (London: G. Bell and Sons, 1920), 1:164.

8. Michel Foucault, *Language, Counter-Memory, Practice*, ed. Donald F. Bouchard, trans. Donald F. Bouchard and Sherry Simon (Ithaca, N.Y.: Cornell University Press, 1977), 92. Subsequent references are given in the text.

9. Northrop Frye explores parallels as well as contrasts between these two works in "Quest and Cycle in Finnegans Wake," *Fables of Identity: Studies in Poetic Mythology* (New York: Harcourt, Brace, & World, 1963), 256–64.

10. Michael Polanyi, *Knowing and Being* (Chicago: University of Chicago Press, 1969), 128.

11. Michael Polanyi and Harry Prosch, *Meaning* (Chicago: University of Chicago Press, 1975), 97.

12. Glasheen, *Third Census*, 288.

13. I use *theme* differently from Clive Hart, who defines themes as "major narrative and allegorical elements of the book [*Finnegans Wake*], such as 'Eating the god,' 'homosexuality,' 'ritual murder.'" I do not believe that allegory functions significantly in the *Wake*, nor do I see themes as significant in advancing narration. Also, exemplifying the text's themes as does Hart causes the *Wake* to sound more like a first cousin to Frazer's *The Golden Bough* than its more distant relation. See *Structure and Motif*, 20.

14. Two especially helpful studies of how networking operates are David Hayman's "Nodality and the Infrastructure of *Finnegans Wake*," *James Joyce Quarterly* 16 (1978/1979): 135–49, and Clark's "Networking in *Finnegans Wake*."

15. See Hart's "An Index of Motifs in *Finnegans Wake*," *Structure and Motif*, 211–47, and Hayman's "Nodality."

16. See Matthew J. C. Hodgart and Mabel P. Worthington, *Song in the Works of James Joyce* (New York: Columbia University Press, 1959) and Ruth Bauerle, *The James Joyce Songbook* (New York: Garland Publishing, 1982).

17. See, for instance, Michael H. Begnal and Grace Eckley, *Narrator and Character in Finnegans Wake* (Lewisburg, Pa.: Bucknell University Press, 1975); Hugh Kenner, *Joyce's Voices* (Berkeley and Los Angeles: University of California Press, 1978); Roland McHugh, *The Sigla of Finnegans Wake* (Austin: University of Texas Press, 1976); and John Paul Riquelme, *Teller and Tale in Joyce's*

Fiction: Oscillating Perspectives (Baltimore: Johns Hopkins University Press, 1983).

18. Suzette Henke describes ALP's "lisping narrative" as "filled with fluid 'l' and 'f' sounds and with open vowels that suggest the yonic spaces of female interiority" (*Politics of Desire*, 198).

19. For an analysis of how alpha and omega function in *Finnegans Wake*, see chapter 1, "Twists of the Teller's Tale," in Riquelme's *Teller and Tale*, 1–47.

Chapter 10

The Letter: Desire as Trope

And if *literal* means "to the letter," the literal becomes the most problematically figurative mode of all.

—Barbara Johnson

Joycean critics have noted the interpenetration of time and space in *Finnegans Wake.* Margot Norris observes, for example,

> Joyce's reasons for linking Anna Livia and the river so steadfastly are probably also multiple. For one thing, the association allowed him to treat time and space as versions of each other—an antinomy that he wanted to reconcile in the manner of Nolan opposites and that he therefore invested in Shem (time) and Shaun (space). Merging Isabel and Kate with Anna Livia as her young and old versions, Joyce makes the chronological development of the female from young girl to old woman correspond to the topological course of the river from spring to delta. The river is an element in the mighty oppositions Joyce invests in ALP and HCE: river/ land, midget/ giant, female/male.[1]

As river, ALP flows. Through metaphor, her river flow is the flow of language ("the languo of flows,"[2] [621.22]), the flow of time, the flow of desire, the flow of memory. She measures change: from her source as spring to her development as stream to her maturity as river to her resolution into sea; from cloud to rain drops to flowing stream and river to condensation into cloud. Her cyclic course loops in two long ovals: from earth to sky back to earth and from spring to river to sea back to spring. This motion monitors continual change, continuing constancy. ALP, as time, is movement, an image of movement, a movement-image.

In *Cinema* 1: The Movement-Image, Gilles Deleuze is concerned with cinema, with that instant when the image became loosed from immobility to take its place in the flow of movement:

> Movement, as physical reality in the external world, and the image, as psychic reality in consciousness, could no longer be opposed. The Bergsonian discovery of a movement-image, and more profoundly, of a time-image, still retains such richness today that it is not certain that all its consequences have been drawn.[3]

Continuing to discuss Bergson's discovery in relation to cinema, Deleuze writes:

> not only is the instant an immobile section of movement, but movement is a mobile section of duration, that is, of the Whole, or of a whole. Which implies that movement expresses something more profound, which is the change in duration or in the whole. To say that duration is change is part of its definition: it changes and does not stop changing. (*Cinema*, 8)

According to Deleuze, then, the notions of whole and movement are constructed by irony. Movement is the synthesis of "immobile" instants; duration is constructed by "mobile" movements; the "whole" is constructed through the changes in duration it undergoes.

The notion of the whole as constructed by the changes in duration it undergoes not only describes ALP as river, but it also recalls some notions about fragments developed in the previous chapter. The fragment, I observed there, is the *Wake*'s working unit, the whole becoming the interaction of those fragments as the reader/writer constructs that interaction. These ideas bear on Deleuze's continuing discussion of Bergson, who, like Joyce, was concerned with the nature of wholes. "Many philosophers," writes Deleuze, "had already said that the whole was neither given nor giveable: they simply concluded from this that the whole was a meaningless notion. Bergson's conclusion is very different: if the whole is not giveable, it is because it is the Open, and because its nature is to change constantly, or to give rise to something new, in short, to endure" (*Cinema*, 9). The notion of whole which Deleuze presents links both with the Joycean whole constituted of permutations on fragments and the *Wake*'s work with desire:

If one had to define the whole, it would be defined by Relation. Relation is not a property of objects, it is always external to its terms. It is also inseparable from the open, and displays a spiritual or mental existence. Relations do not belong to objects, but to the whole, on condition that this is not confused with a closed set of objects. By movement in space, the objects of a set change their respective positions. But, through relations, the whole is transformed or changes qualitatively. We can say of duration itself or of time, that it is the whole of relations. (*Cinema*, 10)

Although *Finnegans Wake* moves in space/time differently than do films, its movement is closely related to theirs. As a "thought experiment" in measuring the degree to which Deleuze's words apply to the *Wake*, one may reread his seven sentences above, substituting, first, *desire* for *relations* and, second, *the fragment as network for connections* for *relations*.

Like *Cinema 1*, *Finnegans Wake* is interested in film. In fact, in the summer of 1923, when Joyce was in the early stages of planning the *Wake*, he made the following entry in one of his notebooks:

cinegraphist/leitmotivs and décor idéal/Proust—max[imum] text—min[imum] action/ Cine [—maximum action—minimum text].[4]

David Hayman comments that "though these are the only conceptual notes I have found, there are other references to the movies and their stars in the early notebooks."[5] That Joyce carried this interest in film into the *Wake* is evidenced in excerpts, all showing the *Wake*'s treatment of "movies" as "movement." ALP is described as "in gait a movely water" (318.01). HCE is named a "Moviefigure on in scenic section" (602.27). Issy is shown "at the movies swallowing sobs and blowing bixed mixcuits over 'childe' chaplain's 'latest' " (166.13–14). Concluding his self-defense after Justius's (Shaun's) attack, Mercius (Shem) "thank[s] Movies from the innermost depths of my still attrite [but not contrite] heart" (194.02).[6] Discussing the invention of the printing press as part of the transition into the Prankquean and Jarl van Hoother tale, one of the *Wake*'s narrators declares, "The movibles are scrawling in motions, marching, all of them ago, in pitpat and zingzang for every busy eerie whig's a bit of a torytale to tell" (20.21).

And another of the *Wake*'s narrators gives this direction to readers: "if you are looking for the bilder deep your ear on the movietone!" (62.09). A second way that film enters the *Wake* is through its cinematiclike procedures in treating "images": cutting, fadeout, juxtaposition, blurred focus, and so on. But in addition to applying these techniques to "visual" "images," Joyce applies them to words themselves as he dissolves their "outlines" through puns, portmanteau constructions, homophony, and other "cutting" techniques.

Movies, movement, time, duration, whole: this is the melange through which we are approaching desire. But we have not yet arrived, *Wake*an desire exhibiting several components not yet identified. The movement of movies is time; movies move time for their duration, and the "whole" we experience in viewing them is duration. That whole-as-duration we experience as affirmation, even in painful reconstructions of human interaction as, for example, representations of the horrors of the Holocaust. Such affirmation affirms in several senses: in enunciating an historical or fantasized event, the film proclaims its possibility, against which we as viewers measure our responsibility, accepting or rejecting our role in the possibility. But in addition to such affirmation, a very different kind exists, which Michel Foucault describes in the context of discussing the role of transgression,

> to measure the excessive distance that it opens at the heart of the limit and to trace the flashing line that causes the limit to arise. Transgression contains nothing negative, but affirms being—affirms the limitlessness into which it leaps as it opens this zone to existence for the first time. But correspondingly, this affirmation contains nothing positive: no content can bind it, since, by definition, no limit can possibly restrict it. (*Language*, 35–36).

An affirmation containing nothing negative or positive but instead affirming the possibility resulting from the erasure of discarded limits: this is very much the kind of affirmation that *Finnegans Wake* makes. Like movement, time, duration, and a sense of the whole, affirmation is part of *Wake*an desire. Throughout *Finnegans Wake*, affirmation and chaos chase each other's tails, forming another of the giant polarities that move the text. Rather than "durable" knowledge, what the text shows us is a multitude of perspectives that compete to the point of chaos. But when readers reach that point, we begin to discover/create patterns of connectedness. This dynamics is similar to a position Nietzsche describes: "It is not the object of perspectives 'to know but to schematize—to impose upon chaos as much regularity and form as our practical needs require.' "[7] Joseph Valente maintains that both Nietzsche and Joyce

> wanted to discredit static, universal forms and to reanimate the play of appearances, of style, which they associated with the ancient Greek artificers, Homer and Daedalus. To accommodate contingencies within dynamic and always provisional or self-deconstructing systems was, they believed, to affirm the life-process itself.
>
> Paradoxically, Nietzsche's philosophy of the "dangerous maybe" and Joyce's aesthetic of incertitude both culminate in an exuberant "yes." This yes, embracing the absence of absolute meaning or value, becomes its own bond, taking all meaning and value upon itself.[8]

Concerned especially with *Ulysses*, Valente is referring to Molly's *yes* ending that text, but the *yes* of *Finnegans Wake* is closely related. Molly's *yes* is the nonpositive and nonnegative affirmation of the process of becoming; the *Wake* says *yes* through its version of the eternal return, manifested in so many ways, as for instance its "end" recycling to "begin" again and its play with variations on motifs, which in their returns are always "the seim" and always "anew."

But affirmation and chaos are never far apart. Deleuze, too, works with these notions, relating them to the *Wake:*

> We know, for example, that certain literary procedures (the same holds for other arts) permit several stories to be told at once. This is, without doubt, the essential characteristic of the modern work of art. It is not at all a question of different points of view on one story supposedly the same; for points of view would still be submitted to a rule of convergence. It is rather a question of different and divergent stories, as if an absolutely distinct landscape corresponded to each point of view. There is indeed a unity of divergent series insofar as they are divergent, but it is

always a chaos perpetually thrown off center which becomes one only in the Great Work. This unformed chaos, the great letter of *Finnegans Wake,* is not just any chaos: it is the power of affirmation, the power to affirm all the heterogeneous series.[9]

Like Valente, Deleuze notes the Joyce-Nietzsche relationship:

> The secret of the eternal return is that it does not express an order opposed to the chaos engulfing it. On the contrary, it is nothing other than chaos itself, or the power of affirming chaos. There is a point where Joyce is Nietzschean when he shows that the *vicus of recirculation* can not affect and cause a "chaosmos" to revolve. To the coherence of representation,[10] the eternal return substitutes something else entirely—its own chaodyssey (*chao-errance*). Between the eternal return and the simulacrum, there is such a profound link that the one cannot be understood except through the other. Only the divergent series, insofar as they are divergent, return: that is, each series insofar as it displaces its difference along with all the others, and all series insofar as they complicate their difference within the chaos which is without beginning or end. (*Logic,* 264)

Through synthesis I arrive at this formulation: through the divergent stories the *Wake* as "great letter" tells, the "vicus of recirculation," which is the "seim anew," affirms chaos through presenting a sense of the whole as experienced duration in which time moves images through the play of spaces. As river, ALP images the flow of time; as female, ALP in her young form as Issy embodies desire, and in her mature form as HCE's wife, she figures the memory of embodied desire. ALP is time, desire, memory.

As a figure of figure, ALP is one structure of the dreamer's dream. Flowing below the level of signifier, her waters match the description Deleuze and Guattari, following Lyotard, give of desire in the dream process:

> Lyotard shows that what is at work in dreams is not the signifier but a figural dimension underneath, which gives rise to configurations of images that make use of words, making them flow and cutting them according to flows and points that are not

linguistic and do not depend on the signifier or its regulated elements. . . . It is not the figures that depend on the signifier and its effects, but the signifying chain that depends on the figural effects—this chain itself being composed of asignifying signs— crushing the signifiers as well as the signifieds, treating words as things, fabricating new unities, creating from nonfigurative figures configurations of images that form and then disinte- grate. . . . The pure figural elements—the "figure-matrix"— Lyotard correctly names desire. (*Anti-Oedipus*, 243–44)

Deleuze and Guattari maintain that Lyotard's account of desire is accurate insofar as he identifies desire as figural, arising from "non- figurative figures," or biology. They agree that desire is synonymous with a "fundamental *yes*" (*Anti-Oedipus*, 244) but declare that Lyotard followed the Freudian error of limiting the field of desire to the fam- ily, which they view as "the familialist reduction." Properly under- stood, according to Deleuze and Guattari, desire is a vast drift, "great decoded flows" instead of "little streams in mommy's bed" (*Anti- Oedipus*, 270). Building on Freud's breakthrough in understanding that desire is "no longer in relation to objects, aims, or even sources (territories), but [is] an abstract subjective essence—libido or sexual- ity" (270), Deleuze and Guattari formulate desire as production rather than the Freudian (and Lacanian) lack: "desire is a machine, a synthe- sis of machines, a machinic arrangement—desiring-machines. The order of desire is the order of *production*; all production is at once desiring-production and social production" (*Anti-Oedipus*, 296). In *Finnegans Wake* Joyce, like Deleuze and Guattari, figures libidinal and social desire as sharing the same production-economy, though with- out their Marxist assumptions, when he repeatedly shows the pur- suits of war and sexual contestation, the building of civilizations and the building of sexual desire as figuring each other.

While it may appear that Joyce, like Freud, territorializes desire within the Oedipal family, that is not the case. Consider the almost endlessly ramifying senses in which the "family" in *Finnegans Wake* constitutes a family. In what senses do these *Wake*an families coin- cide: Mr. and Mrs. Porter with their three children Buttercup, Jerry, and Kevin; HCE and ALP with Shem, Shaun, and Issy; Anna Livia Plurabelle and her 111 river children; Humphrey Chimpden Ear- wicker and his family. That is, to what extent is Mr. Porter identifiable with HCE and Humphrey Chimpden? To what extent is Mrs. Porter identifiable with ALP and Anna Livia? These names are signifiers, below which move their figurations which we "know" as images "told" in words. These names are ciphers which we may fill to some level with their images, but their images-as-words always escape translation into the pictorial. They are giant landscapes seen darkly by night, in dream; figures of the genital family of penis, uterus, testicles, clitoris; the social family of mother, father, sons and daughter; the natural family of river and mountain, cloud and land; the signifying family of chora, thetic, semiotic, symbolic and jouissance; the signifying family of trace, supplement, spacing, dissemination, and play. While oedipal elements appear at one level of the notion of family, they disappear through other figuration at different levels. The father's desire for his daughter becomes the thetic's desire for controlling jouissance becomes the land 's desire for rain. These figures move more comfortably in the realm Deleuze and Guattari designate as schizoanalysis than they do in Freudian psychoanalysis: "schizoanalysis attains a nonfigurative and nonsymbolic unconscious, a pure abstract figural dimension ('abstract' in the sense of abstract painting), flows-schizzes or real-desire, apprehended below the minimum conditions of identity" (*Anti-Oedipus*, 351). Desire in Deleuze and Guattari's sense is the productive force behind making connections; it "constantly couples continuous flows and partial objects that are by nature fragmentary and fragmented" (*Anti-Oedipus*, 5). This is not only the desire of Anna Livia for new banks and of HCE to see himself found guiltless; it is also the desire of readers of *Finnegans Wake* to connect fragment with fragment, chaos with chaos. Once connected the fragment is (not) fragment; chaos is (not) chaos. I want to return for a moment to a formulation by Deleuze considered earlier.

> The secret of the eternal return is that it does not express an order opposed to the chaos engulfing it. On the contrary it is nothing other than chaos itself, or the power of affirming chaos. There is a point where Joyce is Nietzschean when he shows that the *vicus of recirculation* can not affect and cause a "chaosmos" to revolve. To the coherence of representation, the eternal return substitutes something else entirely—its own chaodyssey. (*Logic*, 264)

In *Finnegans Wake* the eternal return manifests itself so continuously that readers may be tempted to suppose that it denies the surrounding chaos. But what happens instead is that by "recirculating" as a difference of the same, each fragment, each motif, each "family" member affirms that chaos: the sea into which Anna Livia rushes, helpless; the series of "old addresses" to which Shaun has attempted delivery of the letter and failed; the attempt of Nuvoletta to capture the attentions of the Mookse and the Gripes. And what is the affirmation of chaos as eternal return, the "seim anew," but the "chaodyssey" of desire. In the circulation of desire engulfed by chaos, "Time itself is affirmed in relation to movement" (*Logic*, 276).

As Deleuze and Guattari write,

> Desire does not lack anything; it does not lack its object. It is, rather, the *subject* that is missing in desire, or desire that lacks a fixed subject; there is no fixed subject unless there is repression. Desire and its object are one and the same thing: the machine, as a machine of a machine. Desire is a machine, and the object of desire is another machine connected to it. (*Anti-Oedipus*, 26)

As they understand desire, and as *Finnegans Wake* works with it,

> Desire does not take as its object persons or things, but the entire surroundings that it traverses, the vibrations and flows of every sort to which it is joined, introducing therein breaks and captures—an always nomadic and migrant desire. (*Anti-Oedipus*, 292)

For Deleuze and Guattari as for the *Wake*, desire is measured by sexuality, and "sexuality is everywhere" (293).

What relationship exists between desire in *Finnegans Wake*, with its compelling parallels to desire as Deleuze and Guattari delineate it, and Lacanian desire? Some of Lacan's formulations have the familiarity of aphorisms: "man's desire finds form" "as desire of the Other"; "desire begins to take shape in the margin in which demand becomes separated from need" (*Écrits*, 311).[11] Lacan's notion of desire must be understood in relation both to his conception of the unconscious as "neither primordial nor instinctual" (*Écrits*, 170) but as marked by the signifier received as "the discourse of the Other"[12] and also in relation to his notion of the signifier. For Lacan, "Language is what alienates human desire such that 'it is from the place of the Other that the subject's message is emitted.'" The juncture between language and desire is the phallus, "'the privileged signifier of that mark where logos is joined together with the advent of desire.'"[13] While declaring that a signifier "is what represents a subject for another signifier" (*Écrits*, 316), Lacan maintains "the supremacy of the signifier in the subject."[14] How are we to understand the notions of signifier and subject when each is so implicated in the other? Barbara Johnson suggests this reading:

> The signifier for which the other signifier represents a subject thus acts like a subject because it is the place where the representation is "understood." The signifier, then, situates the place of something like a reader. And the reader becomes the place where representation would be understood if there were any such thing as a place beyond representation; the place where representation is inscribed as an infinite chain of substitutions whether or not there is any place from which it can be understood. ("Frame of Reference," 345).

On the one hand we have the Lacanian series: reader as place where representation is inscribed as an infinite chain of substitutions; the subject as written by the signifier; language alienating desire such that the subject's message issues from the place of the Other; language as joined to desire by the phallus or object of desire; desire as the remainder in subtracting need from demand; desire as desire of the Other; the unconscious as neither primordial nor instinctual but instead "the discourse of the Other"—at which point we have come full circle back to the reader as locus of an impossible representation. On the other we have Deleuze and Guattari's series: in inverse order, it involves desire as productive of the real; desire as lacking a fixed subject; desire as the vast drift of sexuality; the unconscious as non-figurative and nonsymbolic, "a purely abstract figural dimension" (*Anti-Oedipus*, 351). Deleuze and Guattari's desire moves the energies of sexuality to produce the world of time-space experience; Lacan's desire, joined by the phallus to language, speaks from the place of the Other, displacing one signifier by another through substitution or metaphor, through combination or metonymy. Deleuze and Guattari's desire is the subject-less production of its object; Lacan's desire is the object-less movement of the signifier in the subject. For both, the base of desire is sexuality.

As signifier, *desire* in its various forms occurs thirteen times in *Finnegans Wake:*

sweeten sensation that drives desire (18.26)

indicating that the words which follow may be taken in any order desired (121.13)

he passing out of one desire into its fellow (125.08)

Well, I saith: Angst so mush: and desired she might not take it amiss if I esteemed her but an odd (145.5–7)

In the Dee dips a dame and the dame desires a demselle (226.16)

Dear (name of desired subject, A.N.) (280.09)

With best from cinder Christinette if prints chumming, can be when desires Soldi, for asamples (280.23)

Is the Co-Education of Animus and Anima Wholly Desirable? (307.03)

The desire of Miriam is the despair of Marian (366.35)

Desire, for hire, would tire a shire (502.32)

Magravius threatens to have Anita molested by Sulla, an orthodox savage . . . who desires to procure Felicia for Gregorius, Leo, Vitellius and Macdugalius (573.5–8)

Totumvir and esquimeena, who so shall separate fetters to new desire, repeals an act of union to unite in bonds of schismacy (585.24–26)

Cumulonubulocirrhonimbant heaven electing, the dart of desire
has gored the heart of secret waters. (599.26)

Of these thirteen instances, *desire* issues seven times from HCE, four
times from Issy, and twice on behalf of writing (as subject for writing
[307.04] and as ordering of reading/writing [121.13]). HCE's desires
range from the vast drift of undirected desire he felt before settling
on a sexual partner (18.26) to desire for ALP (585.25 and 599.26) to
desire for Issy (125.08 and 573.07) to desire leading to the "crime"
(366.35 and 502.32). Issy's desires range from desire to be joined with
her twin (226.16) to desire for her "prince charming" (280.23) to her
desire to be considered to know socially correct forms (145.06 and
280.09). The desire of Issy and HCE is linked by the phallus to the
word; concerning the Letter as signifier, desire is productive, that
which produces both subject as well as the ordering of the subject.

Desire as productive meets desire as displaced signifier in the
"limon" who uncovers the "letter" in the litter or, perhaps, the literal:

> in the course of deeper demolition unexpectedly one bush-
> man's holiday its limon threw up a few spontaneous fragments
> of orangepeel, the last remains of an outdoor meal by some un-
> known sunseeker or placehider *illico* way back in his mistridden
> past. (110.27–31)

This "limon" that finds is also the "leman" that answers ("When the
Answerer Is a Leman" [302.R1] and "To what mine answer is a le-
mans" [373.23]). The Oxford English Dictionary, second edition,
gives three possibilities for "leman": a lover or sweetheart; of or about
Christ or the Virgin, in religious language; and an unlawful lover,
applied chiefly to females.

"Limon," French for mud, is also related through contiguity to
"lemmas," which O Hehir and Dillon gloss through the Greek *lemma*
as "anything received; gain, credit, profit; (Logic): premise; title or
argument of an epigram; burden."[15] "Lemmas" occurs twice in the
Wake:

> Lucihere.! I fee where you mea. The doubleviewed seeds. Nun,
> lemmas quatsch, vide pervoys akstiom, and I think as I'm suqeez
> in the limon (295.36–296.03)

and

> Well, Sir Arthur. Buy Patersen's Matches. Unto his promisk
> hands. Blown up last Lemmas by Orchid Lodge. Search Un-
> claimed Male. (420.36–421.02)

The second use, associated with the date of Lammas or 1 August,
concerns us less than the first, where "lemmas" occurs in conjunction
with "quatsch," which O Hehir and Dillon gloss as deriving from the
Latin *quatio*, to shake or to agitate (269),[16] and McHugh as coming
from the German for "nonsense" (*Annotations*, 296). A variant of
"lemmas quatsch" is "lebbensquatsch," which occurs as one of
Shem's marginal comments in the Children's Studies chapter: "I'll
go for that small polly if you'll suck to your lebbensquatsch" (270.L1).
McHugh gives the following associations with the term: *Leben* is German for life; *lebban* is Arabic for milk; and the term suggests the
British lemon squash (a sweet fruit drink) (*Annotations*, 270).

But Joyce complicates the already complex relationship between
"limon" and "leman" by substituting "woman squash" for
"lebbensquatsch" and "lemmas quatsch." That curious phrase occurs
three times, each arising in the context of The Four's impotent desire,
which counterpoints the achieved desire of Tristram and Iseult:

> Luke and Johnny MacDougall and all wishening . . . for four far-
> back tumblerfuls of woman squash (386.6 and 10)

> As the holymaid of kunut said to the haryman of Koombe. For
> his humple pesition in advices. Women. Squash. Part. Ay, ay
> (390.31–33)

> It was too bad entirely! All devoured by active parlourmen, laud-
> abiliter, of woman squelch. (392.35–36)

"Woman squash" is "lebbensquatsch" is "lemmas quatsch" is "leman" is "limon." Working backwards, mud or the clay of life is the
sweetheart/Christ-like or Virginal/illicit lover is the subject for exploration and possibly subsidiary proposition in the male dream/gaze is
the agitating burden and shaken credit is the milk of life is the life
force is (not) nonsense. This displacement of signifier by signifier

puts the reader in the (chaotic) place where representation would be understood—via Lacan—if there were any such thing as a place beyond representation; the reader as that place where representation is inscribed as the infinite chain of substitutions. Woman inscribes, answers, and discovers fragments (the "limon" and her "orange-peel"); woman is that out of which issues the primordial mud of life, the life book; woman is virgin and whore and sweetheart ("leman"); woman is question and proposition ("lemmas"); woman is the milk and honey of life ("lebbensquatsch").[17]

Out of this litter of fragments, this littoral zone of flows, this literal "comicalbottomed copsjute (dump for short)" (110.26), rises the Letter, which is not one, though when we encounter the phrase we tend to identify it with ALP's letter in book IV. Issy writes letters: the socially "correct" letter beginning "Dear (name of desired subject, A.N.)" and ending "From Auburn chenlemagne" (280.09–29); the love letter beginning "I know, pepette, of course, dear, but listen, precious!" and ending "So long as the lucksmith. Laughs!" (143.31–148.32); the love letter beginning "Come, smooth of my slate, to the beat of my blosh" and ending "it's the surplice money . . . what buys the bed while wits borrows the clothes" (279.F1); and the "spoken" letter to Jaun beginning "Meesh, meesh, yes, pet. We were too happy" and ending "and listen, with supreme regards, Juan, in haste, warn me which to ah ah ah ah" (457.25–461.32). Besides Issy's four written/spoken letters, there is the Boston "transhipt" letter to "Maggy," of which Issy's is a variant, beginning "Dear whom it proceded to mention Maggy" and concluding with its PS (111.10–20). The children's nightletter to their parents announces their intended takeover of adult power (308); Anna Livia calls for "a brandnew bankside" (201). The Shem/Dolph letter begins "Dear and he went on to scripple gentlemine born, milady bread, he would pen for her" and concludes "From here Buvard to dear Picuchet" (301.10–302.10). There's the reported letter of "the secretary bird" (369.25–370.14), a variant of the Boston "transhipt" letter that conflates the bird with Pandora with the Liffey and voices concerns for husband and children. There is Shaun's letter that opens with "To the Very Honourable The Memory of Disgrace, the Most Noble, Sometime Sweepyard at the Service of the Writer," in which HCE speaking through Shaun indicts himself on a number of sexual counts (413.3–26). And, penul-

timate in the text, is the ALP letter beginning "Dear. And we go on
to Dirtdump. Reverend. May we add majesty" and ending

> The herewaker of our hamefame is his real namesame who will
> get himself up and erect, confident and heroic when but, young
> as of old, for my daily comfreshenall, a wee one woos.
>   Alma Luvia, Pollabella.
> P.S. Soldier Rollo's sweetheart. And she's about fetted up now
> with nonsery reams. And rigs out in regal rooms with the ritzies.
> Rags! Worns out. But she's still her deckhuman amber too.
> (619.12–19)

ALP wants to defend and clear the charges from HCE's good
"name"; through Shaun, HCE reveals his guilt; Shem puts his ser-
vices as writer at ALP's disposal; Issy wants both to reflect social
order and to attract "prints chumming"; ALP wants new banks for
her riverself; the Boston "transhipt" letter writer confirms the social
order by using its forms; the children want their parents' preroga-
tives. Written and spoken, these letters manifest desire. The desire
of the Issy and HCE/Shaun letters links with the word through the
phallus as object of desire. In the hen and ALP and Shem letters,
desire produces the subject (HCE) as well as the ordering of the
subject. What Barbara Johnson writes of Poe's "Purloined Letter"
holds for all these letters:

> The letter as a signifier is thus not a thing or the absence of a
> thing, not a word or the absence of a word, not an organ or the
> absence of an organ, but a *knot* in a structure where words,
> things, and organs can neither be definably separated nor com-
> patibly combined. ("Frame of Reference," 345)

But what Lacan writes of Poe's "Purloined Letter" does not hold for
the *Wake* letters, which neither are "the true subject of the tale" nor
do they "have a course which is proper to [them]." These letters do
not contain a signifier that "has no more signification," nor do they
"always arrive[s] at [their] destination."[18] ALP's letter ending *Finnegans Wake* arrives to readers but not to HCE and those judging him.
That it has not arrived at its "destination" is indicated by Anna Livia's

words to her "man of the hooths" following the letter, that he should "watch would the letter you're wanting be coming may be" (623.29–30). Not only because letters do not always arrive at their destination, thus exhausting their capacity for signification, but also because of their capacity for endless connectedness and thus "circulation," the letters/Letter can not contain signifiers having no more signification. Instead, the signifiers have always more and more signification. Nor do the letters, in their "circulation," have a "proper course" to follow. Shaun attempts delivery at addresses no longer current; but the letters have only "currency." And, finally, the letters/Letter are not the "true subject" of *Finnegans Wake*, which indeed has no "true subject," not through lack, but through the subject-less production of their achievement, the endless production of signification via the endless knots of linked and connected signifiers.

Do the *Wake*'s letters/Letter then stand in the relation that Derrida posits about Lacan's account of Poe's "The Purloined Letter"?

> what occurs in the psychoanalytical deciphering of a text when the deciphered (text), already explains itself? When it reveals a great deal more (a debt acknowledged more than once by Freud)? And above all when it also inscribes in itself the scene of deciphering? When it deploys more force in staging and carries the process down to the very last word—for example, truth?[19]

Like Poe's "The Purloined Letter," *Finnegans Wake* "explains itself" through the work it asks of the reader, guiding that work through such "asides" to the reader as "deep your ear on the movietone" (62.09). In the *Wake*, this coincides with its "also inscrib[ing] in itself the scene of deciphering." And the *Wake* "carries the process down to the very last word," whose "truth," is *the*, which, as the text's ultimate "word," denies, through the deferral its use necessitates, the notions of determinate truth and finality.

The *Wake*'s "Great Work," to return to Deleuze's phrase, its status as letters/Letter, is the voicing of desire. It is desire that produces the letters/Letter of *Finnegans Wake*. If delivered, the Letter obviates desire in that HCE's—and our—need for justification and redemption is answered. But if the Letter is always expected, letters continue to be written. Writing letters expresses desire, expresses the human:

And watch would the letter you're wanting be coming may be. And cast ashore. That I prays for be mains of me draims. Scratching it and patching at with a prompt from a primer. And what scrips of nutsnolleges I pecked up me meself. Every letter is a hard but yours sure is the hardest crux ever. Hack an axe, hook an oxe, hath an an, heth hith ences. But once done, dealt and delivered, tattat, you're on the map. Rased on traumscrapt from Maston, Boss. After rounding his world of ancient days. Carried in a caddy or screwed and corked. On his musgisstosst surface. With a bob, bob, bottledby. Blob. When the waves give up yours the soil may for me. Sometime then, somewhere there, I wrote me hopes and buried the page when I heard Thy voice, ruddery dunner, so loud that none but, and left it to lie till a missmiss coming. So content me now. Lss. (623.29–624.06)

NOTES

1. Margot Norris, "Anna Livia Plurabelle: The Dream Woman," in *Women in Joyce*, ed. Suzette Henke and Elaine Unkeless (Urbana: University of Illinois Press, 1982), 198–99.

2. Bernard Benstock suggests that the Language of Flowers is the base motif here and that flow or flux is an extension by way of Quinet's four flowers (private correspondence).

3. Gilles Deleuze, *Cinema* 1: The Movement-Image, trans. Hugh Tomlinson and Barbara Habberjam (London: Athlone Press, 1986), preface to the French edition. Subsequent references are given in the text.

4. Hayman, *"Wake" in Transit*, 159. Hayman explains that he added the bracketed material in Joyce's notebook entry in his "attempts to flesh out what appears to be Joyce's meaning" (159 n. 7).

5. Hayman, *"Wake" in Transit*, 159.

6. Stephen Greenblatt explains the "late-medieval clerical preoccupation with the distinction between *attrition* and *contrition*. The former was a change in behavior caused by the buffets of fortune and the hope of escaping punishment through a prudent repentance; the latter was a more authentic repentance rooted not in calculation but in grief." *Shakespearean Negotiations* (Berkeley and Los Angeles: University of California Press), 194 n. 13.

7. Joseph Valente quotes here from Nietzsche's *The Will to Power*. Cited in Valente, "Beyond Truth and Freedom: The New Faith of Joyce and Nietzsche," *James Joyce Quarterly* 25 (1987): 90.

8. Valente, "Beyond Truth and Freedom," 88–89.

9. Gilles Deleuze, *The Logic of Sense*, trans. Mark Lester with Charles Stivale, ed. Constantin V. Boundas (New York: Columbia University Press, 1990), 260. Subsequent references are given in the text.

10. Deleuze thus challenges Umberto Eco's view of *Finnegans Wake* as "a representation of the chaos and the multiplicity within which the author seeks the most congenial models of order." See Eco's *Aesthetics of Chaosmos*, 63.

11. Barbara Johnson reads the second quotation in this way: "Desire is what is left of the 'demande' when all possible satisfaction of 'real' needs has been subtracted from it." See Johnson, "The Frame of Reference," Davis and Schleifer, *Contemporary Literary Criticism*, 344.

12. Lacan, "Seminar on 'The Purloined Letter,'" 304.

13. Barbara Johnson quotes and translates from Lacan's *Écrits*, (French edition, 690 and 692), in "Frame of Reference," 344, 345. Subsequent references to Johnson's essay are given in the text.

14. Lacan, "Seminar on 'The Purloined Letter,'" 306.

15. O Hehir and Dillon, *Classical Lexicon*, 269.

16. O Hehir and Dillon, *Classical Lexicon*, 269.

17. Sexist and stereotyped as they are, these images of "woman" can perhaps be best understood as projections of "the nocturnal male psyche haunted by actions and urges" (Hayman, *"Wake" in Transit*, 154).

18. Lacan, "Seminar on 'The Purloined Letter,'" 311, 317–18.

19. Jacques Derrida, "The Purveyor of Truth," trans. Willis Domingo, James Hulbert, Moshe Ron, and R.-R. L. *Yale French Studies* 52 (1975): 32.

References

Abel, Reuben. *Man Is the Measure.* New York: Free Press, 1976.

Adams, Hazard. *Antithetical Essays in Literary Criticism and Liberal Education.* Tallahassee: Florida State University Press, 1990.

———. *Philosophy of the Literary Symbolic.* Tallahassee: Florida State University Press, 1983.

Arnason, H. H. *History of Modern Art.* New York: H. N. Abrams, 1968.

Atherton. James S. *The Books at the Wake.* Carbondale: Southern Illinois University Press, 1959.

Attridge, Derek. "The Backbone of Finnegans Wake: Narrative, Digression, and Deconstruction." *Genre* 17 (1984): 375–400.

———. "What Constitutes Narrative in *Finnegans Wake.*" Paper presented at the Thirteenth International James Joyce Symposium, Dublin, June 1992.

Bakhtin, Mikhail. *Rabelais and His World.* Trans. Helene Iswolsky. Cambridge: MIT Press, 1968.

Bauerle, Ruth. *The James Joyce Songbook.* New York: Garland Publishing, 1982.

Beckett, Samuel. "Dante . . . Bruno. Vico..Joyce." In Samuel Beckett et al., *Our Exagmination Round His Factification for Incamination of Work in Progress,* 1-22. Paris: Shakespeare & Co., 1929.

Begnal, Michael H., and Grace Eckley. *Narrator and Character in Finnegans Wake.* Lewisburg, Pa.: Bucknell University Press, 1975.

Behler, Ernst. "Das Fragment." In *Prosa kunst ohne Erzählen.* ed. Klaus Weissenberger, 125–45. Tübingen: Niemeyer, 1985.

Benstock, Bernard. *Joyce-Again's Wake.* Seattle: University of Washington Press, 1965.

Benstock, Shari. "Apostrophizing the Feminine in Finnegans Wake." *Modern Fiction Studies* 35 (1989): 587–614.

———. "The Letter of the Law: *La Carte Postale* in *Finnegans Wake.*" *Modern Philology* 63 (1984): 163–85.

Bishop, John. *Joyce's Book of the Dark.* Madison: University of Wisconsin Press, 1986.

Blake, William. *The Four Zoas.* In *The Complete Poetry and Prose of William Blake.* Rev. ed., ed. David V. Erdman, 300–407. Berkeley and Los Angeles: University of California Press, 1982.

Bruno, Giordano. *Cause, Principle, and Unity.* Trans. Jack Lindsay. Westport, Conn.: Greenwood Press, 1962.

Burke, Kenneth. *A Grammar of Motives.* New York: Prentice-Hall, 1945.

Burton, Robert. *The Anatomy of Melancholy*. Ed. Rev. A. R. Shilleto. 3 vols. London: G. Bell and Sons, 1920.

Byron, George Gordon. *Don Juan*. Ed. T. G. Steffan et al. New York: Viking Penguin, 1988.

Clark, Hilary. "Networking in Finnegans Wake." *James Joyce Quarterly* 27 (1990): 745–58.

Deleuze, Gilles. *Cinema* 1: The Movement-Image. Trans. Hugh Tomlinson and Barbara Habberjam. London: Athlone Press, 1986.

———. *The Logic of Sense*. Ed. Constantin V. Boundas; trans. Mark Lester with Charles Stivale. New York: Columbia University Press, 1990.

Deleuze, Gilles, and Felix Guattari. *Anti-Oedipus: Capitalism and Schizophrenia*. Trans. Robert Hurley, Mark Seem, and Helen R. Lane. New York: Viking Press, 1977.

de Man, Paul. "Semiology and Rhetoric." *Allegories of Reading*, 3–19. New Haven: Yale University Press, 1979.

De Quincey, Thomas. *Confessions of an English Opium Eater*. Ed. Alethea Hayter. New York: Viking Penguin, 1971.

Derrida, Jacques. "Differance." In *Speech and Phenomena*, trans. David B. Allison, 129–60. Evanston: Northwestern University Press, 1973.

———. *Glas*. Trans. John P. Leavey, Jr., and Richard Rand. Lincoln: University of Nebraska Press, 1986.

———. *Of Grammatology*. Trans. Gayatri Chakravorty Spivak. Baltimore: Johns Hopkins University Press, 1976.

———. *Positions*. Trans. Alan Bass. Chicago: University of Chicago Press, 1981.

———. *The Post Card*. Trans. Alan Bass. Chicago: University of Chicago Press, 1987.

———. "The Purveyor of Truth." Trans. Willis Domingo, James Hulbert, Moshe Ron, and R.-R. L. *Yale French Studies* 52 (1975): 31– 113.

———. "The Supplement of Copula: Philosophy before Linguistics." In *Margins of Philosophy*, trans. Alan Bass. Chicago: University of Chicago Press, 1982.

———. *The Truth in Painting*. Trans. Geoff Bennington and Ian McLeod. Chicago: University of Chicago Press, 1987.

———. "White Mythology: Metaphor in the Text of Philosophy." In *Margins of Philosophy*, trans. Alan Bass. Chicago: University of Chicago Press, 1982.

Devlin, Kimberly J. " 'See ourselves as others see us': Joyce's Look at the Eye of the Other." *PMLA* 104 (1989): 882–93.

———. *Wandering and Return in Finnegans Wake*. Princeton: Princeton University Press, 1991.

Di Bernard, Barbara. "Alchemical Number Symbolism in Finnegans Wake." *James Joyce Quarterly* 16 (1979): 433–46.

Eckley, Grace. *Children's Lore in Finnegans Wake*. Syracuse: Syracuse University Press, 1985.

Eco, Umberto. *The Aesthetics of Chaosmos: The Middle Ages of James Joyce*. Trans. Ellen Esrock. Cambridge: Harvard University Press, 1989.

————. *The Role of the Reader*. Bloomington: Indiana University Press, 1979.

Ellmann, Richard. *James Joyce*. New York: Oxford University Press, 1959.

————. "Joyce and Politics." In *Joyce & Paris: 1902. . . . .1920–1940. . . . .1975*, eds. J. Aubert and M. Jolas, 31–32 plus panel response to Ellmann, 101–23. Lille: Publications de l'Université de Lille 3 / CNRS, 1979.

Epstein, Edmund. *The Ordeal of Stephen Dedalus*. Carbondale: Southern Illinois University Press, 1971.

Flaubert, Gustave. *The Temptations of St. Anthony*. Trans. Lafcadio Hearn. New York: Alice Harriman, 1910.

Foucault, Michel. *Language, Counter-Memory, Practice*. Ed. Donald F. Bouchard; trans. Donald F. Bouchard and Sherry Simon. Ithaca, N.Y.: Cornell University Press, 1977.

Frye, Northrop. *Anatomy of Criticism*. Princeton: Princeton University Press, 1957.

————. "Quest and Cycle in Finnegans Wake." In *Fables of Identity: Studies in Poetic Mythology*. New York: Harcourt, Brace, & World, 1963.

Gillespie, Michael Patrick. *Reading the Book of Himself: Narrative Strategies in the Works of James Joyce*. Columbus: Ohio State University Press, 1989.

Glasheen, Adaline. *Third Census of Finnegans Wake*. Berkeley and Los Angeles: University of California Press, 1977.

Gordon, John. *Finnegans Wake: A Plot Summary*. Syracuse: Syracuse University Press, 1986.

Greenblatt, Stephen. *Shakespearean Negotiations*. Berkeley and Los Angeles: University of California Press, 1988.

Hart, Clive. *A Concordance to Finnegans Wake*. Minneapolis: University of Minnesota Press, 1963.

————. *Structure and Motif in Finnegans Wake*. Evanston, Ill.: Northwestern University Press, 1962.

Hartman, Geoffrey H. *Saving the Text*. Baltimore: Johns Hopkins University Press, 1981.

Hayles, N. Katherine. *Chaos Bound: Orderly Disorder in Contemporary Literature and Science*. Ithaca, N.Y.: Cornell University Press, 1990.

Hayman, David, ed. *A First-Draft Version of Finnegans Wake*. Austin: University of Texas Press, 1963.

————. "Nodality and the Infrastructure of Finnegans Wake." *James Joyce Quarterly* 16 (1978/1979): 135–49.

————. *The "Wake" in Transit*. Ithaca, N.Y.: Cornell University Press, 1990.

Heath, Stephen. "Ambiviolences: Notes for Reading Joyce." In *Post-Structuralist Joyce*, ed. Derek Attridge and Daniel Ferrer, 31–68. Cambridge: Cambridge University Press, 1984.

Henke, Suzette A. *James Joyce and the Politics of Desire*. New York: Routledge, 1990.

Herring, Phillip F. *Joyce's Uncertainty Principle*. Princeton: Princeton University Press, 1987.

Hodgart, Matthew J. C., and Mabel P. Worthington. *Song in the Works of James Joyce*. New York: Columbia University Press, 1959.

Hood, A. B. E., ed. and trans. *St. Patrick: His Writings and Muirchu's Life.* London: Phillimore and Co., 1978.

Jakobson, Roman. "The Metaphoric and Metonymic Poles." In *Critical Theory Since Plato,* ed. Hazard Adams, 1113–16. New York: Harcourt Brace Jovanovich, 1971.

Johnson, Barbara. "The Frame of Reference: Poe, Lacan, Derrida." In *Contemporary Literary Criticism,* 2d ed., ed. Robert Con Davis and Ronald Schleifer, 322–50. New York: Longman, 1989.

———. "Rigorous Unreliability." *Critical Inquiry* 11 (1984): 278–85.

Josipovici, Gabriel. *Writing and the Body.* Princeton: Princeton University Press, 1982.

Joyce, James. *Finnegans Wake.* New York: Viking Press, 1939.

———. *Letters of James Joyce.* Vol. 1, rev. ed., ed. Stuart Gilbert. Vols. 2 and 3, ed. Richard Ellmann. New York: Viking Press, 1966.

———. *The James Joyce Archive: A Facsimile of Drafts, Typescripts, and Proofs for Finnegans Wake, Book II, Chapter 1, and Book IV.* Ed. Michael Groden; assoc. eds. Hans Walter Gabler, David Hayman, A. Walton Litz, and Danis Rose. Arranged by Danis Rose with the assistance of John O'Hanlon. New York: Garland Publishing, 1977.

———. *A Portrait of the Artist as a Young Man.* New York: Viking Press, 1956.

———. *Ulysses.* New York: Random House, 1961.

Joyce, Stanislaus. *My Brother's Keeper.* London: Faber & Faber, 1958.

Kenner, Hugh. *Joyce's Voices.* Berkeley and Los Angeles: University of California Press, 1978.

Kristeva, Julia. *Desire in Language.* Ed. Leon S. Roudiez; trans. Thomas Gora, Alice Jardine, and Leon S. Roudiez. New York: Columbia University Press, 1980.

———. "Joyce 'The Gracehoper' or the Return of Orpheus." In *James Joyce: The Augmented Ninth,* ed. Bernard Benstock, 167–80. Syracuse: Syracuse University Press, 1988.

———. *Language: The Unknown.* Trans. Anne M. Menke. New York: Columbia University Press, 1989.

———. *Revolution in Poetic Language.* Trans. Margaret Waller. New York: Columbia University Press, 1984.

———. "The System and the Speaking Subject." *Times Literary Supplement,* 1249–50. 12 October 1973.

Lacan, Jacques. "The Agency of the Letter in the Unconscious or Reason since Freud." In *Ecrits,* trans. Alan Sheridan, 146–78. New York: W. W. Norton, 1977.

———. "Seminar on 'The Purloined Letter'." Trans. Jeffrey Mehlman. In *Contemporary Literary Criticism,* 2d ed., ed. Robert Con Davis and Ronald Schleifer, 301–20. New York: Longman, 1989.

Levin, Harry. *James Joyce: A Critical Introduction.* Norfolk, Conn.: New Directions, 1941.

McCarthy, Patrick. *The Riddles of Finnegans Wake.* Rutherford, N.J.: Associated University Press, 1980.

McFarland, Thomas. *Romanticism and the Forms of Ruin.* Princeton: Princeton University Press, 1981.

McHugh, Roland. *Annotations to "Finnegans Wake."* Baltimore: Johns Hopkins University Press, 1980.

———. *The Sigla of Finnegans Wake.* Austin: University of Texas Press, 1976.

Mellard, James. *Doing Tropology.* Urbana: University of Illinois Press, 1987.

Mercanton, Jacques. "The Hours of James Joyce." In *Portraits of the Artist in Exile,* ed. Willard Potts, 206–52. Seattle: University of Washington Press, 1979.

Norris, Christopher. *Deconstruction: Theory and Practice.* London: Methuen, 1982.

Norris, Margot. "Anna Livia Plurabelle: The Dream Woman." In *Women in Joyce,* ed. Suzette Henke and Elaine Unkeless, 197–213. Urbana: University of Illinois Press, 1982.

———. *The Decentered Universe of Finnegans Wake.* Baltimore: Johns Hopkins University Press, 1976.

———. "Joyce's Heliotrope." In *Coping with Joyce: Essays from the Copenhagen Symposium,* ed. Morris Beja and Shari Benstock, 3–24. Columbus: Ohio State University Press, 1989.

O Hehir, Brendan. *A Gaelic Lexicon for Finnegans Wake.* Berkeley and Los Angeles: University of California Press, 1967.

O Hehir, Brendan, and John Dillon. *A Classical Lexicon for Finnegans Wake.* Berkeley and Los Angeles: University of California Press, 1977.

Peake, C. H. *James Joyce: The Citizen and the Artist.* Stanford: Stanford University Press, 1977.

Polanyi, Michael. *Knowing and Being.* Chicago: University of Chicago Press, 1969.

Polanyi, Michael, and Harry Prosch, *Meaning.* Chicago: University of Chicago Press, 1975.

Preminger, Alex, ed. *Princeton Encyclopedia of Poetry and Poetics,* enlarged ed. Princeton: Princeton University Press, 1974.

Rabelais, François. *Gargantua and Pantagruel.* Trans. Sir Thomas Urquhart and Peter le Motteux. New York: E. P. Dutton, 1929.

Riquelme, John Paul. *Teller and Tale in Joyce's Fiction: Oscillating Perspectives.* Baltimore: Johns Hopkins University Press, 1983.

Rose, Danis, and John O'Hanlon. *Understanding Finnegans Wake.* New York: Garland Publishing, 1982.

Sheridan, Richard Brinsley. *The Rivals.* Ed. C. J. Price. New York: Oxford University Press, 1968.

Solomon, Margaret C. *Eternal Geomater.* Carbondale: Southern Illinois University Press, 1969.

Spoo, Robert. "Preparatory to Anything Else . . . ." *James Joyce Quarterly* 27 (1990): 721–23.

Tindall, W. Y. *James Joyce: His Way of Interpreting the Modern World.* New York: Charles Scribner's Sons, 1950.

Tyler, Anne. *The Accidental Tourist.* New York: Knopf, 1985.

Ulmer, Gregory L. "The Post-Age." *Diacritics* 11, no. 3 (Fall 1981): 39–56.

Valente, Joseph. "Beyond Truth and Freedom: The New Faith of Joyce and Nietzsche." *James Joyce Quarterly* 25 (1987): 87–103.

Vico, Giambattista. *The New Science.* Trans. Thomas Goddard Bergin and Max Harold Fisch. Ithaca, N.Y.: Cornell University Press, 1968.

White, Hayden. *Metahistory.* Baltimore: Johns Hopkins University Press, 1973.

———. *Tropics of Discourse.* Baltimore: Johns Hopkins University Press, 1978.

Index

Adams, Hazard, 116, 142
Affirmation, 7, 127, 128, 135, 184, 190–92, 195
ALP, 22, 41–45, 48, 51, 52, 53n.9, 56, 61, 62, 67n.4, 76, 88, 91, 100, 105, 112–13, 116, 118, 121, 123, 124, 132, 137, 141, 183, 186n.18, 187–89, 192–94, 198, 200, 201
Anagram, 70, 72, 74, 79n.6, 101, 155
Anatomy of Melancholy, The, 164, 165
Anna Livia, 44, 112, 137, 168, 169, 172, 174, 181–84, 187, 193–95, 200, 201, 203n.1
Archdruid, 59, 64, 117, 130, 132, 137, 139, 147–57, 159
Aristotle, 60, 74, 134n.6, 136
Art, 8, 18, 27, 32, 33, 37, 48, 61, 158n.6, 162, 191
Ass, 50, 59, 67n.6
Association, as a metonymic logic, 139, 140, 153
Attridge, Derek, 10n.8, 157
Aufhebung, 39, 52n.3, 79–80n.7
Autobiographical material, Joyce's use of, 143, 144, 158n.6, 165

Bakhtin, Mikhail, 53n.6
Balkelly, 137, 139, 151, 154, 155
Beckett, Samuel, 27, 86, 108n.17, 129
Behler, Ernst, 161
Benstock, Bernard, 24n.11, 67n.11, 203n.2
Benstock, Shari, 24n.19, 107n.3
Benveniste, Emile, 66n.3, 134n.6
Berkeley. *See* Archdruid

Birth, in Vico cycle, 14, 100, 101, 126
Bishop, John, 6, 39, 108n.12
Blake, William, 17, 35, 117, 142
Body, and writing, 52n.1; for Bakhtin, 53n.6; in *FW*, 7, 36, 40–44, 48, 51, 52, 96, 126; in Kristevan senses, 35, 39–40
Bruno, Giordano, 33, 59–61, 77, 136, 172
Buckley, and the Russian general, 104, 113, 120, 138, 152
Burke, Kenneth, 111, 112
Burrus, and Casseous, 59, 63

Chaos, in *FW*, 5, 7, 11, 120, 123, 135, 159, 190–92, 194, 195, 204n.10
Chaos theory, 129–33
Character, in *FW*: function of, 7, 13, 48, 99, 105, 112, 113, 116, 118, 136, 165, 172, 175; nature of, 63, 65, 67n.4, 86, 92
Children's Games chapter, 7, 70, 74, 76, 78, 79n.1, 152
Chora, and thetic, 6, 13, 14, 17–20, 22, 23n.7, 34, 44–46, 48, 55, 66, 194
Chuff. *See* Glugg
Clark, Hilary, 113, 114, 185n.14
Clustering, as a metonymic logic, 137, 138, 146, 153
Coherence, functioning of, 3, 4, 11, 12, 16–18, 20, 29, 30, 68n.13, 113, 135, 166, 192, 194
Collideorscape, 16, 30, 31, 125
Comic, the, in relation to the sacred, 101, 104–5. *See also* Humor

Contraries, coincidence of: in Bruno, 60, 61; for Joyce, 31, 34, 35, 36, 61
Copula, the, 3, 61, 117, 134n.6
Crime in the park, 29, 141, 153
Cyclicity, relation: to *différance*, 98, 101; to irony, 121; to the life span, 172, 173; to sexuality, 77, 179; to time, 176, 179

Deconstruction, 4, 9n.5, 86, 88
Deleuze, Gilles, and Felix Guattari, 78, 185n.5, 187–89, 191–97, 202, 204n.10
De Man, Paul, 78
Derrida, Jacques, 4, 7, 40, 55, 57, 60–61, 63, 65, 66n.1, 67n.5, 69, 71–78, 79n.5, 79–80n.7, 81–95, 97–99, 101–6, 107n.7, 108n.11, 134n.6, 157, 202
Desire, 78, 131, 166; and ALP, 42, 43; and the body, 36, 69, 73; as cycle, 119; and heliotrope, 79n.1; for Issy, 41, 47; and Jarl van Hoother, 120; as trope, 7, 97, 159, 187–203; and writing, 44, 53n.9, 91, 98, 107n.3
Devlin, Kimberly, 37n.1
Dialectic, role of, in irony, 120, 123
Différance, 7, 55, 57–61, 64–66, 67n.5, 69–71, 74, 77, 79n.6, 79–80n.7, 90, 95, 98, 99, 101, 103, 104
Dissemination, as Derridean term, 7, 56, 65, 73, 74, 77, 79n.5, 82, 88, 133, 194
Dolph, and Kev, 120, 132, 152, 153, 200
Dualism, in Bruno, 34; in Kristeva, 32, 55
Dublin, 175; in city motto, 139; in "Dear Dirty Dublin," 12, 56; in metaphoric logic, 136; as synecdoche, 116, 117, 141

Earwicker, 102, 130, 140, 193
Eco, Umberto, 38n.3, 67n.7, 108n.12, 204n.10

Ellmann, Richard, 8, 28, 38n.3, 108n.17
Encyclopedic form, 164–65, 185n.6
Epstein, Edmund, 23n.5
Excrement, 122, 123

Fall, the, 62, 100, 118, 121, 138, 141, 164, 165, 167, 168, 173
Family, the, 8, 24n.18, 44, 87, 101, 119, 158n.6, 172, 193–95
Fictions, 83; and fictive logic, 142, 143
Film, and cinema, 187–90
Finn, 20, 21, 29, 43, 62, 102, 112, 118, 119, 140, 141, 167, 168, 173
Finnegan, 100, 139-41, 168, 172, 174
566: 58, 62, 119, 140
40: 118
Foucault, Michel, 164, 190
4: 119
Four, The, 13, 50, 58, 76, 92–93, 99, 119, 121, 169–72, 176–77, 181–82, 199
Four Zoas, The, 164–65
Fragment, 198, 200; as structural component, 4, 7, 29, 113, 120, 130, 137, 139, 140, 149, 151, 153, 159–84, 188, 189, 194, 195
Fragmentation, in Joyce and Derrida, 61, 90, 93–95; in Joyce and Kristeva, 30, 31, 34, 38n.7; in Kristeva, 27, 29; as process in reading, 120, 134n.10, 179; in relation to The Four, 58; in Romanticism, 162–63
Freud, Sigmund, 42, 75; and Deleuze and Guattari, 193; and Derrida, 82, 84–87, 95, 97–99, 202
Frye, Northrop, 121, 124, 164, 185n.6
Fuitfiat, 62, 155

Gargantua and Pantagruel, 164, 165
Genotext, 12–14, 23n.3, 34, 55. *See also* Phenotext
Gillespie, Michael Patrick, 5, 9n.3
Glas, 61, 79n.5, 86

Glasheen, Adaline, 19, 51, 102, 118, 134n.9

Glugg, and Chuff, 41, 69, 70, 72, 74, 75, 79n.3, 96, 136, 143

Gordon, John, 128

Gracehoper, and Ondt, 113, 137, 143

Greenblatt, Stephen, 203n.6

Gripes, and Mookse, 13, 21, 59, 63, 114, 120, 174, 195

Hart, Clive, 50, 146, 147, 150–52, 158n.6, 173, 179, 185n.13

Hartman, Geoffrey, 65

Hayles, N. Katherine, 128–32

Hayman, David, 8, 9n.2, 24n.17, 147, 173, 179, 185n.14, 189, 203n.4, 204n.17

HCE, 8, 17–20, 22, 24n.18, 29, 37n.1, 41, 43–46, 48–52, 57, 58, 61, 62, 67n.4, 89, 91, 100, 102, 103, 105, 106, 108n.18, 112, 113, 115, 116, 118, 128, 129, 132, 141, 144, 152–54, 167–69, 171–75, 181, 183, 187, 189, 192–94, 198, 200–202

Heath, Stephen, 128, 142

Heliotrope, 7, 12, 14, 57, 63, 69–78, 79n.1, 81, 141, 152

Henke, Suzette, 53n.5, 186n.18

Herring, Phillip, 9n.5

History: as denial of transcendence, 163; in Derrida, 59; and The Four, 171; and HCE, 41; Irish, 20, 116, 117; for Joyce and Kristeva, 30, 35, 37; for Joyce in FW, 33, 34, 39, 87, 117, 119, 126, 132, 165, 168; in Kristeva, 28, 32, 36; in Vico, 76, 172; and writing, 43

Homonym, phonic, 63, 106

"House That Jack Built, The," 65, 122

Humor, 31, 56, 63, 64, 131, 135, 163, 164. See also Comic, the

Incoherence, 5; Bishop's explanation of, 6; in Derrida, 7, 40, 55–57, 61, 66; as effect of reading FW, 5, 11, 12, 39, 111, 160; and fragments, 160–61; in Kristeva, 6, 16–18, 20–22, 27, 29, 30, 37; as productive of coherence, 4, 9, 52, 159; in Rose and O'Hanlon, 147; and tropes, 78, 111, 113, 116, 129

Indeterminacy, 5, 9n.5, 18, 55, 129, 149, 150

Intonation, 11, 13, 14, 15, 19, 23n.3, 179

Ireland, in FW, 21, 57–59, 62, 128, 136, 140, 141, 144, 148, 150, 153, 155, 157–58n.2, 167, 168

Irony, as trope in FW, 4, 7, 9–10n.8, 112, 120–28, 133, 135, 142–46, 153, 160, 163, 166, 184, 188

Iseult, 76, 120, 121, 132, 199. See also Tristan

Issy, 13, 17, 18, 23n.5, 24n.18, 41–45, 47, 48, 51, 52, 58, 76, 89, 91, 92, 105, 112, 115, 118, 124, 125, 132, 136, 141, 152, 170, 172, 189, 192, 193, 198, 200, 201

Izod, 69–72, 74, 75, 136, 143

Jakobson, Roman, 112

Jarl von Hoother, 50, 100, 117–20, 132, 138, 139, 189

Johnson, Barbara, 66n.2, 187, 196, 201, 204n.11

Josipovici, Gabriel, 52n.1

Jouissance, 44, 47, 48, 92, 194

Jute, and Mutt, 117, 138

Kate, 102, 112, 113, 132, 187

Kev. See Dolph

Kristeva, Julia, 4, 6–7, 12–14, 17, 18, 20–22, 22–23n.2, 23n.3, 24n.14, 27–37, 38n.7, 39, 40, 44, 45, 47–48, 55, 66, 66n.3, 75, 133. See also Chora, and thetic; Genotext; Phenotext; Semiotic, the; Symbolic, the

Lacan, Jacques, 52, 84, 112, 195–97, 200–202

Laughter: in FW, 28, 31, 37, 56, 65, 104, 105, 123; in Kristeva, 27–28,

Laughter (*continued*)
30, 31, 37, 47. *See also* Comic;
Humor
Leman, 198–200
"Lemmas quatsch," 199
Letter, the, 7, 18, 24–25n.19, 40–43,
48–52, 53n.9, 63, 83, 88, 89, 100,
101, 106, 107, 107n.3, 115, 116,
124–27, 132, 135, 137, 159, 170,
187, 192, 195, 198, 200–203
Levin, Harry, 22n.1
Lewis, Wyndham, 17, 136
Literal, 52n.1; and figurative, 3, 127,
128, 198, 200
Logic, tropic, 7, 68n.14, 135–57. *See
also* Irony; Metaphor; Metonymy;
Synecdoche
Lyotard, Jean-François, 192, 193

McCarthy, Patrick, 79 nn.1,6
McFarland, Thomas, 162
McHugh, Roland, 21, 63, 171, 174,
199
Macrocosm, and microcosm in *FW*,
11, 36, 53n.5, 74, 124, 127, 162,
177, 184
Maggy, 49, 51, 52, 125, 200
Magritte, René, 108n.9
Materialism, for Derrida, 60; in
Nietzsche, 142
Mellard, James, 112
Memory, and ALP, 187, 192; and
writing, 41–44, 63, 81
Message/sending, 89, 97, 101, 106
Metalanguage, and *FW*, 6, 9–10n.8,
27; and Kristeva, 32, 37
Metaphor, 41, 49, 52n.1, 61, 69,
107n.1, 124, 125, 126, 128, 133, 167,
172, 173, 176, 187, 196; in Hayles,
128; and heliotrope, 69–78, 79n.1;
in language, 56; as logic, 4, 7, 9–
10n.8, 135–36, 146, 152–53; and
The Post Card, 82, 83, 89, 93–94, 98,
101, 106; role of, for coherence in
FW, 112, 113, 120, 160, 166, 168;
and transcendence, 163

Metonymy, 49, 124–28, 133, 196; as
logic, 4, 7, 112–16, 135, 137–40,
146, 153–54, 156; role of, for coher-
ence in *FW*, 160, 166–68; in *The
Post Card*, 101–2; and transcen-
dence, 163
Microcosm. *See* Macrocosm
Mimesis, in modern poetic texts, and
Kristeva, 27
Mimetic language, 111, 133n.1
Modernism, 9, 23n.6
Mookse. *See* Gripes
Moore, Thomas, 95, 167
Motif: and Hart, 50; and *The Post
Card*, 84; as unit in *FW*, 4, 12, 20,
102, 107n.6, 116, 138–39, 155, 171,
173–79, 184, 191, 195, 203n.2
Mutt. *See* Jute
Myth, 39, 167; *FW* as, 8, 87; relation
to history, 33, 34, 35, 117, 132, 138

Narrative events, 67n.4; as part of
linear metonymic logic, 138–40,
146–50, 154–55, 157
Negativity, Kristevan, 30, 33–36; for
Joyce, 78
Networks, as units in *FW*, 7, 113–14,
163–64, 168, 173, 189
Nietzsche, Friedrich, 95, 101,
108n.11, 142, 163, 191, 192
Night book, *FW* as, 82, 165
Nonsynonymic substitutions for
différance, 56, 57, 61, 65, 66, 71, 82,
113, 135
Norris, Margot, 79n.1, 141, 187
Norwegian ship's captain, 132
Nuvoletta, 58, 59, 136, 195

O'Donnell, Patrick, 133n.1
O'Hanlon, John, 146, 147, 152
O Hehir, Brendan, and John Dillon,
82–83, 125, 127, 159, 198, 199
Ondt. *See* Gracehoper
I: 62, 105, 118
III: 45, 56, 61, 102, 105, 118, 136, 193
II32: 58, 62, 118, 119, 140

Parallax, 28, 49, 52

Pattern: and chaos theory, 131–32; in FW, 11, 14, 23n.8, 179, 191; lack of consistent role of, in FW, 17, 19, 64–65; in motifs, 173, 177–78; oppositional nature of, in FW, 17; and tropes, 142

Peake, C. H., 145

Phenotext, 12, 14, 23n.3, 34, 55. See also Genotext

Plato, 60, 81; in The Post Card, 84–87, 90–91, 95, 97–99, 103

Play, and incoherence, 5, 39, 49; as Derridean term, 7, 56, 64–65, 68n.14, 73–74, 194

Polanyi, Michael, 166

Polyphony, 27, 28, 31, 37, 47

Polysemy, 57, 61, 70, 71, 73, 77

Portmanteau words, 56, 63, 114

Post Card, The, 7, 42, 79n.5, 81–107, 107n.3

Postmodernism, 8

Poststructuralism, 129

Prankquean, 12, 50, 100, 117–20, 132, 138–40, 189

Prosch, Harry. See Polanyi, Michael

"Purloined Letter, The," and FW, 202

Quinet flower passage, 12, 102, 169, 173, 175–77, 179, 203n.2

Rainbow Girls, 118, 136, 152

Recursive symmetry, 130–33

Repetition: as structuring principle in FW, 11, 146, 155; and chora, 13, 14; for Kristeva, 21; in recursive symmetry, 131

Representation, in Deleuze, 192, 194; for Eco, in FW, 204n.10; in Hayles, 128; in Johnson, 196; in Kristeva, 32, 35, 36; for Lacan, 200

Rhythms: aural, 19; as component of voice, 181, 184; in FW, 102, 122, 161; and genotext, 14, 23n.3, 31; for Kristeva, in FW, 47; in motifs,

173, 177, 179; role of, in FW, 27; semiotic, 15, 20

Riquelme, John Paul, 186n.19

Rivals, The, 15

Rose, Danis, 146, 147, 152

Russian general, the, 104, 113, 118, 120, 138, 152

Sacred, the, inversions of, in FW, 27, 57, 63, 104–5, 121–23, 172; and the comic, 101; and laughter, 28, 30, 37

St. Patrick, 21, 59, 64, 117, 132, 137, 139, 147–49

Saussure, Ferdinand de, 56

Seim anew, 35, 77, 79n.6, 98, 102, 175

Semiotic, the, 12, 14–22, 22–23n.2, 23 nn. 3, 7, 24n.10, 27, 29, 30, 34, 39, 44, 46, 48, 53n.5, 55, 61, 66, 181, 194. See also Symbolic, the

7: 105, 106, 118, 119

Sexist, Joyce's treatment of women and writing as, 53n.9, 204n.17

Sexuality, 117, 195; in the Children's Games chapter, 143, 152; in Deleuze and Guattari, 193, 195–97; and The Four, 92, 171; and Issy, 41; as metaphor, 90, 101; relation with heliotrope and numbers 2 and 3, 14, 70–78, 79 n.3; as theme, 172; and transgression in FW, 28

Shaun, 18, 22, 23n.5, 24n.18, 24–25n.19, 27, 37, 41–44, 46–52, 53n.6, 57, 58, 59, 61, 63, 81, 84, 87, 89–92, 100, 101, 104, 106, 112, 114, 115, 124, 132, 136, 140, 141, 143, 145, 146, 149, 167, 174, 177, 179, 181, 187, 189, 193, 195, 200–202

Shem, 12, 18, 20, 23n.5, 24n.18, 27, 37, 41–44, 46, 48, 50, 53n.6, 58, 59, 61, 63, 70, 81, 89, 96, 101, 104, 106, 112, 114–16, 119, 122, 124, 126, 132, 136, 137, 140, 141, 143–45, 149, 174, 177, 179, 181, 187, 189, 193, 199–201

6: 119

Solomon, Margaret, 155

Spacing, as Derridean term, 7, 56, 63, 68n.13, 72–74, 79n.5, 90, 194
Spoo, Robert, 116
Stereotyping in Joyce's treatment of minorities and women, 23n.6, 204n.17
Subject, the: for Aristotle, 136; for Deleuze and Guattari, 195, 197; in *FW*, 4, 7, 22–23n.2, 44, 53n.9, 67n.4, 138; for Hayles, 128; for Kristeva, 6, 17, 22, 28, 30–32, 34–36, 40, 55, 66; for Lacan, 196
Supplement: as Derridean term, 7, 52, 56, 60, 67n.5, 74, 90, 194; in *FW*, 59, 63, 72–73, 93
Sycamore, 168–73, 175
Symbolic, the, 12, 14–22, 22–23n.2, 23n.3, 24n.10, 27, 29–32, 34, 36, 38n.7, 39, 40, 44, 46, 48, 55, 66, 194. *See also* Semiotic, the
Synecdoche, 4, 7, 9–10n.8, 40, 52n.1, 75–78, 101, 106, 112, 116, 117–21, 124–27, 128, 133, 135, 140–42, 146, 150, 152, 159, 160–63, 166, 177, 184

Tailor, Kersse the, and the Norwegian ship's captain, 120, 138, 140
Temptations of St. Anthony, The, 164–65
10: 62, 105, 118
Text: in Derrida's sense, 55, 56, 66, 66n.1, 68n.13, 69, 74, 81; in Kristeva's sense, 22–23n.2
Theme in *FW*, 57, 87, 100, 115, 138, 145, 168–69, 172–75, 179, 185n.13
Theology, 36, 73, 77, 131
Thetic. *See* Chora
3: 118
Thunderclaps, 123
Tindall, W. Y., 22–23n.8
Trace, as Derridean term, 7, 52, 56, 61–63, 67n.10, 68n.13, 72, 74, 79n.5, 90, 101, 104, 190, 194
Transcendence, denial of, in *FW*, 60, 163, 164

Transgression: for Foucault, 190; in *FW*, 11, 46, 64; for Kristeva, 23n.7, 36
Transitions in *FW*, 139, 140, 189
Tristan, 76, 120, 121, 160, 170. *See also* Iseult
Tropes, 129, 184; in *FW* and *The Post Card*, 82, 101, 103, 105, 107; and incoherence, 3, 4, 9–10n.8, 78, 129; and incoherence, in *FW*, 91, 123, 127, 133. *See also* Irony; Metaphor; Metonymy; Synecdoche
Tropic language, 111, 133n.1
2: 118
283: 62, 119

Ulmer, Gregory, 82, 83, 87, 88, 94, 103
Ulysses, 5, 16, 18, 23n.4, 28, 53n.6, 86, 108n.13, 118, 191
Unconscious, the, 55, 76, 107n.3, 194–96
Unity, and opposition, 29, 31, 34, 35, 38n.7, 61, 77, 105, 125, 165, 176, 191; in Archdruid and Patrick exchange, 150; for Bruno and Derrida, 60, 77

Valente, Joseph, 191, 192
Vico, Giambattista, 76, 117, 123, 172; Vico cycle, 14, 23–24n.8, 57, 100, 126–27
Voice, 11, 13, 14, 17, 19, 46, 52, 141, 154; of ALP, 112, 181–84; as fragment, 161, 163; as unit for analysis, 179, 181–84
Void, 3, 9, 106, 107, 129

Washerwomen, 112, 116, 174, 177, 181–84
Weaver, Harriet Shaw, 100, 157–58n.2, 159, 160, 162, 184n.1
White, Hayden, 112
"White Mythology," 7, 70, 74, 78, 107n.1

Whole, the, 59, 77, 86, 116–17, 128, 160, 163–64; for Joyce, 38n.7; in relation to desire, 7, 188–90, 192; as synecdoche, in *FW*, 120, 127, 135, 139–40, 146, 157, 161–62, 166; undercut, in *FW*, 61

Writing/reading, 8, 90–94, 97, 106, 107n.8